D1029340

Women Composers and Hymnists
A Concise Biographical Dictionary

by

Gene Claghorn

The Scarecrow Press, Inc.
Metuchen, N.J., and London
1984

Library of Congress Cataloging in Publication Data

Claghorn, Charles Eugene, 1911-
   Women composers & hymnists.

   Bibliography: p.
   1. Women hymn writers--Biography. 2. Women composers--
Biography. 3. Hymns--Bio-bibliography. I. Title.
BV325.C58 1984   783'.02'60922 [B]   83-20429
ISBN 0-8108-1680-6

To Charles & Holly

CONTENTS

Acknowledgments   vi

Introduction   vii

Index of Women Composers   xi

The Dictionary   1

Bibliography   271

The author wishes to thank the following persons for their help:

Jane Shaffer, Reference Librarian at the Cocoa Beach (Florida) Public Library for her assistance in obtaining reference books from the State Library at Tallahassee.

Joan E. Wilson and her committee in supplying information on Christian Science hymnists.

Andrew J. Hayden of Tonbridge, Kent, England for supplying the death dates of many English hymnists.

The American Society of Composers, Authors and Publishers for supplying birth and death dates of their members.

Richard E. Holtz, Territorial Music Director of the Salvation Army, Atlanta, Georgia for information on their hymnists.

W. Thomas Smith, Executive Director of The Hymn Society of America, Wittenberg University, Springfield, Ohio for birth and death dates.

This book is the first and only comprehensive biographical dictionary of women hymnists and composers of church and sacred music covering all leading Protestant denominations, many Roman Catholics and a few Jewish hymnists. It contains the concise biographies of 155 women composers and 600 women hymnists. The biographies are very brief, as many of the women were single or housewives who wrote published hymns; few were noted poets found in various biographical dictionaries or encyclopedias. These women do deserve recognition for their efforts; their names are known to posterity through published hymnals of various churches. Much of the information obtained was from newspaper obituaries, church and cemetery records, and personal letters from the women composers and hymnists, or their children. Only a small portion of the information is drawn from other publications.

This volume is a very valuable reference work for school, college, and public libraries and for various churches. Pastors, priests, church organists and choir directors will be interested in this book, as well as all people seeking musical biographies. But most important of all, the book contains hard-to-find reference material for libraries.

The book comprises concise biographies of women composers and hymnists from the twelfth century to modern times. Most of the women included were born in the British Isles, Canada, Ireland, Germany and the United States, with a few women born in France, Italy, the Scandanavian countries and other nations.

Women hymnists have written some other fascinating and extraordinary verses. Julia Carney, a schoolteacher in Boston, in 1845 wrote:

> Little drops of water,
> Little grains of sand,
> Make the mighty ocean
> And this beauteous land.

Another is the Irish hymnist and poet, Cecil Frances Alexander, who wrote:

> All things bright and beautiful,
> All creatures great and small,
> All things wise and wonderful,
> The Lord God made them all.

Her book, Hymns for Little Children (1848), was so popular that by 1896 it reached a 69th edition! A British writer has used all four lines as titles for his novels.

We are all familiar with "America the Beautiful" by Katharine Lee Bates. In 1893 she visited the Columbian Exposition in Chicago and decided to travel west and visit Pike's Peak, Colorado, where she was so impressed with the beauty of the view that she wrote her famous hymn:

> O beautiful for spacious skies,
> For amber waves of grain,
> ... From sea to shining sea.

The second and third lines above appeared on the 18 cent U.S. postage stamp in 1981.

Of course, some composers and hymnists encountered difficulties. Elizabeth Stirling studied piano and organ and at age twenty became organist at All Saints Poplar, in England. While she was in her thirties she attended Oxford University and in 1856 passed the examination for the degree of Mus. Bac. and composed the work, Psalm 130 for five voices with orchestra, which Oxford University accepted as satisfactory. But they refused to grant the degree which she had earned, stating they could not give a degree to a woman!

When Emily Woodmansee joined a group of Saints traveling west, she had no oxen and no covered wagon, and no money to buy same, so she agreed to pull a handcart the whole trip. Those pioneer women were rugged! Yes, Emily pulled her belongings in a handcart for one thousand miles, dear soul! Of her pilgrimage to Salt Lake City in

1856 she said, "I never knew what trouble was until I became a Mormon."

In 1877 Mary Lathbury, of East Orange, New Jersey, wrote what are probably the most beautiful words ever written on the subject of approaching death:

> Day is dying in the west,
> Heaven is touching earth with rest.
> Wait and worship while the night
> Sets her evening lamps alight
> Through all the sky.

Some critics may dispute my statement, saying it is just an "Evening Hymn" and was written as such. But I believe my evaluation confirmed in the third stanza:

> When forever from our sight
> Pass the stars, the day, the night,
> Lord of angels, on our eyes
> Let eternal morning rise, and shadows end.

In 1839, Mary Duncan of Melrose, Scotland, wrote a child's prayer which has never been surpassed, by man or woman. It was used extensively in England and Scotland, but not in America:

> Jesus, tender Shepherd, hear me,
> Bless thy little lamb tonight;
> Through the darkness be thou near me,
> Keep me safe till morning light.

How much better than the common American prayer, "If I should die before I wake, I pray to God my soul to take." The above hymn appears in the Episcopal Hymnal (1940), and should be in all American hymnals. I wish to give thanks to Mary Lathbury and Mary Duncan for writing two of the most beautiful verses in the English language.

Gene Claghorn
Cocoa Beach, Florida

INDEX OF WOMEN COMPOSERS

American

Adams, Carrie
Ahlwen, Elsie
Alcott, Louisa
Arbuckle, Dorothy
Ashford, Emma
Bainbridge, Katherine
Beach, Amy
Berkey, Georgia
Bitgood, Roberta
Bond, Carrie
Bonds, Margaret
Booth, Evangeline
Branscombe, Gina
Briel, Marie
Brock, Blanche
Brown, Margaret
Buchanan, Annabel
Burkalow, Anatasia
Butt, Thelma
Byles, Blanche
Caldwell, Mary
Camp, Mabel
Capers, Valerie
Cassel, Flora
Cawthorn, Janie
Coates, Dorothy
Cooper, Rose
Currie, Nancy
Daniels, Mabel
Davis, Hazel
Davis, Katherine
Deacon, Mary
Dittenhaver, Sarah

Drury, Miriam
Dungan, Olive
Eakin, Vera
Faircloth, Alta
Forsyth, Josephine
Foster, Fay
Freeman, Carolyn
Fryxell, Regina
Fuller, Esther
Gates, Ellen
Gay, Annabeth
Glasser, Victoria
Glen, Irma
Goodman, Lillian
Hanna, Ione
Hokanson, Margarthe
Imelda-Teresa, Sister
Irwin, Lois
James, Dorothy
Jolley, Florence
Kinscella, Hazel
Klotz, Leora
Knapp, Phoebe
Lang, Margaret
Larsen, Libby
Leech, Lydia
Lemmel, Helen
Lillenas, Bertha
Lockwood, Charlotte
McAllister, Louise
McCaw, Maxine
McCollin, Frances
Marshall, Jane
Marth, Helen
Meyer, Lucy
Miller, Anne

Miller, Lillian
Moody, May
Morris, Lilia
Morse, Anna
Murphy, Annie
Musgrave, Thea
Nevin, Alice
Newell, Laura
Ortlund, Elizabeth
Parente, Elizabeth
Parker, Alice
Patterson, Joy
Patterson, Wiley
Patton, Abby
Paul, Doris
Perkins, Emily
Porter, Ethel
Posegate, Maxcine
Rittenhouse, Elizabeth
Rounsfell, Carrie
Saunders, Carrie
Scott, Clara
Seaver, Blanche
Shearer, Winifred
Siedhoff, Edna
Smith, Eleanor
Smith, Ruby
Spaeth, Harriett
Steele, Helen
Stutsman, Grace
Thomas, Edith
Tourjee, Lizzie
Upton, Anne
Warren, Della
Weaver, Mary
Wesson, Jan
Williams, Marian
Williams, Frances
Wilson, Emily
Winter, Gloria
Worth, Amy
Zoeckler, Dorothy

Canadian

Clarkson, Edith

Dutch

Booth, Cornelie

French

Beaumesriel, Henriette
Grandval, Marie
La Guerre, Elizabeth

English

Barker, Elizabeth
Barnard, Charlotte
Booth-Hellberg, Lucy
Browne, Mary
Edwards, Alice
Flower, Eliza
Gibbs, Ada
Gipps, Ruth
Hammond, Mary
Havergal, Frances
Hornabrook, Mary
Hutton, Laura
Kingham, Millicent
Potter, Doreen
Rendle, Lily
Rhodes, Sarah
Scott, Lesbia
Sharpe, Evelyn
Sidebotham, Mary
Smyth, Ethel
Spratt, Ann
Stainer, Rosalind
Stirling, Elizabeth
Stock, Sarah
Streatfield, Charlotte
Tiddeman, Maria

German

Bingen, Hildegard of
Kock, Minna
Prussia, Princess of
Reichardt, Luise

Irish

Cuthbert, Elizabeth
Holmes, Augusta
Maconchy, Elizabeth
Piggot, Jean

Italian

Aleotti, Raffaela
Caccini, Francesca
Coccia, Maria
Leonarda, Isabella

Polish

Janotha, Natalia

Scotch

Masson, Elizabeth
Nairne, Baroness

South African

Gerstman, Blanche

Spanish

Martinez, Marianne

Swedish

Aulin-Valborg, Laura

THE DICTIONARY

ADAMS, CARRIE B. WILSON (1859-1940)
Remember now Thy Creator

Composer, organist, and choir director, she was the daughter of David Wilson, a singing teacher, and was born at Oxford, Ohio on July 28, 1859. She studied music with her
father, and at age seven she was in a choir at a convention
in Millville, Ohio under the direction of Dr. Horatio R. Palmer. In 1880 she married bassist Allyn G. Adams and they
settled in Terre Haute, Indiana where he went into business.
She served as director, chorister, and organist for the choirs
of the First Congregational Church and the Central Christian
Church. Her first anthem was published in 1876. She composed four anthem books, two sacred cantatas--Redeemer the
King and Easter Praise--and anthems for the Choir Music
Journal. She wrote for The Choir Herald, published by
E. S. Lorenz.

ADAMS, JESSIE (1863-1954)
"I feel the winds of God today."

Born at Ipswich, Suffolk, England on September 9, 1863, she
was a progressive teacher and a leader of the local adult
school in Frimley, England. She was a member of the Society of Friends (Quakers) and died at York, England on
July 15, 1954. Her hymn appeared in Christian Worship--
A Hymnal (1953).

ADAMS, SARAH FLOWER (1805-1848)
"Nearer, my God to Thee, nearer to Thee!"

"Part in peace; Christ's life was peace."

Daughter of Benjamin Flower (editor of The Cambridge Intelligencer) she was born at Great Harlow, Essex, England
on February 22, 1805. Her father was imprisoned at New-
gate for six months for criticizing the political conduct of
the Bishop of Llandaff. While there he was visited by an
admirer, Eliza Gould, a schoolteacher from Devonshire,
whom he married upon his release from prison. In 1834
Sarah married William B. Adams, an engineer and inventor.
She contributed poems and hymns to the Monthly Repository
(1834-35), edited by the Rev. William J. Fox, a Unitarian
pastor. Sarah desired to be an actress, and appeared as
Lady Macbeth at the Richmond Theatre in London (1837) in
a successful performance. She found the work so strenuous,
however, that she gave up the stage to continue her writing.

2 / Adams, Sarah Flower

Rev. Fox published Hymns and Anthems (1840-41) to which
Sarah contributed 13 hymns; her sister Elizabeth wrote 63
out of 150 tunes in the collection. Elizabeth died of tuberculosis in 1846, and Sarah of the same disease in London on
August 14, 1848. Her first hymn (above) appears in The
American Service Hymnal (1968); Baptist (1973); Broadman
(1977); Christian Worship (1953); Christian Science (1937);
Episcopal (1940); Lutheran (1941); Methodist (1966); Presbyterian (1955); Songs of Praise (1931); and the Pilgrim Hymnal (1958).

AGNEW, EDITH JOSEPHINE (b. 1897)
   "When Jesus saw the fishermen."

The daughter of Ella Dunlap and Clinton Agnew, she was
born at Denver, Colorado on October 13, 1897 and was educated at Park College, Parkville, Missouri (A. B., 1921),
New Mexico Highlands University, Las Vegas, New Mexico
and at Western State College, Gunnison, Colorado. After
teaching in Delta, Colorado (1921-24), at Logan Academy,
Logan, Utah (1924-28), and other schools, she worked with
the Presbyterian Board of National Missions (1945-50) and
with the Presbyterian Board of Christian Education as editor of Opening Doors (1950-57), then taught again at the
Delta High School in Delta, Colorado (1957-62).

   Edith Agnew wrote numerous books, The Songs of
Marcelind (1936), Hand on My Shoulder (1953), People of
the Way (1959), Treasures for Tomas (1964), etc. In February 1982 she was living in a Presbyterian Home in Santa
Fe, New Mexico and was writing a history of the Presbyterian Church. [Letter from the Delta High School, Delta,
Colorado.]

AHLWEN, ELSIE R. (b. 1905)
   Tune--PEARLY GATES

A composer, she was born at Örebro, Sweden and came to
the United States as a young woman. After studying at the
Moody Bible Institute in Chicago, she became an evangelist
and worked with the Swedish-speaking people in Chicago.
Later she toured the United States singing and preaching.
She married Daniel A. Sundeen and continued her ministry,
finally retiring to live in Manchester, New Hampshire.
While Miss Ahlwen wrote the tune, it is based on an old

Swedish melody, and it may be said it was adapted by her.
It was used with the hymn "Love divine, so great and wondrous," in Hymns for the Living Church (1974).

AIRD, MARION PAUL (1815-1898)
    "Had I the wings of a dove, I would fly."

Born in Glasgow, Scotland, she later resided in Kilmatnock.
Her poems and hymns were published between 1846 and 1853.
She was a Presbyterian and died on January 30, 1898.

AKERMAN, LUCY EVELINA METCALF (1816-1874)
    "Nothing but leaves, the spirit grieves
    Over a wasted life."

Daughter of Thomas Metcalf, she was born at Wrentham,
Massachusetts on February 21, 1816 and married Charles
Akerman of Portsmouth, New Hampshire. A Unitarian, her
hymn appeared in the Christian Observer (1858) and in the
Scottish Family Treasury (1859). She died at her home in
Providence, Rhode Island on her birthday, February 21,
1874. More recently, her hymn appeared in the Baptist
Hymnal (1973).

AKERS, DORIS MAE (b. 1922)
    "There's a sweet, sweet spirit in this place."

Born in Brookfield, Missouri on May 21, 1922, she wrote
her first gospel song when she was only ten years old. Despite the lack of formal musical training, she has directed
choirs in various cities in the United States. She was the
director of the Skypilot Choir in Los Angeles, California in
the 1950s. Later she resided in Columbus, Ohio and was a
member of the Full Gospel Church. She sang with Jim
Bakker's PTL Club on programs from Charlotte, North Carolina. [Supplied by Lou Willadsen of Cocoa Beach. Florida.]
Her hymn appeared in the Baptist (1973); Hymns for the Family of God (1976); and the New Broadman (1977) hymnals.

ALCOTT, LOUISA MAY (1832-1888)
    "O, the beautiful old story!"

Daughter of Abigail May and A. Bronson Alcott, the educator

and author, she was born at Germantown (now in Philadelphia), Pennsylvania on November 29, 1832. The family
moved to Boston in 1834, where her father opened a "free-
thinking" school. In 1840 they moved to Concord, Massachusetts, where her father became friends with Ralph Waldo
Emerson, Margaret Fuller, Nathaniel Hawthorne and Henry
D. Thoreau. With such brilliant conversations in the house,
she was tutored by her father and these learned ladies and
gentlemen. She served as a nurse in the Civil war and is
best known for her novels Little Women (1868-69), which
sold millions of copies, Little Men (1871) and Jo's Boys
(1886). She died at Boston on March 6, 1888. Her hymn
above was included in The New Hymn and Tune Book (Unitarian, 1914) and her hymn, "A little kingdom I possess" in
the Union Hymnal (Jewish, 1932 & 1957).

ALDERSON, ELIZA SIBBALD DYKES (1818-1889)
        "Lord of Glory, who has bo't us
        With Thy lifeblood as the price. "

Granddaughter of the Reverend Thomas Dykes of Hull, England, and the daughter of William H. Dykes, Manager of the
Yorkshire District Bank at Hull, she was born there on August 16, 1818. She was the sister of the Rev. Dr. John
Bacchus Dykes, the famous hymnist. In 1850 she married
the Rev. W. T. Alderson, Chaplain of the West Riding House
of Correction in Wakefield, England where he served for 43
years (1833-76). She published Twelve Hymns (no date).
Her hymns were published in the Appendix to Hymns Ancient
and Modern (1868) and in other hymnals with tunes composed
by her brother. She died at Heath, near Wakefield, England
on March 18, 1889 and was buried at Kirkthorpe, in Yorkshire, England where her husband had ministered. More recently her hymn appeared in The Lutheran Hymnal (1941).

ALEOTTI, RAFFAELA (b. 1570-d. after 1638)
        Cantiones sacrae

Composer, daughter of Giovanni Battista Aleotti (1546-1636),
the architect who designed the Teatro Farnese at Parma,
she was born at Ferrara, Italy. A pupil of Ercole Pasquini
and Allessandro Milleville, she published her compositions
in book form at Venice in 1593. Other compositions were
published that same year by Vittoria Aleotti, who could have
been the sister of Raffaela, or this may have been her pen-

name. Later Raffaela entered the Convent of San Vito at Ferrara where she served as Prioress. She died at Ferrara some time after 1638.

ALEXANDER, CECIL FRANCES HUMPHREYS (1818-1895)
"There is a green hill far away. "

The daughter of John Humphreys, she was born at Redcross Parish, County Wicklow, Ireland in 1818 although some references say 1823. She wrote The Burial of Moses and books of verse: Verses for Holy Seasons (1846), Hymns for Little Children (1848), Hymns Descriptive and Devotional (1858), The Legend of the Golden Prayers (1859), etc. From Hymns for Little Children come her famous lines:

> All things bright and beautiful,
> All creatures great and small,
> All things wise and wonderful,
> The Lord God made them all.

That book was so popular that by 1896 it reached a 69th edition. On October 15, 1850 she married an Anglican rector, William Alexander, who became Bishop of Derry and Raphoe in 1867 and Archbishop of Armagh in 1896, a year after her death. She died at Londonderry, North Ireland on October 12, 1895. Her hymns appear in the American (1968); Baptist (1973); Broadman (1977); Episcopal (1940); Family of God (1976); Joyfully Sing (1968); Lutheran (1941); Methodist (1966); Pilgrim (1958); Presbyterian (1955); and in numerous other hymnals.

ALEXANDER, HELEN C. (MRS. C. M. ALEXANDER) see HELEN C. A. DIXON

ALLDREDGE, IDA ROMNEY (1892-1943)
"They the builders of the nation. "

The daughter of Miles and Catherine Cottam Romney, she was born at Colonia Juarez, Mexico on January 7, 1892. In 1912 she moved to Douglas, Arizona and married Lew Alldredge, who was engaged in the mercantile business. Later they moved to Mesa, Arizona, and she died at Phoenix, Arizona on June 14, 1943. Her hymn appeared in Hymns (1948) of the Church of Jesus Christ of Latter-day Saints.

ALSTYNE, FRANCES VAN see CROSBY, FANNY

ANDERSDATTER, ELLE (1600-c. 1650)
"I hoppet sig min fralsta själ fönöjer."
"In hope my soul, redeemed to bliss unending."

Daughter of Andrew Andersdatter of Denmark, she wrote
several hymns. One hymn "Eja, mit hjert a ret inderlig
jubilerer" acrostically spelled her name. It is quoted in
N. N. Skaar's Norsk Salmehistorie Vol. L Her hymn above
appeared in The Lutheran Hymnal (1941).

ANDERSON, MARIA FRANCES HILL (1819-1895)
"Our country's voice is pleading."

The daughter of Thomas Fenimore Hill of Exeter, England,
she was born at Paris, France on January 30, 1819 and
raised in the Church of England. In April 1847 she married
George W. Anderson, professor at the University of Lewisburg (now Bucknell) in Lewisburg, Pennsylvania and then she
became a Baptist. They had one son and one daughter. He
became pastor of the Lower Merion Baptist Church in Bryn
Mawr, Pennsylvania in 1858. In 1869 he received an honorary D. D. degree from Madison College (now Colgate) in Hamilton, New York, from which he had graduated in 1844.
Later he was editor of the Philadelphia Christian Chronicle.
Her hymn appeared in the Baptist Harp (1849) and in the
Methodist Protestant (1921); Augustana Lutheran; Concordia
(Lutheran); Presbyterian (1927); Evangelical United Brethren
and other hymnals. She published Baptists in Sweden (1861).
She died on October 13, 1895 and was buried in Lower Meri-
on Baptist Church Cemetery, on property adjacent to Bryn
Mawr College. [Information from Nancy S. Weyant, Head,
Reference Department, Bucknell University; also from Mrs.
Hill's granddaughter, Mrs. Elizabeth Bliss Divine of Anna-
polis, Maryland.]

ANNE SOPHIA see HESSE DARMSTADT, COUNTESS OF

ARBUCKLE, DOROTHY FRY (b. 1910)
Anthem--"The Church Wherein I Worship."

Composer, hymnist, and pianist, she was born at Eldred,

Illinois on January 23, 1910 and educated at Northwestern University, Evanston, Illinois. She was a teacher, librarian, church organist, and choir director. As of March 1982 she was enjoying her retirement.

ARMES, SIBYL LEONARD (b. 1914)
    "How gracious are thy mercies, Lord. "

Born in Gatesville, Texas on January 16, 1914, she was educated at Mary Hardin-Baylor College (B. A. , 1934) and later received an honorary Lit. D. degree there. She married Woodson Armes, secretary of the Christian Education Commission of the Baptist General Convention of Texas. She has written twelve hymns and several books, I Shall Meet Tomorrow Bravely, Serene in the Storm, The Radiant Trail, Devotions for Dynamic Living and Devotions from a Grateful Heart. Her hymn appeared in Baptist Hymnal (1975) and the New Broadman Hymnal (1977).

ARMITAGE, ELLA SOPHIA BULLEY (1841-1931)
    "Eternal love, whose law doth sway. "

The granddaughter of the Rev. Thomas Raffles, D. D. , she was born at Liverpool, England on March 3, 1841 and was one of the first students at Newnham. In 1874 she married the Rev. E. S. Armitage, later Theological Professor at the Congregational United College, Bradford. Her main interests were archaeology, history, and education. After serving on the school boards of Rotherham and Bradford and on the West Riding Educational Committee, she was assistant commissioner to the Royal Commission on Secondary Education and lectured at Manchester University which gave her an honorary degree for her archaeological work. Sixteen of her original hymns were published in her book, The Garden of the Lord (London, 1861). She wrote, "I believe I was intended by nature for an archaeologist, but life has made me a hymn-writer, and I shall be content to be known as such when my archaeology is forgotten. " Later her hymns were published in the Congregational Church Hymnal (1887); the Methodist Free Church Hymnal (1889); and the English Baptist Hymnal (1961). She died on March 20, 1931.

ARMSTRONG, FLORENCE CATHERINE (1843-1890)
    "O to be over yonder. "

Daughter of William Armstrong, M. D., of Collooney, County Sligo, Ireland, she was born on March 18, 1843. Her hymn was published in the British Herald in February 1865, and later appeared in several hymnals. Her hymn appeared again in her book, The King in His Beauty and Other Poems in 1875. She died on January 9, 1890.

ARNER, BETTY ANNE J.   see   CAMPION, JOAN

ARNOTT, CATHERINE CAMERON BONNELL (b. 1927)
     "God, who stretched the spangled heavens."

Daughter of the Rev. John Sutherland Bonnell, minister of the Fifth Avenue Presbyterian Church in New York City, she was born at St. John, New Brunswick, Canada on March 27, 1927. She earned a Ph. D. in Sociology and under her professional name, Dr. Catherine Cameron, taught at La Verne College in La Verne, California, specializing in family problems. Her hymn appeared in the Baptist (1975); Broadman (1977); and Family of God (1976) hymnals.

ASHFORD, EMMA LOUISE HINDLE (1850-1930)
     Sacred cantata-- The Prince of Peace

A composer, she was born at Newark, Delaware on March 27, 1850 and was taught by her father, who was a music teacher. She sang in the local church choir and also played the guitar. In 1864 the family moved to Plymouth, Massachusetts, then to Seymour, Connecticut, where she became organist at St. Peter's (Episcopal) Church. In 1867 she married John Ashford and they moved to Chicago where she was contralto in the quartet of St. James (Episcopal) Church during the time Dudley Buck was organist and director there. Later they moved to Nashville, Tennessee, where they had charge of music in a Presbyterian Church and the Jewish Temple simultaneously. Later she became connected with the Lorenz Publishing Company of Dayton, Ohio. She composed over 250 anthems, 50 sacred solos, 24 sacred duets, trios, and cantatas, and over 200 organ voluntaries. She also wrote numerous gospel songs and Ashford's Organ Instructor. Her hymn tunes EVELYN and SUTHERLAND appeared in the Methodist Hymnal (1911).

AUBER, HENRIETTE (1773-1862)
"Our blest Redeemer, ere he breathed
His tender, last farewell. "

The great-great granddaughter of Pierre Aubert, a French
Huguenot who fled from Normandy, France in 1685 after the
Revocation of the Edict of Nantes whereby Protestantism in
France became a crime, she was born in London on October
4, 1773. Some hymnals give her Christian name as Harriet,
but the records at Somerset House show it as Henriette.
She was the daughter of the vicar of Tring, Herts., and was
raised in the villages of Broxbourne and Hoddesdon. The
hymn above was written for use on Whitsunday; fifty days
after Easter, and was included in her Spirit of the Psalms
(1829), then in Hymns Ancient and Modern, Public School
Hymn Book (1919), etc. She died at Hoddesdon on January
20, 1862 near what is now the conference centre of High
Leigh. Some of her versions of the Psalms were included
in Charles H. Spurgeon's Our Own Hymnbook (1866) for use
in his Baptist Tabernacle. Her hymn, "Praise our great
and gracious Lord" is in the Christian Science Hymnal (1937),
and the above hymn in the Baptist (London, 1961); Songs of
Praise (1931); and the Episcopal (1940) hymnals.

AULIN-VALBORG, LAURA (1860-1928)
Christmas Hymn

Composer and pianist, she was born at Gävle, Sweden, on 9
January 1860, and was the sister of Tor Aulin, composer,
conductor, and violinist. She studied at the Stockholm Conservatory (1877-82) and won the Jenny Lind award for two
years' study in Paris with Godard and Massenet. Her
"Christmas Hymn" was composed for mixed chorus and organ. She was a pianoforte teacher in Orebo, Sweden and
died there on 11 January 1928.

AYERS, MINNY M. H. (d. 1942)
"I walk with Love along the way. "

She joined the Church of Christ, Scientist on June 1, 1917.
Her hymn appeared in the Christian Science Hymnal (1937).
She died on December 23, 1942.

BACHE, SARAH (1771-1844)
   "'See how He loved,' exclaimed the Jews."

She was a relative of the Carpenters, who ran a school in
Birmingham, England for many years. Her hymn appeared
in the Exeter Collection, published in 1812 by Dr. Lant Carpenter, a Unitarian Minister in Exeter and later in Bristol,
England. Her hymn also appeared in Martineau's Hymns for
the Christian Church and Home and in the Belfast Collection
of 1886.

BAILLIE, JOANNA (1762-1851)
   "Clothed in majesty sublime."

Daughter of Dr. James Baillie, a Scotch Presbyterian Minister, she was born at the Manse of Bothwell, Lanarkshire,
Scotland on September 22, 1762, but raised in Hamilton.
She lived in London after 1784. Her hymn appeared in her
Fugitive Verses, published in 1840. She published other
volumes of plays and poetry. She died at Hampstead, England on February 23, 1851.

BAINBRIDGE, KATHARINE (1863-1967)
   "God answers prayer."

Composer and hymnist, she was born at Basingstoke, England on June 30, 1863 and educated at Hardwicke College in
Australia. She was a member of the National League of
American Pen Women and a life member of the Poetry Society of Southern California. She composed the music for this
hymn. She died on February 12, 1967 in her 104th year.

BAIRD, CATHERINE (b. 1895)
   "O love, revealed on earth in Christ."

Born at Sydney, Australia in 1895, she was of Scottish descent on her father's side and Manx descent on her mother's
side. After serving as a Salvation Army officer in South
Africa, she was assigned to the U. S. A. Central Territory
with offices in Chicago, Illinois where she was editor of The
Young Soldier. Later she was editor of the International
Young Soldier, then editor of The Warrior, and in 1953 she
became Literary Secretary at International Headquarters in
London, England. She rose to Colonel in The Salvation Army,

and was the author of a number of books, including The Sword of God, Of Such is the Kingdom, The Banner of Love and Evidence of the Unseen. She wrote a number of songs which appeared in The Musical Salvationist, including the one above which appeared in the March-April 1950 issue and in The Song Book of the Salvation Army (1953). Catherine Baird is still living. [Letter dated 2/7/83 from Richard E. Holz, Territorial Music Director, The Salvation Army, Atlanta, Georgia.]

BAKER, AMY SUSAN, LADY (1847-1940)
"We are only little workers."

Born at Chuton Glen, near Christchurch, Hants, England on August 22, 1847, she married the Rev. Sir T. H. B. Baker, Bart., of Ranston, Dorset on December 30, 1875. He died in 1900. She also wrote "True friends help each other." Her hymns appeared in Lays for the Little Ones (1876); Hymns and Songs (1876); Mrs. Brock's Children's Hymn Book (1881); the Congregational Church Hymnal (1887); etc. She died on January 26, 1940.

BALFOUR, CLARA LUCAS LIDDELL (1808-1878)
"Come, gentle daughters of our land."

Born at New Forest, Hampshire, England on December 21, 1808, she was raised in London. In 1827 she married James Balfour of the Ways and Means Office in the House of Commons and they lived at Chelsea in London. She became a temperance lecturer at the Greenwich Literary Institution in 1841 and was an active temperance advocate for over thirty years. Author of over 40 books, she wrote Moral Heroism (1846); Women of Scripture (1847); Women and the Temperance Movement (1849); Working Women (1854); A Mother's Sermon (1862); Bible Patterns of Good Women (1867); Women Worth Emulating (1877); etc. Her book Whisper to the Newly Married (1850) reached 23 editions. She was elected President of the British Women's Temperance League in May 1877 and died at Croydon, England on July 3, 1878.

BANCROFT, CHARITIE LEES SMITH (1841-1923)
"The King of glory standeth."

Daughter of the Rev. Sidney Smith, D.D., rector of Drumragh,

County Tyrone, Ireland, she was born at Bloomfield, Merrion, County of Dublin, Ireland on June 21, 1841. In 1869 she married Arthur E. Bancroft. She published her poems and hymns in Within the Veil (1867) and her hymn appeared in Lyra Britannica (1867) and Hymns and Songs of Praise (New York, 1874). After her husband died she became Mrs. De Chenez. More recently her hymn appeared in the Presbyterian Hymnal (1933).

BARBAULD, ANNA LAETITIA AIKIN (1743-1825)
   "Praise to God, immortal praise. "

   "Come, says Jesus' sacred voice. "

Daughter of the Reverend John Aikin, she was born at Kibworth-Harcourt, Leicestershire, England on June 20, 1743. She was tutored by Dr. Philip Doddridge, and in 1774 she married a French Protestant minister, the Reverend Rochemont Barbauld; together they ran a boarding school at Palgrave in Suffolk. Her hymns were published in Hymns in Prose for Little Children, London (1825), by her niece, Lucy Aikin. She died at Stoke Newington, England on March 9, 1825. More recently her hymn (first one above) appeared in The Lutheran Hymnal (1941).

BARBER, MARY ANN SERRETT (1800-1864)
   "Prince of Peace, control my will. "

Daughter of Thomas Barber, she was born in England and wrote many poems and hymns for the Church of England Magazine. She wrote several books. Her autobiography, Bread Winning: or, The Ledger and the Lute was published in 1865 after her death. She died on March 9, 1864. Her hymn appeared in the Methodist Hymnal (1911).

BARCLAY, MARGARET (b. 1923)
   "Each morning brings us fresh outpoured. "

Born in England, she was an English translator on the staff of the World Council of Churches (1947-53) and translated hymns from the German and one Chinese hymn into English for Cantate Domino (1951). After 1953 she was a translator with the High Authority of the European Coal and Steel Community, a branch of the Common Market, in Luxembourg.

She was elected a Fellow of the Institute of Linguists in London. Her hymn, a translation, appeared in The Pilgrim Hymnal (1958).

BARKER, ELIZABETH RAYMOND HALKETT (1829-1916)
    Tune--PARACLETE

Composer, daughter of William Halkett of Aylestone Hall, Leicester, England, she studied music under G. A. Löhr. In 1853 she was married to the Rev. F. Barker of Oriel College. Later she became acquainted with Dr. John Mason Neale (1818-1866). In 1867 she joined the Roman Catholic Church. Her tune appeared in the English Methodist Hymn-Book (1935).

BARNARD, CHARLOTTE ARLINGTON (1830-1869)
    Tunes--BROCKLESBURY and BARNARD

A composer and songwriter, she was born at London, England on December 23, 1830 and was married to Charles C. Barnard on May 18, 1854. Between 1858 and her death in 1869, she wrote about 100 songs and ballads under the pen-name "Claribel." She published Thoughts, Verses and Songs and Songs and Verses. Brocklesbury is a town near Dover, England, where she died on January 30, 1869. She is buried in the cemetery of St. James' Church. Her tune has appeared in hymnbooks with the hymn "Jesus, Tender Shepherd, hear me," and with "Savior, Who Thy flock are feeding," in The Baptist Hymnal (1973). Her tunes appeared in Hymns for the Living Church (1974). Her best-known popular song was "Come Back to Erin." One of her popular songs is worth repeating here:
        I cannot sing the old songs,
        I sung long years ago,
        For heart and voice would fail me,
        And foolish tears would flow.

BARNARD, WINIFRED EVA (b. 1892)
    "Let us sing our song of praise."

Born at Twickenham, Middlesex, England, she was educated at Orme Girls' School in Newcastle, Staffordshire and at Strand Green and Hornsby High School in London. After serving as assistant head of a nursery school at Bow (1928-30), she was co-head of the Kingsley Hall Nursery School at

Dagenham (1930-39) and continued as head during the war years after it was removed to Gloucestershire to protect the small children. Later she was head of the nursery school department at a private school at Beckenham, Kent, England. She wrote Tales to Tell Little Children (series of books) and also Song and Picture Book (in a series). A member of the Church of England, her hymns appeared in Infant Praise (1964) and other hymnals.

BATES, KATHERINE LEE (1859-1929)
"O beautiful for spacious skies,
For amber waves of grain."

"Dear God, our Father, at Thy knee confessing,
Our sins and follies, close in Thine embrace."

Daughter of a Congregational Minister, she was born at Falmouth, Massachusetts on August 12, 1859 and was graduated from Wellesley College (B. A., 1880). She taught at the high school in Natick, Massachusetts and at Dana Hall, then at Wellesley (1886-1925). In 1893 she visited the Columbian Exposition in Chicago and decided to travel west and visit Pike's Peak, Colorado, where she was so impressed with the beauty of the view that she wrote her famous hymn, which appeared in The Congregationalist. She also wrote the hymn, "The kings of the East are riding" (1914) and was the author or co-author of about 20 books or collections, including a History of American Literature (1908) and a book of poems, The Pilgrim Ship (1926). She died at Wellesley, Massachusetts on March 28, 1929. The first hymn above appeared in the American (1968); Baptist (1973); Broadman (1977); Christian (1953); Family of God (1976); Joyfully Sing (1968); Methodist (1966); and Presbyterian (1955) hymnals and The Pilgrim Hymnal (1958).

BAUM, MARIA LOUISE (d. 1941)
"Put on the whole armor of pure consecration."

She came to Boston about 1900, when she joined a Christian Science Church. She worked for the Christian Science Monitor. Her hymn above was based on Ephesians 6:11-17 and I Chronicles 29:11. Seven of her hymns appeared in the Christian Science Hymnal (1937). She died on April 27, 1941.

BAXTER, LYDIA (1809-1874)
"Take the name of Jesus with you. "

She was born in Petersburgh, New York on September 2,
1809 and married a Mr. Baxter. She and her sister helped
form a Baptist Church in Petersburgh. Her poems and
hymns were published in Gems by the Wayside in 1855 and
in Pure Gold in 1871. She died in New York on June 22,
1874. Her hymn appeared in The American Service Hymnal
(1968); Baptist (1973); Broadman (1977); Family of God (1976);
Methodist (1966); and Presbyterian (1955) hymnals together
with five recordings listed by Phonolog Reports of Los Angeles, California (1978).

BEACH, AMY MARCY CHENEY (1867-1944)
Mass with Orchestra

Born at Henniker, New Hampshire on September 5, 1867,
she was a composer, hymnist, pianist, and songwriter.
She studied with her mother, also with E. Perabo, K. Baer-
man (piano) and Junius W. Hill (harmony). After making
her debut as a pianist in Boston in 1883 she made many appearances as a soloist with various orchestras and toured
Europe in 1910. She married Dr. Henry Harris Aubrey
Beach, the singer. She served as President of the Board
of Councillors of the New England Conservatory in Boston,
Massachusetts and composed Mass with Orchestra, Mass in
e; Gaelic Symphony and various orchestral works and several sacred songs. She died in New York City on December
27, 1944.

BEALE, MARY CRADDOCK (1632-1697)

The daughter of the Rev. Craddock, Minister at Walton-on-
Thames, England, her versions of the Psalms were included
in Samuel Woodford's Paraphrases in English Verse upon the
Books of the Psalms (1667). She died at Pall-mall.

BEAUMESRIEL, HENRIETTE ADELAIDE VILLARD DE (1758-
1813)
Oratorio--Les Israelites poursuivis par Pharaon

Composer and singer, born at Paris, France on 31 August
1758, she was a pupil of C. F. Clement and made her debut

in Sylvie (by Berton & Trial) at the Paris Opera in 1766.
Her one-act opera, Tibrille at Delie, ou Les Saturnales,
was the third opera by a woman performed at the Academie
Royale de Musique on 15 January 1784 (see Mme la Guerre).
Her oratorio (above) was sung at the Concert Spirituel on 8
December 1784. She died at Paris in 1813.

BEHN, APHRA JOHNSON (1640-1689)
    "And forgive us our trespasses. "

Daughter of John and Amy Johnson, she was born at Wye,
Kent, England on July 10, 1640 and was raised in the West
Indies where her stepfather was Lieutenant General of Surinam. She returned to England about 1658 after England
turned over Surinam to the Dutch. She married a Dutch
merchant named Behn, but by 1666 she was a widow. King
Charles II of England sent her to Antwerp as a spy, but she
only sent intelligence information to London which was ridi-
culed. She was about to marry Van der Aalbert when he was
stricken with a fever in Amsterdam and died, so she returned to London and became England's first woman professional writer to earn her own living by her pen. She wrote
novels and several dramas and comedies which were produced
in England. Her hymn appeared in the Penguin Book of Res-
toration Verse (c. 1969). She died at London, England on
April 16, 1689 and was buried in the Cloisters at Westminster Abbey.

BELL, M. BETTE (d. 1923)
    "Press, on, dear traveler, press thou on. "

She studied with Mary Baker Eddy in Boston, Massachusetts
in 1885 and 1886 and her hymn first appeared in the Christian Science Journal in April 1886. She became a resident
of Chicago, Illinois and was a Christian Science practitioner
there and also a teacher (1892-1915). Her hymn appeared in
the first edition of the Christian Science Hymnal (1892) and
in the 1937 edition.

BELL, MAUD ALMA (1868-1957)
    "Father, all-seeing, friend of all creation. "

During World War I she worked in the Ministry of Health in
London, England and for Serbian Relief. She was noted for

her water colors of London. She published her poems and hymns in London Songs (1924) and her hymn above appeared in Songs of Praise (1931) and in the Baptist Hymn Book (1962).

BERG, KAROLINA VILHELMINA SANDELL (1832-1903)
"O Father, Thy kingdom is come upon earth. "

Daughter of Jonas Sandell, a Lutheran pastor, she was born at Froderyd, county of Jönköping, Sweden on October 3, 1832. She started writing her poems and hymns in 1858, after the death of her beloved father, and was greatly influenced by the evangelist preacher Carl Olaf Rosenius, a disciple of the British Methodist, George Scott. She wrote some 650 poems and hymns, many of which were set to music by the guitarist Oskar Ahnfelt and published at the expense of Jenny Lind in Ahnfelt's Sanger. In 1861 she married Carl Oscar Berg, Roumanian Counsel-General in Sweden. She published Tales for the Sunday School, and was known as the "Fanny Crosby of Sweden." She died at Stockholm, Sweden on July 27, 1903. Her hymns appeared in the Christian Science Hymnal (1937); the New Broadman Hymnal (1977); and Hymns for the Family of God (1976).

BERGEN, ESTHER CATHRYN KLAASSEN (b. 1921)
"Rejoice, all ye people, your mighty anthems raise. "

"Thank the Lord with a joyful heart. "

Translator and versifier. Born at Morden, Manitoba, Canada on June 21, 1921, she was educated at the Mennonite Collegiate Institute in Gretna, Manitoba; at the Normal School in Winnipeg; and the Mennonite Brethren Bible College in Winnipeg, Manitoba, where she taught for a year. She became dean and registrar at the Canadian Mennonite Bible College. In 1952 she was married to Nenno Bergen, and they served as missionaries in Mexico (1956-69). Later they lived in Herbert, Saskatchewan, Canada. Her hymns appeared in the Baptist (1975) and Broadman (1977) hymnals.

BERKEY, GEORGIA GUINEY
Tune--DWELL IN ME

A composer, her tune for "Dwell in me, O blessed Spirit, "

first appeared in the Sunday School Hymnal for the Evangelical and Reformed Churches, Heidelberg Press, Philadelphia 1899. She married a Mr. A. G. Berkey. More recently her tune appeared in the 1941 edition of The Hymnal. The hymn was written by Martha J. Lankton.

BERTRAM, MARY ANN (1841-1864)
"Bending before Thy throne on high. "

She was the wife of the Rev. Robert A. Bertram, a Congregational Minister in St. Helena, Manchester, Barnstaple and Nottingham, England. Her hymn appeared in his The Cavendish Hymnal of 1864, prepared for the use of the congregation of Cavendish Chapel in Manchester, England.

BEVAN, EMMA FRANCES SHUTTLEWORTH (1827-1909)
"Rise, ye children of salvation. "

The daughter of the Rev. Philip N. Shuttleworth, Warden of New College, Oxford, England and Bishop of Chichester, she was born at Oxford on September 25, 1827. A member of the Church of England, she married R. C. L. Bevan of the Lombard Street banking firm in London in 1856. As a translator and versifier, in 1858 she published her translations from the German in Songs of Eternal Life and in 1859 Songs of Praise for Christian Pilgrims. She died at Cannes, France. More recently her hymn appeared in The Lutheran Hymnal (1941), and another hymn, "Sinners, Jesus will receive, sound this word of grace to all, " in The New Broadman Hymnal (1977); and the Baptist Hymnal (1975).

BINGEN, HILDEGARD, ABBESS OF (1098-1179)
"You beautiful faces
Beholding God and building in the dawn
How noble you are. "

Composer and hymnist, known as the "Sybil of the Rhine, " was born at Böckelheim near Kreuzmach, West Germany. While Abbess of Bingen, Rhineland-Palatinate, West Germany, she wrote 35 antiphons, 18 responses, 6 sequences, and 10 hymns. Seventy-seven of her chants were included in her cycle Symphonia Armonic celestium revelationium (Symphony of the Harmony of the Heavenly Relations), known as Scivias. The above is a quote from her Song No. 38, extolling women.

Thirteen of her chants were addressed to Saint Ursula and fifteen to the Virgin Mary. She is the only woman composer of the Middle Ages whose music has survived. She died at Rupertsberg, near Bingen, Rhineland. She is referred to in a number of publications as "Saint Hildegard," although she has never been created a Saint.

BITGOOD, ROBERTA (b. 1908)
"The greatest of these is love."

Conductor, composer, hymnist, violist, and organist, she was born at New London, Connecticut on January 15, 1908 and was graduated from the Connecticut College for Women; Columbia University (M. A.) in New York City; and Union Theological Seminary (M. S. M.; S. M. D.). She was a violist at Redlands University Community Symphony in California, the Detroit Women's Symphony in Michigan, the Saginaw (Michigan) Symphony and then Director of Music at Bloomfield College and Seminary in New Jersey (1936-47). Also she was organist at Temple Sharey Tefilo, East Orange, New Jersey (1943-47), and Temple Beth El in Riverside, California (1958-60). She composed the music for the above chorale. She married Bert Wiersma and as of March 1982 was the first woman President of the American Guild of Organists and was residing in Quaker Hill, Connecticut. [Information from Frances & Royal Bitgood of East Lyme, Connecticut.]

BLACK, MARY ANNE MANNING (1855-1882)
"There's a fold, both safe and happy."

The elder daughter of John Manning, Justice of the Peace in Nottingham, England, she was born there on October 10, 1855. In September 1879 she married Arthur Black. A member of the Church of England, she wrote a number of hymns before her marriage, and the above hymn was written after the death of her sister in 1878. It is included in W. R. Stevenson's School Hymns (1880).

BLAIR, HENRIETTA ELIZABETH see FANNY J. CROSBY

BODE, ALICE MARY (1849-1924)
"Once pledged by the cross."

Daughter of John E. Bode (1816-1874), Rector of Westwell, Oxon, Oxfordshire, she was born there on May 11, 1849. He became Rector at Castle Camps, Cambridgeshire, England in 1860. Her hymn was written in 1901 at Notting Hill, London and published in Hymns Ancient and Modern (1904). She was a member of the Church of England, and died on July 31, 1924.

BÖHMER, MARIA MAGDALENA (1675-1744)
"Regardless now of things below."

The sister of Just Henning Böhmer, Professor of Law at Halle University, she was born in Hamburg, Germany and never married. Her hymn was freely translated by John Wesley and appeared in Hymns and Sacred Poems (1740).

BOHEMIA, ELIZABETH STUART, QUEEN OF (1596-1662)
"This is joy, this is true pleasure,
If we best things make our treasure,
And enjoy them at full leisure."

A granddaughter of Mary, Queen of Scots, and daughter of King James VI of Scotland (afterwards James I of England), and Anne of Denmark, she was born at Falkland Castle in Fifeshire, Scotland in August 1596. In February 1613 she married Frederick V, Palatine Elector, and resided at Heidelberg, Germany. He was elected King of Bohemia on August 26, 1619 and they arrived at Prague (now in Czechoslovakia) on October 31, 1619. But the Protestant forces of the king were defeated by the Catholic League at the Battle of Prague on November 8, 1620 and Frederick and Elizabeth fled to Brandenburg, then to The Hague, The Netherlands, where they lived in exile. Her husband died on November 29, 1632. During her 40 years in exile, under the protection of the Prince of Orange, she lived in moderate circumstances, without the retinue of 440 servants, but remained cheerful, wrote poetry, and was known as the "Queen of Hearts" because of her charming personality. Finally her nephew, King Charles II, allowed her to return to England in 1661, and she died at Westminster on February 13, 1662. Seven of her thirteen children predeceased her. Her daughter, Sophia, married Ernest Augustus, Elector of Hanover, and was the mother of King George I of England.

BONAR, JANE CATHERINE LUNDIE (1821-1884)
"Fade, fade, each earthly joy,
Jesus is mine. "

She was born at the Kelso Manse on the Tweed River near
Melrose, Scotland in December 1821 where her father, Rev.
Robert Lundie, was the parish minister. Her elder sister,
Mary, married the Rev. William W. Duncan, a Presbyterian
minister. Jane Catherine married the famous hymnist Dr.
Horatio Bonar in 1843. Her hymns appeared in Dr. Bonar's
Songs for the Wilderness (1843-44) and in his Bible Hymn
Book (1845). She died in Edinburgh, Scotland on December
3, 1884. Her hymn (above) appeared in The American Ser-
vice Hymnal (1968); and The Baptist Standard Hymnal (1973).

BOND, CARRIE JACOBS SMITH (1862-1946)
"God remembers when the world forgets. "

Composer, hymnist, songwriter, and publisher, she was born
at Janesville, Wisconsin on August 11, 1862. When she was
only seven years old she was badly scalded, and never fully
recovered from the trauma. In 1880 she married E. J.
Smith and they had one son, but were later divorced. In
1887 she married Dr. Francis Bond who took up his medical
practice in the small mining town of Iron River, Michigan.
Then tragedy struck--the mines closed, they had no income,
Dr. Bond slipped on an icy pavement, and fell. He died
five days later (1895). She moved to Chicago with her nine
year old son and for the next six years lived on one meal
a day. During this time she wrote 32 songs although she
had no musical training whatsoever. She formed the Bond
Shop and printed her own songs. With an income of less
than $8. 00 per month, she managed somehow. To increase
her income she sang her own songs in night clubs in Chicago.
About 1901 she published Seven Songs which included "I Love
You Truly. " It sold over one million copies. While staying
at the Mission Inn at Riverside, California in 1909 she drove
up to Mount Rubidoux to see the sunset and wrote "The End
of a Perfect Day" which sold over five million copies in its
first wave of popularity. In 1932, in a fit of depression,
her only child committed suicide. But despite all her trage-
dies, she felt she had a good life. She was entertained in
The White House by President and Mrs. Theodore Roosevelt
and she was thrilled when she heard the soldiers singing
"The End of a Perfect Day" in camps during World War I.
She died at Hollywood, California on December 28, 1946.

BONDS, MARGARET (1913-1972)
    Arrangement--"Lord I just can't keep from crying. "

Black composer, arranger, conductor, pianist, and writer,
she was born at Chicago, Illinois on March 3, 1913 and was
educated at Northwestern University, Evanston, Illinois (B. M. ;
M. M.), Juilliard in New York City, and studied privately.
She won scholarships from the National Association of Negro
Musicians, Julius Rosenwald, the Rodman Wanamaker Award,
etc.   She toured as a pianist and served as Chairman of
Afro-American Music for the Eastern Region and on the National Association of Negro Musicians.   She composed Mass
in d and other works.   She made numerous arrangements of
negro spirituals--"I'll reach to heaven, " "Ezekiel saw the
wheel, " etc.

BOOTH, CORNELIE IDA ERNESTINE SCHOCH (1864-1919)
    "Bring to the Saviour thy burden of grief. "

Composer, hymnist and songwriter, one of three talented
sisters, she was the daughter of a Dutch military colonel,
and was born in The Netherlands on October 13, 1864.   Upon
his retirement from military service he joined The Salvation
Army and was given the rank of Colonel responsible for its
work in Holland.   Her sisters were married to Lt. Colonel
Fritz Malan and Commissioner W. Elwin Oliphant.   Cornelie
was married to Herbert Booth in Congress Hall, Clapton.
Her compositions "A Perfect Trust" with its refrain "O for
a deeper ...   O for a perfect trust in the Lord!" and "Holy
Spirit, seal me I pray" appeared in Songs of Peace and War
at the time of her marriage.   Her hymn above appeared in
Canadian War Cry (1893); The Musical Salvationist (April
1894); and in The Song Book of the Salvation Army (1930).
Her hymn "Have you heard the angels singing?" appeared in
the 1953 song book.

BOOTH, EVANGELINE CORY (1865-1950)
    "Dark shadows were falling, my spirit appalling. "

Composer and hymnist, she was born at Hackney, England,
a suburb of London on December 25, 1865, the seventh of
eight children of Catherine Mumford and William Booth,
founders of the Salvation Army.   She was raised a Methodist,
self educated in music, and was selling the War Cry on the
streets at age fifteen.   She composed several Salvation Army

hymns, the best known being "The Word of God." She became Field Commander of Canada at Toronto, Ontario in
1896 and the American Commander-in-Chief in 1904 and a
United States citizen in 1923. Upon her retirement in 1939
she resided at Hartsdale, New York until her death on July
17, 1950. Her hymns appeared in The Song Book of The
Salvation Army (1953).

BOOTH-CLIBBORN, CATHERINE (1858-1955)
    "O spotless Lamb, I come to Thee."

The third of eight children and eldest daughter of Catherine
Mumford and William Booth, founders of The Salvation Army,
she was born at Gateshead, England on September 18, 1858.
Catherine was an evangelistic preacher and was a pioneer in
Army work in France and Switzerland. She preached that
"Christ is the Son of man, and unless He was so He could
not have brought healing to the broken hearts of men." She
preached in the streets of Paris, and in cafes and dance
halls, and wherever she could be heard. She was mobbed
and robbed, and suffered vile threats. She was condemned
by the Roman Catholic church, and imprisoned in Neuchâtel.
In time she was accepted, even by the Catholic priests, who
admired her sanctified courage. She became known as "Le
Maréchale," a term of affection by the masses.

On February 8, 1887 she married Arthur S. Clibborn,
and he changed his name to Booth-Clibborn. The Booth-
Clibborns resigned their commissions in January, 1902, but
le Maréchale continued her preaching. She died on May 9,
1955, in her 97th year. Her hymn above appeared in the
War Cry (October 28, 1882); in Salvation Music, Vol. 2
(1899); and in The Song Book of the Salvation Army (1899).
Her hymn "O Lamb of God, Thou wonderful Sin-bearer" appeared in The Musical Salvationist (June 1888), and in The
Song Book of the Salvation Army (1899 & 1953 editions).

BOOTH-HELLBERG, LUCY MILWARD (1868-1953)
    "Sins of years are all numbered."

Composer and hymnist, the youngest child of William and
Catherine Booth, she was born at 1 Cambridge Lodge Villas,
Hackney, London, England on April 28, 1868. As a young
woman, she suffered several periods of illness, during which
time she wrote lyrics and composed the melodies for them.

After spending some time in The Salvation Army, she married Emanuel D. Hellberg, a Swedish officer in the Army. They worked together in India, Switzerland, and France. He changed his name to Booth-Hellberg. After his death in 1909, Mrs. Booth-Hellberg continued as a territorial commander in Denmark, South America, and in Norway. When her mother was dying, at Clacton-on-Sea, England, Lucy stayed up all night with her mother, who told Lucy to love backsliders, and to pray for sinners. Upon returning by train to London, she wrote her hymn, and later set the words to music. She died on July 18, 1953. Her hymn appeared in The Musical Salvationist (November 1890) and in The Song Book of the Salvation Army (1899; 1953).

BOOTH-TUCKER, EMMA MOSS (1860-1903)
"O my heart is full of music and of gladness. "

Fourth child of Catherine and William Booth, she was born at Gateshead, England on January 8, 1860. At that time Mr. Booth was superintendent minister of the Methodist New Connexion. She traveled with her parents to different parts of England during the time Mr. Booth was an evangelist preacher, and from 1865 in London where he held his revival meetings. Mr. Booth established training homes for men and women to study to be officers in The Salvation Army, and Emma was appointed Training Home Mother. On April 10, 1888 Emma married Frederick St. George de Lautour Tucker, and he changed his name to Booth-Tucker. Some five thousand people attended the wedding in Congress Hall, Clapton. The Booth-Tuckers traveled to India, Ceylon, and to the United States to continue their missionary work. She was known as the Consul. Emma was killed in a railway accident at Deak Lake, near Marceline, Missouri on October 28, 1903. Her hymn appeared in The War Cry (August 10, 1895); in The Musical Salvationist (October 1896); and in The Song Book of the Salvation Army (1899; 1953).

BORTHWICK, JANE LAURIE (1813-1897)
"Be still, my soul; the Lord is on thy side. " (Original hymn by Katharine von Schlegel)

"Come, labor on. Who dares stand idle on the harvest plain?"

Translator and versifier, she also wrote some original hymns (the second one above is an original). She was born in Edinburgh, Scotland on April 9, 1813. Her hymns were translated with her sister, Sarah B. Findlater, and published in Hymns from the Land of Luther (between 1854 and 1884). Their hymns were published in Thoughts for Thankful Hours (1857). She died at Edinburgh on September 7, 1897. More recently her hymns appeared in the American (1968); Christian Science (1937); Episcopal (1940); Lutheran (1941); Methodist (1966); Presbyterian (1955); Songs of Praise (1931) hymnals and in The Pilgrim Hymnal (1958).

BOURDILLON, MARY COTTERILL (1819-1870)
    "Blessed Jesus, wilt Thou hear us?"

Daughter of the Reverend Joseph Cotterill, sometime rector of Blakeney, Norfolk, England and Jane Boak Cotterill, the hymnist, she was born at Ampton, Suffolk, England on August 30, 1819. She was a member of the Church of England and married E. D. Bourdillon. Her hymns appeared in A Mother's Hymns for Her Children (1849). She died at Dresden, Germany on February 19, 1870.

BOURIGNON, ANTOINETTE (1616-1680)
    "Venez, Jesus mon salutaire."
    "Come, Saviour Jesus, from above."

A child of wealthy parents, she was born at Lisle, France on January 13, 1616. On two occasions her parents tried to force her into a marriage she did not desire, and she fled from her home. After her father died in 1648, leaving her a considerable fortune, and desiring to do good with the money, she took charge of a foundling hospital in 1653. She joined the order of Augustines in 1667, but later renounced Roman Catholicism and attracted great attention by her discourses and tracts. She was hounded and persecuted and fled from place to place and finally found peace in The Netherlands. She died at Franeker, Friesland on October 30, 1680. Her writings were published in 19 volumes at Amsterdam, The Netherlands (1686). Her book, The Light of the World, was translated into English and had a wide sale in Britain. Her hymn appeared in the Methodist Hymnal (1911) and The Song Book of the Salvation Army (1953).

BOYE, BRIGITTE KATERINE JOHANSEN HERTZ (1742-1824)
"Han er opstanden! Store Bud!"
"He is risen! Glorious Lord!"

"O Lue fra Guds Kjaerlighted. "
"Holy Spirit, God of Love, Who our night dost brighten. "

The daughter of Jens Johansen and Dorothea Henriksdatter, she was born at Gentofte, Denmark on March 7, 1742. Her father was in royal service and Brigitte was the eldest of seven children. In 1763 she married Herman Hertz, forester of Vordingborg, and within five years she bore him four children. During this time she studied German, French, and English and translated many poetic works. Prince Frederick of Denmark decided to issue a new hymnal, and instructed his secretary, O. H. Guldberg to compile one. In 1773 he issued a call to the public to write hymns. Brigitte started writing hymns for the new hymnal when her husband became ill and lost his job. She applied for help to Guldberg, who brought the matter to the attention of Prince Frederick. The Prince ordered both of her sons educated at the crown's expense, and after her husband died, she received maintenance expenses for three years. Together with Guldberg and Bishop L. Harboc, she published in 1778 Salmebog, eller en Samling af gamle... ("A hymn-book, or a collection of old and new hymns, for the honour of God, and the edification of His church"). The collection contained 124 original hymns by her and 24 of her translations. In that same year she married Hans Boye, an employee in the customs house in Copenhagen, Denmark. She died on October 17, 1824. Her hymns appear in The Lutheran Hymnal (1941).

BRADFORD, ELLEN K. (b. 1850)
"Oh, tender and sweet was the Master's voice. "

Apparently the daughter of Arial C. Keith, she was born at Palmer, Massachusetts about 1850. Her hymns were published in Ira D. Sankey's Gospel Hymns and in his Sacred Songs and Solos (1881). We have been unable to locate her place and date of death, but she did reside in Palmer, Massachusetts prior to her marriage to N. K. Bradford. More recently her hymn appeared in the Baptist Hymnal (1973). [Information from Malcolm D. Gibb, Principal, Faith Baptist Church, Palmer, Massachusetts in a letter dated July 6, 1982.]

BRADFORD, LOUISE LARKINS (b. 1924)
"Our God, the great Provider. "

Born at New York, New York on January 25, 1924, she was graduated from Western College for Women at Oxford, Ohio and received her M. A. from Radcliffe in Cambridge, Massachusetts. She married S. Sydney Bradford. She taught choral music at Emma Willard School in Troy, New York, at Kent Place School in Summit, New Jersey and at Roland Park Country School in Baltimore, Maryland. In May 1982 she was living in Philadelphia, Pennsylvania. Her hymn, "How lovely is the House of God" and the one above appeared in Twelve New Hymns for Children, published by The Hymn Society of America (1965).

BRANDENBURG, LUISE HENRIETTE, ELECTRESS OF (1627-1677)
"Jesus meine Zuversicht. "
"Jesus, my Redeemer lives. "
"Jesus Christ, my sure Defence. " (Various translations).

Daughter of Friedrich Heinrich, Prince of Nassau-Orange and Stadtholder of the United Netherlands, she was born at 'S Gravenhage (The Hague) on November 27, 1627. She was a member of the Reformed (Dutch) Church. On December 7, 1646 she married, at The Hague, Friedrich Wilhelm Hohenzollern, Elector of Brandenburg. After her father died in June, she and her husband lived in his castle at Cleve, where their first child, Wilhelm Heinrich, was born in May 1648. In that autumn she and her husband set off for Berlin, but the severe winter storms were too much for their infant son, and he died at Wesel in 1649. It was almost six years before they had another son, and it looked like the Hohenzollern family line would perish. It was at this time she reportedly wrote her hymn, in despair. Her second son was born in 1655 but died in 1674. Her third son, born at Königsberg on July 11, 1657, later became Friedrich I, King of Prussia. Her fourth son was born in 1666. Her hymn appeared in the Crüger-Runge Gesang-Buch (1653) and later in the Moravian Hymn Book (1769); A. T. Russell's Psalms and Hymns (1851); the Ohio Lutheran Hymnal (1880); and other hymnals. She died at Berlin, Germany on June 18, 1667. More recently her hymn appeared in the Evangelical and Reformed Church Hymnal (1941).

BRANSCOMBE, GINA (1881-1977)
Chorale--The Lord is our fortress

Composer, conductor, educator and songwriter, she was
born at Picton, Ontario, Canada on November 4, 1881 and
was educated at the Chicago Musical College (B. M.), Whitman College (hon. M. A.), and studied privately with Engel-
bert Humperdinck in Germany, among others. She headed
the piano department of Whitman College Conservatory (1907-
09), and married John F. Tenney. She conducted the Branscombe Choral, State Chorus of New Jersey, Contemporary
Club Choral in Newark, New Jersey, MacDowell Choral in
New Jersey, etc. She composed Pilgrims of Destiny (a cantata, 1928) and other pieces. She died in New York City on
July 21, 1977.

BRAUNSCHWEIG, ELISABETH, DUCHESS OF (1510-1558)
"Joyful I will be and bless His holy name. "

Daughter of Joachim I of Hohenzollern, Elector of Brandenburg, and Princess Elisabeth, sister of Christian II, King
of Denmark, at age 15 she married Erich I, Duke of
Braunschweig-Calenberg, who was 40 years her senior.
She bore him three daughters and one son. Elisabeth and
her brother, Joachim II, turned Protestant, and her husband,
Eric I remained neutral. Her husband died in 1540, and
since her son, Erich II, was only twelve years old, she was
named Regent. After her son became Erich II in 1546, she
married Poppo, Duke of Henneberg, a staunch Lutheran.
But after the battle of Mühlberg in April of 1547, when the
Protestants were defeated, Erich II restored the Catholic
faith to his country to the horror and despair of his mother.
But the Protestants won the battle of Sievershausen in 1553,
and at the Peace of Augsburg in 1555 the Lutherans gained
legal status. One price of the peace was the expulsion of
Elisabeth, who left Munden for Hanover with her daughter
Katherine. After she left Braunschweig she wrote her hymns
of joy, even though her household of 200 servants had van-
ished and her income was cut off. After three years she
was allowed to return home to her son's castle where she
died on May 25, 1558. Her hymns appeared in "Lieder der
Herzogin Elisabeth, " Zeitschrift der Gesellschaft für nieder-
sächische Kirchengeschichte, XIX (1914) 147-208.

BRAWN, MARY ANN (1828-1903)
"O Thou who art in every place. "

Daughter of the Rev. Samuel Brawn, for 51 years the pastor
of the Baptist Chapel at Loughton, Essex, England, she was
born there on August 15, 1828. Her hymn appeared in the
Rev. Samuel Green's Domestic Worshipper (1850). Another
hymn, "O Father, we are weak," appeared in the Methodist
Sunday School Hymn Book (1879). She died on December 16,
1903.

BRECK, CARRIE ELLIS (1855-1934)
    "Face to face with Christ, my savior. "

She was born in Walden, Vermont on January 22, 1855 and
spent her childhood there. Later she lived in New Jersey,
married Frank A. Breck and resided in Portland, Oregon.
They had five daughters and she was an active member of
the Presbyterian church. Another hymn, "Ev'ry prayer will
find its answer," appeared in the Baptist Hymnal (1973) and
"There was one who was willing to die in my stead" appeared
in the American Service Hymnal (1968). One recording of
"Help somebody today" appeared in Phonolog Reports of Los
Angeles. The above hymn appeared in the Baptist (1975);
Broadman (1977); Family of God (1976); and American (1968)
hymnals with seven recordings listed in Phonolog Reports.
She died at Portland, Oregon on March 27, 1934.

BREWER, EDITH GADDIS (d. 1951)
    "Prayer with our waking thought ascends,
    Great God of light. "

She joined the Church of Christ, Scientist on November 5,
1909 and her hymn appeared in the Christian Science Hymnal
(1937). She died on May 11, 1951. Two of her hymns appeared in the hymnal.

BRIEL, MARIE (1896-1960)
    Ritual music for The Holy Communion

Composer and organist, she was born at Peru, Illinois on
February 14, 1896 and educated at Northwestern University
School of Music (Mus. B., 1919; Mus. M., 1925), Evanston,
Illinois. She taught at Marionville College in Missouri, at
Iowa Wesleyan College at Mt. Pleasant, Iowa; Columbia School
of Music in Chicago; American Conservatory of Music in
Chicago; and at the National College of Education in Evanston,

Illinois. She was organist-director of the Methodist Episco-
pal Church in Wilmette, Illinois. Her music appeared in the
Methodist Hymnal (1935). She was married to J. William
Humphries and she died on May 24, 1960. [Information
from Patrick M. Quinn, University Archivist, Northwestern
University Library, Evanston, Illinois.]

BROCK, BLANCHE KERR (1888-1958)
　　"He's a wonderful savior to me."

Composer and pianist, she was born at Greenfork, Indiana
on February 3, 1888 and educated at the American Conservatory of Music in Chicago, Illinois and at the Indianapolis
Conservatory in Indianapolis, Indiana. She was a solo pianist with evangelistic preachers. Her husband, Virgil P.
Brock, wrote hymns and she composed the music for them.
She died at Winona Lake, Indiana on January 3, 1958.

BRONTË, ANNE (1820-1849)
　　"Believe not those who say
　　The upward path is smooth."

The sister of Charlotte and Emily Brontë, she was born at
Haworth on January 17, 1820 and baptized at Thornton, Eng-
land. She was raised in the Church of England (Episcopal),
and is best known for her novels Agnes Grey (1847) and The
Tenant of Wildfell Hall (1848). She died on May 28, 1849.
Her sister, Charlotte, wrote "On the Death of Anne Brontë":

　　　　There's little joy in life for me,
　　　　And little terror in the grave;
　　　　I've lived the parting hour to see,
　　　　Of one I would have died to save.

Anne's hymn appeared in Songs of Praise (1931).

BRONTË, CHARLOTTE (1816-1855)
　　"The human heart has hidden treasures."

The daughter of Maria Branwell and Patrick Brunty (who
changed his name to Brontë), she was born at Thornton,
Yorkshire, England on April 21, 1816 and was the sister of
Anne and Emily Brontë. She was raised a Methodist, and on
June 29, 1854 she married the Reverend Arthur B. Nicholls

and they resided at Haworth. She is best known for her
novel, Jane Eyre (1847). She died at Haworth, England on
March 31, 1855. In a letter to George H. Lewes, after
Lewes criticized Charlotte Brontë's portrayal of Mrs. Pryor
in Shirley, as recorded in The Life of Charlotte Brontë
(1857) by Elizabeth Cleghorn Gaskill, she wrote the very
famous lines: "I can be on guard against my enemies, but
God deliver me from my friends. "

BRONTË, EMILY JANE (1818-1848)
"No coward soul is mine. "

The sister of Anne and Charlotte Brontë, she was born at
Thornton, England on July 30, 1818 and baptized there. She
is best known for her novel, Wuthering Heights (1847). She
died on December 19, 1848. Emily's hymn appeared in
Songs of Praise (London 1931).

BROOK, FRANCES (b. 1870)
"O Lord, with Thee 'tis but a little matter. "

The daughter of the Rev. James Brook, M. A. of Helme
Edge, Meltham, Huddersfield, she was born at Bath, England. A member of the Church of England, she also wrote
"There is singing in the Homeland" and other hymns which
were published in the Church Missionary Hymn Book (1899).
She was living in Scarborough, Yorkshire, England in the
early 1920s.

BROTHERTON, ALICE WILLIAMS (1850-1930)
"Consider the lillies, how stately they grow. "

She was born in Cambridge City, Indiana. "I found the marriage of her parents, Ruth H. Johnson to Alfred B. Williams
in 1843. Alice's own marriage to William E. Brotherton of
Cincinnati, Ohio was on October 18, 1876 ... She was a
member of one of Cambridge City's most extraordinary fam-
ilies--with a brilliant record of accomplishment for four generations. I didn't realize she wrote hymns, all references
stress her teaching of Shakespeare and her work for Century
Magazine and the Atlantic Monthly. " [Letter from Pauline
Montgomery, Conklin House, Cambridge City, Indiana, February 1982.] Her hymn first appeared in Horder's Worship
Song (1905).

BROWN, ANN (b. 1908)
    "Grace, love, and peace abide. "

Daughter of Mary Rives and Wiley B. Brown, she was born
at Meridian, Mississippi on February 20, 1908 and raised in
Shreveport, Louisiana where she graduated from Centenary
College summa cum laude (1927). She was a school teacher
in Shreveport and in 1936 married Walter Hines Sims, composer and hymnist. They moved to Nashville, Tennessee
where she became head of the Latin Department of Montgomery Bell Academy. Her hymn appeared in the Baptist
Hymnal (1956) of which her husband was an editor.

BROWN, JEANNETTE ELOISE PERKINS (1887-1960)
    "Thanks be to God for blessings. "

Born at Grand Island, Nebraska, she was educated at Bradford College for Girls in Boston, Massachusetts and was
married to Edward B. Brown. She published As Children
Worship (1936) and A Little Book of Singing Graces (1946)
which included the above hymn. In addition she collected
and edited A Little Book of Bedtime Songs and contributed
to Songs for Early Childhood and Songs and Hymns for Primary Children.

BROWN, LEILA JACKSON (b. 1930)
    "Listen to our prayer. "

Translator and versifier (text from India). She was born
at Grand Rapids, Michigan on May 31, 1930 and studied at
the American Conservatory of Music in Chicago and at Al-
bion College (BA., 1952). She served as a Methodist missionary in India and taught in the secondary schools in Luck-
now (1952-55) and at Ipoh, Perak, Malaysia (1956-59) and at
Petaling, Jaya, Selanar, Malaysia (1961-65). Cooperative
Recreation Service of Delaware, Ohio has published collections of oriental folk music which she was instrumental in
assembling, Joyful Songs of India (1956), and with Don Smith,
Malaya Sings (1956 & 1967). Her hymn appeared in the
Methodist Hymnal (1966).

BROWN, MARGARET WISE (1892-1952)
    "Jesus calls me, I must follow,
    Follow Him today. "

A composer born in New York City on May 23, 1892, she
was educated at Hollins College in Hollins, Virginia. The
words and music for the above hymn were written with Howard L. Brown (1889-1965). She wrote childrens' books,
hymns, and songs and died at Nice, France on November 11,
1952. Her hymn appeared in Joyfully Sing--A Hymnal for
Juniors (1968).

BROWN, MARY (1856-1918)
     "It may not be on the mountain's heights,
     Or over the stormy sea...
     I'll go where you want me to go, dear Lord. "

Born at Natick, Rhode Island, on May 19, 1856, she taught
school in Norwich, Connecticut and over twenty years in
Jewett City, Connecticut. "I was given your letter at church
yesterday as I had known Mary Brown. She and her family
lived for many years in my grandfather's two-family house
and they were friends as well as neighbors. She was an active member of the Baptist Church and a Sunday School teacher. The Christian Endeavor Consecration hymn was first
published by Silver Burdett & Co. 1892 in a songbook, Our
Best Endeavor, with music by Charles E. Prior, a local organist, and the title "Go Stand and Speak. " In a 1904 hymnal
it was titled "I'll Go Where You Want Me to Go" with the
tune by Carrie Rounesfell. I am sure Mary Brown would be
happy to know that her little poem was still speaking to people after nearly a hundred years. " [Letter dated March 22,
1982 from Mrs. Lillian Cathcart, Jewett City, Connecticut.]
Mary Brown died at Jewett City on January 22, 1918 during
the terrible World War I flue epidemic. Her hymn appeared
in the American (1968); Baptist (1973); and Family of God
(1976) hymnals.

BROWN, PHOEBE HINSDALE (1783-1861)
     "I love to steal awhile away. "

Daughter of George Hinsdale, she was born at Canaan, New
York on May 1, 1783 and left an orphan at age two. She
was eighteen years old before she learned to read. Always
poor, she did not improve her lifestyle by marrying a jour-
neyman painter, Timothy H. Brown, who took her to Ellington, Tolland County, Connecticut. Here she wrote some
poems which appeared in the Religious Intelligencer at New
Haven, Connecticut, which was published by her brother,

Nathan Whiting Hinsdale.   Here she also wrote her "Twilight
Hymn" about loving to steal away from her household chores
to her garden to pray.   Later she and her husband were living in Monson, Massachusetts when the evangelist Ashael Nettleton came to town.   He later wrote that "I found Mrs.
Brown living in a very humble cottage. "   Nettleton published
four of her hymns, including the one above, in his Village
Hymns (1824).   Other hymns she wrote appeared in S. C.
Brace's Parish Hymns (Philadelphia, 1843).   She lived in
Monson from 1820-50, then moved to Henry, Illinois.   Her
son, Dr. Samuel R. Brown, a Congregational Minister, the
first missionary from America to Japan, went out there under the auspices of the Reformed (Dutch) Church.   Phoebe
Brown died at Marshall, Illinois on October 10, 1861.   More
recently her hymn appeared in the Methodist (1955); Evangelical Lutheran; Augustana Lutheran; Concordia (Lutheran);
Presbyterian USA (1933); Brethren; Baptist (1958); Mennonite
and other hymnals.

BROWNE, MARY ANNE (1812-1844)
        Tune--PLYMOUTH or BROWNE

A composer, she was born in England and was a relative of
the noted poet Felicia Browne Hemans.   She composed her
tune PLYMOUTH for the hymn "The breaking waves dashed
high" by Mrs. Hemans about the Pilgrims landing at Plymouth, Massachusetts in 1620.   Her tune appeared in New
Hymn and Tune Book (Unitarian, 1914).

BROWNING, ELIZABETH BARRETT (1809-1861)
        "Since without Thee we do no good. "

Daughter of Mary Graham and Edward Moulton, who later
changed his name to Barrett, she was born at Coxhoe Hall,
parish of Kelloe, Durham, England on March 6, 1806 and in
1846 she married the poet Robert Browning.   Her hymn appeared in Hymns Ancient and Modern (1875).   She died at
Florence, Italy on June 30, 1861.   More recently her hymn
appeared in the Methodist Hymnal (1925).

BUCHANAN, ANNABEL MORRIS (1888-1983)
        Tune--LAND OF REST

A composer, she was born at Groesbeck, Texas on October

22, 1888 and was graduated from the London Conservatory of Music in Dallas (1907) and attended the Guilmant Organ School in New York City. She taught music in Oklahoma and Texas for eight years, then at Stonewall Jackson College in Abington, Virginia for three years. In 1912 she married John Preston Buchanan. She was president of the Virginia Federation of Music Clubs (1927-30), co-founder of the Virginia State Choral Festival and director of the White Top Music Festival and Conference (1931-41). Her tune is a harmonization of an old Scottish or North English tune and was the setting for the hymn "Jerusalem, my happy home," in The Pilgrim Hymnal (1958). She died at Paducah, Kentucky on January 6, 1983, where she resided, and was buried in Marion, Virginia. [Letter from Mack H. Sturgill of Marion, Virginia.]

BUCHANAN, VIOLET NITA CRITCHETT (1891-1975)
"O day of joy and wonder."

The daughter of Sir Anderson Critchett, M. D., she married Andrew Sinclair Buchanan and they resided in London, England. She was a member of the Church of England. She wrote numerous hymns which appeared in various hymn books. The hymn above appeared in the Anglican Hymn Book (1965). She died on July 26, 1975.

BUELL, HARRIETT EUGENIA PECK (1834-1910)
"My Father is rich in houses and lands."

She was born in Cazenovia, New York on November 2, 1834. One summer in 1878, while at the Thousand Island Park in upper New York State, she wrote the hymn "Child of a King" and sent it to the Northern Christian Advocate in Syracuse, New York, which published the poem. It was first sung as a hymn in the Manlius Methodist Church in Manlius, New York. She died at Washington, D. C., on February 6, 1910. Her hymn appeared in Hymns for the Living Church (1974) and in the Baptist Hymnal (1975).

BULMER, AGNES COLLINSON (1775-1837)
"Thou who hast in Zion laid."

Born in London, England on August 31, 1775, she was raised a Methodist and in 1793 she was married to Joseph Bulmer.

Her hymns appeared in the Supplement to the Wesleyan Hymn Book (1830) and her own book, Messiah's Kingdom, was published in 1833. She died on August 30, 1837. More recently her hymn appeared in The Liturgy & Offices of Worship (Moravian).

BURKALOW, ANATASIA VAN (b. 1911)
"Almighty God, who made all things. "

Composer and hymnist, daughter of Mable R. Ramsay and James T. van Burkalow, she was born at Buchanan, New York on March 16, 1911 and educated at Hunter College (B. A., 1931) and Columbia University (Ph. D. , 1934) in New York City. She was a member of the faculty of Hunter College in New York City (1938-75), and was professor of geology and geography. "I have been organist and choir director in several New York City churches, though I gave up that work in 1965 because of the pressure of my college duties. For my choir I made numerous special arrangements and some original compositions, but none of these have been published.... Four of my hymns have been published by The Hymn Society of America. " [Letter dated 4/29/82 from Miss van Burkalow from New York City. Her article, "60 Years of The Hymn Society of America 1922-82" was published in The Hymn (January 1982), pages 12-15.] "High time it is to seek the Lord" was published in 15 New Bible Hymns (1966), two hymns in 16 New Hymns on the Stewardship of the Environment (1973) and the above hymn in New Hymns for America (1976), all published by The Hymn Society of America. She is a Methodist.

BURKE, CHRISTIAN CAROLINE ANNA (1857-1944)
"Lord of life and King of glory. "

Born at Camberwell, London, England on September 18, 1857, her poems were published in numerous magazines and she collected them in The Flowering of the Almond Tree and Other Poems (1896; 1901). Her hymn above appeared in The Treasury, London, February 1904. She died at Saffron Walden, Essex, England on March 4, 1944. More recently her hymn appeared in the English Baptist Hymn Book (1962) and in Hymns for the Living Church (1974).

BURLINGHAM, HANNAH KILHAM (1841-1901)
"Christ the Author of our peace. "

Translator and versifier, her translations appeared in Reid's
Praise Book in 1872 and in other hymnals. She was the
eldest daughter of Henry Burlingham of Evesham, England,
and was born there. She died at Eversham on May 15, 1901.

BURMAN, ELLEN ELIZABETH (1837-1861)
    "Teach me to live! 'tis easier far to die. "

She was born at Stratford-on-Avon, England on July 11, 1837.
Her hymn was written in 1860 and included in Shepp's Songs
of Grace and Glory in 1872.

BURROWES, ELIZABETH HAVENS (1885-1975)
    "God of the ages, by whose hand. "

Born in Detroit, Michigan on January 13, 1885, she married
Paul deNyse Burrowes and they lived in Englewood, New Jersey and raised five children. Later they moved to Berkeley,
California where she became a Presbyterian Elder and active
in St. John's Presbyterian Church in Berkeley. Her hymn
was published in World Order Hymns by The Hymn Society
of America (1958). She was the author of two books and
numerous poems and hymns. She died at Berkeley, California on March 27, 1975. More recently her hymn appeared
in The Book of Hymns (United Methodist, 1966); The Lutheran
Book of Worship (1978); and the Presbyterian hymnal.

BUTLER, MARY MAY (1841-1916)
    "Looking upward every day. "

    "O help me, Lord, this day to be. "

A granddaughter of Bishop Samuel Butler of Litchfield, England, she was the daughter of Thomas Butler, M. A. , Rector
at Langar, Notts, and Prebendary of Clifton in Lincoln Cathedral. Her hymns appeared in Mrs. Brock's Children's Hymn
Book (1881). She was the sister of Samuel Butler who wrote
The Way of All Flesh and other books. Mary founded the St.
Saviour's Home for girls in Shrewsbury. The above hymn
was written for the confirmation of her niece and was published in the English Baptist Hymn Book (1962).

BUTT, THELMA VAN EYE (1905-1972)
    "How wonderful. "

Composer, hymnist, and publisher, she was born at Crowley, Louisiana on December 17, 1905 and was educated at Southwestern Institute in Louisiana. There was one recording of her hymn listed in Phonolog Reports (1978). She died on January 17, 1972.

BYLES, BLANCHE DOUGLAS (1892-1979)
Tune--THY GREAT BOUNTY

A composer, daughter of Mary Baker and Enoch A. Douglas, she was born at Sterling, Connecticut on August 14, 1892 and was educated at Brown University, Providence, Rhode Island (A. B. , 1914) and became a school teacher at the Norwich Free Academy at Norwich, Connecticut. As a composer and organist, she had no formal training, but played the organ at a small Baptist church where she was raised, and later sang in choirs of the Madison Avenue Methodist Church and the Episcopal Chapel of the Intercession in New York City. Later she was a church organist in Los Angeles for six years. Ten of her hymns were published in the Modern Youth Hymnal. She was married to Howard T. Byles who was serving as a Lieutenant Colonel in the U. S. Army at Fort Douglas, Utah in 1945. They had one son and one daughter. Her hymn tune appeared in the Evangelical and Reformed Church Hymnal (1941). She died on May 10, 1979. [Letter from Sandra Clifford Valletta, Brown University, Providence, Rhode Island.]

BYRNE, MARY ELIZABETH (1880-1931)
"Be thou my vision, O Lord of my heart. "

Born at Dublin, Ireland on July 1, 1880, she was educated at the University of Ireland (M. A. , 1905) and became a researcher on the Board of Intermediate Education. Her treatise on England in the Age of Chaucer was awarded the chancellor's gold medal by the Royal University. Her hymn was translated by her from the ancient Irish and versified by Eleanor M. Hull. She died at Dublin on January 19, 1931. Her hymn appeared in the Broadman (1977); Christian Worship (1953); Hymns for the Family of God (1976); and Methodist (1966) hymnals; The Hymn-book Presbyterian (1955) and The Pilgrim Hymnal (1958).

CACCINI, FRANCESCA (1588-1640)
Sacred opera--Il martirio di Sant' Agata

Composer, singer, and harpsichordist, the daughter of Giulio Caccini, singer and composer, she was born at Florence, Italy on 18 September 1588 and studied under her father. She was married to Giovanni Battista Signorini and they had two daughters. She collaborated with Giovanni Battista da Gagliano on her sacred opera (above) which was produced at Florence on 10 February 1622. She was the first woman composer of an opera-ballet, La liberazione di Ruggiero dall' isola d'Alcina (words by Ferdinando Saracinelli), which was produced at the Tuscan court at the Villa Poggio Imperiale, near Florence, on 2 February 1625. She died at Lucca, Italy about 1640.

CADDELL, CECILIA MARY (1813-1877)
"Behold the lilies of the field. "

"Dear Saint, who on thy natal day. "

"Hail, Mary, only sinless child. "

Nine of her hymns appeared in H. Formby's Catholic Hymns in 1853. She wrote numerous books, including Blind Agnese; or, the Little Spouse of the Blessed Sacrament (Dublin, 1856); History of the Missions in Japan and Paraguay (London, 1856); and Wild Times: A Tale of the Days of Queen Elizabeth (1865). More recently her hymns appeared in the Presbyterian Hymnbook (1955).

CAIN, FLORENCE EMILY (1881-1973)
"God of truth from everlasting. "

Daughter of a Methodist circuit rider, she was born at the parsonage in Cicero, Indiana and was educated at DePauw University, Greencastle, Indiana. Later she served as an executive director for the YWCA and was a publicity writer for Stetson University, DeLand, Florida. She was active in the American Association for the United Nations and the League of Women Voters. She composed music for the piano, but we don't know of any published compositions. After her retirement she lived in Glendale, California. She died there on September 13, 1973. Her hymns were published by The Hymn Society of America, the above hymn in Hymns for the 70's (1970) and "O God who made this wonderous world" in The Stewardship of the Environment (Ecology--1973).

CALDWELL, MARY ELIZABETH GLOCKLER (b. 1909)
"Tell us shepherd maids. "

Conductor, organist, hymnist, and composer, she was born
at Tacoma, Washington on August 1, 1909, was graduated
from the University of California at Berkeley (A. B. , 1930)
and studied at the Munich Conservatory (1930-31). On October 14, 1932 she married Philip G. Caldwell. She served
as organist and choir director at the Scotia (N. Y.) Reformed
Church (1933-40), First Baptist Church of Pasadena, California (1941-44), San Marino Community Church from 1948.
She has composed cantatas, and her hymn above had two
recordings listed in Phonolog Reports (1978) of Los Angeles,
California. "I have to admit that your letter provided a bit
of comic relief to our otherwise very businesslike weekly
staff meeting at church! Yes, I'm still very much alive and
am finishing my 34th year as organist at the San Marino
Community Church--I'm still a size 8 and climb mountains
in the summertime as you may see by the enclosed article
which I am sending. " [Letter of February 17, 1982.] Her
first published anthem, The Carol of the Little King has
sold 700, 000 copies, and her second opera, The Gift of Song,
about Franz Gruber, the composer of "Silent Night, " has
been performed over 200 times in America, England, and
Australia, and her third opera, The Night of the Star is about
a young shepherd boy who stayed behind to help an angel with
a broken wing.

CAMP, MABEL JOHNSTON (1871-1937)
"Lift up your heads, Pilgrims aweary. "
Tune--CAMP

Composer, hymnist and pianist, the daughter of a banker,
she was born at Chanute, Kansas on November 25, 1871 and
attended a girl's school in Steubenville, Ohio. She was an
accomplished pianist, had a beautiful contralto voice, and
was also a composer of hymns. She married Norman H.
Camp, an attorney, who, after attending one of Dwight L.
Moody's Union Bible Classes taught by William R. Newell,
was converted to Christianity with Christ as his savior, as
was his wife. He became an evangelist teacher. Her hymns
and hymn tunes were published by the leaders of the Moody
Memorial Church in Chicago. She died in Chicago, Illinois
on May 25, 1937. Her hymns and tunes appeared in the
American Service (1968); Great Hymns of the Faith (1972);
and Hymns for the Living Church (1974).

CAMPBELL, EMMA F. R. (1830-1919)
"What means this eager, anxious throng,
Pressing our busy streets along?...
Voices in accent hushed reply
'Jesus of Nazareth passeth by.'"

Daughter of Abner Campbell, she was born at Newark, New
Jersey on November 16, 1830. Emma and her sister established a private school in Morristown, New Jersey in the
1860s. She was graduated from the Packer Institute for Girls
in Brooklyn in 1859. A spectacular religious revival took
place in Newark in 1864, which Miss Campbell attended, and
there she wrote her hymn, "Jesus of Nazareth passeth by."
Ira D. Sankey, the noted evangelist singer and preacher,
sang the hymn in almost every corner of the world. For
37 years Miss Campbell taught Sunday School in the First
Presbyterian Church in Morristown, New Jersey. Her hymn
was published under the signature "Eta," the Greek letter,
in Song Victories and also in E. P. Hammond's Praises of
Jesus (1864). She published "A New Year Thought" in December 1888, and another hymn, written by request for the
Centennial Celebration of the First Presbyterian Church in
October 1891. She also wrote children's books, Green Pas-
tures for Christ's Little Ones, Paul Preston and Better Than
Rubies. She died at Morristown, New Jersey the week be-
fore February 28, 1919. More recently Ms Campbell's hymn
appeared in The Song Book of the Salvation Army (1953).
[Information from Ms. Shelia Sweeney, Local History Research
Assistant, The Joint Free Public Library of Morristown,
New Jersey.]

CAMPBELL, JANE MONTGOMERY (1817-1878)
"Im Abfabg war's auf Erden."
"We plow the fields and scatter
The good seed on the land."

Translator and versifier, daughter of Rev. A. M. Campbell,
she was born in Paddington, London, England and taught
singing in her father's parish school. Her translations from
the German appeared in the Rev. Charles S. Bere's Garland
of Songs; or an English Liederkranz (1862) and in his Children's Chorale Book (1869). She was a member of the
Church of England (Episcopal) and published a Handbook for
Singers. She died at Bovey Tracey, South Devon, Devonshire, England on November 15, 1878. More recently her
hymn appeared in the Baptist (1973); Christian Worship (1953);

Episcopal (1940); Family of God (1976); Methodist (1966);
Presbyterian (1955) hymnals; Songs of Praise (1931) and The
Pilgrim Hymnal (1958).

CAMPBELL, MARGARET MALCOLM, LADY (1808-1841)
"Praise ye Jehovah, praise the Lord most holy. "

Eldest daughter of General Sir John Malcolm, G. C. B. , who
at the time was a Lieutenant Colonel in the British Army stationed in India, she was born there.   On June 20, 1827 she
married her cousin, Sir Alexander Thomas Cockburn-Campbell who had taken the name Campbell in 1825.   Her hymns
were published in the Plymouth Brethren Psalms and Hymns
(London: Walther, 1842) and in the Free Church Hymn-Book
(1882).   She died at Alphington, near Exeter, England on
February 6, 1841.   Her husband moved to Australia, where
he was resident magistrate at Albany, West Australia, and
died on April 23, 1871.   More recently her hymns appeared
in the Methodist (1955); Evangelical Lutheran; Church of Scotland; Presbyterian Church of Canada; and Moravian hymnals.

CAMPBELL, SUSAN F. (d. 1954)
"In love divine all earthborn fear. "

She joined the Church of Christ, Scientist on June 2, 1911
and her hymn appeared in the Christian Science Hymnal
(1937).   She died on January 22, 1954.

CAMPION, JOAN (b. 1940)
"Creator God, we give You thanks. "

Born Betty Anne J. Arner at Weissport, Pennsylvania on
April 14, 1940, she was educated at Cedar Crest College in
Allentown, Pennsylvania and at Western State College, Gun-
nison, Colorado.   She was employed by the Globe-Times in
Bethlehem, Pennsylvania and by the Times News in Lehigh-
ton, Pennsylvania and worked in public relations.   "Special
Honors: Fellowship, Memorial Foundation for Jewish Cul-
ture.   Under this grant I have written a biography called
Gisi Fleischmann and the Jewish Fight for Survival, about
one of the greatest and least-known heroines of the Holocaust.
I have also written a play about Gisi Fleischmann, Mission
to Fulfill, which is already in print; and a non-fiction novel
about her, In the Lion's Mouth, which will soon be in print.

I also lecture, mostly about Gisi. I changed my name for professional purposes, but also legally. " [Letter from Joan Campion.] Her hymn appeared in The Stewardship of the Environment (Ecology) published by The Hymn Society of America (1973). As of May 1982 she was living in Miami, Florida.

CAPERS, VALERIE (b. 1935)
    Christmas cantata--Sing About Love

Composer, conductor, and pianist, born in the Bronx, New York City on 24 May 1935, and at age six she suffered a streptococcus infection, which started as a strep throat, then entered her blood stream and affected her optic nerve, which blinded her. She earned a reputation as a classical pianist at the New York Institute for the Education of the Blind, and earned her bachelor's and master's degrees at the Juilliard School of Music in New York City (1953-60). Then she taught at the Manhattan School of Music, made several appearances in trios in New York. In 1970 she won a Creative Artists Public Service Fellowship to write her Christmas cantata, which ran two hours and fifteen minutes, and which contained gospel music, Latin rhythms, jazz, and pop music. It was first performed in 1974 at the Central Presbyterian Church in New York City, then the next two years at the Cuyahoga Community College in Cleveland, Ohio and the fourth time at Carnegie Hall in New York City on 18 December 1978. "We believe she is still living. Our records show her address to be ... Avenue, Bronx, New York 10457;' [Letter of 5/26/83 from Deborah G. Davis, Assistant Librarian, Lila Acheson Wallace Library, The Juilliard School.]

CARNEY, JULIA ABIGAIL FLETCHER (1823-1908)
    "Think gently of the erring one. "

Born at Lancaster, Massachusetts on April 6, 1823, she began writing verses as a child and at age fourteen was contributing poems to juvenile magazines. She became a primary schoolteacher in Boston in 1844 and there wrote her famous poem:

        Little drops of water,
        Little grains of sand,
        Make the mighty ocean,
        And this beauteous land.

It was first published in the Boston Primary School Reader in 1845 and more recently in Songs of Praise (1931). In 1849 she married the Rev. Thomas J. Carney, a Universalist minister. She was also a Universalist, and died at Galesburg, Illinois on November 1, 1908. Her hymn above appeared in the Methodist Hymnal (1911). More recently her hymn appeared in the Methodist (1955); Evangelical United Brethren and the Union Hymnal (Jewish).

CARPENTER, MARY (1807-1877)
"To Thee, my God, to Thee"

She was the daughter of Dr. Lant Carpenter, a Unitarian Minister in Bristol, England. Her hymn appeared in her book, Morning and Evening Meditations in 1845, and also in the Belfast Collection of 1886. Another hymn, "Father, here Thy glory praising," appeared in the Supplement of Martineau's Hymns for use at Lewin's Mead Chapel, Bristol in 1849 and 1859.

CARSON, MARTHA (b. 1921)
"Satisfied, I'm gonna walk and talk with my Lord."

"I can't stand up alone."

Hymnist, singer and guitarist, she was born in Neon, Kentucky and first appeared on radio on station WHIS in Bluefield, West Virginia in 1939.

CARY, ALICE (1820-1871)
"Along the mountain track of life."

Elder sister of Phoebe Cary, she was born near Cincinnati, Ohio and published her Poems in 1850. The hymn above appeared in Henry Ward Beecher's Plymouth Collection (1855), and another hymn, "Earth with its dark and dreadful ills," appeared in Hymns and Songs of Praise, New York (1874). Her other hymns appeared in Lyra Sacra Americana (1868) and in the Methodist Sunday School Hymn Book, London (1879). She died at Cincinnati, Ohio on February 12, 1871, five months before the death of her sister.

CARY, PHOEBE (1824-1871)
"One sweetly solemn thought
Came to me o'er and o'er. "

The younger sister of Alice Cary, she was born about eight
miles north of Cincinnati, Ohio on September 4, 1824 and
was the sixth child of seven daughters and two sons. Her
various poems and hymns were published along with those of
her sister, Alice. Phoebe was assistant editor of the Revolution, Susan B. Anthony's suffrage paper. Her hymn above
was called "Nearer Home" and appeared in her book Religious
Poems and Hymns (1852). She died at Newport, Rhode Island on July 31, 1871. More recently her hymn appeared in
The American Service Hymnal (1968); Baptist (1973); and one
recording was listed by Phonolog Reports (1978) of Los Angeles, California. With Dr. C. F. Deems, she compiled
Hymns for All Christians (1869).

CASSADAY, LILLIAN WEAVER (1861-1914)
"O Christians leagued together,
To battle for the right. "

She was active in the Italian Lutheran mission in Philadelphia, Pennsylvania and her hymn first appeared in the Luther League Review (1893), then in the Luther League Hymnal
(New York, 1894), the Lutheran Book of Worship (Philadelphia, 1899), the Common Service Book (1917) and more recently in the Lutheran Service Book and Hymnal (1958).

CASSEL, FLORA HAMILTON (1852-1911)
Tune--CASSEL--"I am a stranger here, within a
foreign land. "
Tune--LAMBDIN--"From over hill and plain. "

Composer, pianist, singer, daughter of the Rev. B. B. Hamilton, a Baptist pastor, she was born at Otterville, Jersey
County, Illinois on August 21, 1852 and raised at Whitehall,
Illinois, where her father was pastor. At age sixteen she
went to live with an aunt in Brooklyn, New York City, where
she studied voice with Madame Hartell. Later she was sent
to the Maplewood Institute at Pittsfield, Massachusetts where
she studied piano, harmony, and composition. After graduation she took charge of the department of music at Shurleff
College in Upper Alton, Illinois and while there married Dr.
E. T. Cassel of Nebraska City, Nebraska. While in Nebraska,

Dr. Cassel practiced medicine in South Bend, Ashland, Edgar, and Hastings. She published a song book, White Ribbon Vibration (1890) which included her song, "Around the World"; it became a Women's Christian Temperance Union song. In 1902 the Cassels decided to move to Denver, Colorado, where her tragic death occurred. [Information from Linda M. Rea, Hastings Public Library, Hastings, Nebraska.] As she placed her foot on the step of her buggy, her dress got caught in the step. Something frightened the horses, and she was dragged to her death on November 17, 1911. Her hymn tunes appeared in the Baptist Hymnal (1956). Her husband wrote the words to her hymn tunes.

CATHEY, MARY JACKSON (b. 1926)
   "God almighty, God eternal. "

She obtained her A. B. from Winthrop College, Rock Hill, South Carolina (1947) and her Master's in Religious Education at the Presbyterian Assembly's Training School in Richmond, Virginia (1953). In 1958 she was married to Henry M. Cathey of Bethesda, Maryland and she became the Director of Religious Education at the Presbyterian Church there. Previously she had held a similar position at the First Presbyterian Church in Anderson, South Carolina. In 1956 her youth hymn, "Come forth, O Christian youth" was published by The Hymn Society of America and the above hymn was published by the Society in Twelve New World Order Hymns and also in the Hymnbook for Christian Worship (1970), the American Baptist/Disciples of Christ hymnbook.

CAWTHORN, JANIE M. (1888-1975)
   "In that beautiful home above. "

Composer and hymnist, she was born at Mt. Carmel, South Carolina on November 27, 1888 and was educated at Harbison College and Teachers' Normal School. She was Superintendent of the Apostolic Church Sunday School for 27 years and an evangelist. Other hymns she wrote were "I see him, " "Won't you come and see the man?, " "Somebody He can use, " and "Call Heaven. " She died on May 21, 1975.

CHANT, LAURA ORMISTON DIBDIN (1848-1923)
   "Light of the world, faint were our weary feet. "

Born at Woolastone, Gloucestershire, England, she later
served as Sister of the Sophia Wards of the London Hospital.
In 1877 she married Thomas Chant, M. R. C. S. of Bridgewater, England. Her hymn, "Beyond the far horizon" appeared in Stopford A. Brooke's Christian Hymns (1891) and
the hymn above in The Methodist Hymn Book (1904). She
died on February 16, 1923.

CHARLES, ELIZABETH RUNDLE (1828-1896)
    "True, the heart grows rich in giving. "

Hymnist, translator, and versifier, daughter of John Rundle,
banker and Member of Parliament, she was born at the Bank,
Tavistock, Devonshire, England on January 2, 1828 and was
a member of the Church of England. In 1851 she married
Andrew P. Charles, barrister at law, and they lived in
Hampstead Heath. Her hymns appeared in her books Voice
of the Christian Life in Song in Many Lands and Ages (1864);
Poems (New York, 1867); and Songs Old and New (1882).
She wrote more than 25 books, the best known in America
being The Chronicles of the Schonberg-Cotta Family (1863),
being the story of Martin Luther's childhood, in which she
remarked:

> To know how to say what others only know how to
> think is what makes men poets or sages, and to
> dare to say what only others dare to think makes
> men martyrs or reformers, or both.

Her books were immensely popular in England and America
and enjoyed a wide sale. She died at Hampstead, England
on March 28, 1896. More recently her hymns appeared in
the Christian Science (1937); Hymns for the Family of God
(1976); and Methodist (1966) hymnals.

CHERRY, CONSTANCE (b. 1953)
    "Proclaim new hope through Christ our Lord. "

Born at Charlotte, Michigan on March 27, 1953, she was
educated at Huntington College, Huntington, Indiana and received her Master's in Music (composition) at Bowling Green
State University, Bowling Green, Ohio (1982). She became
interested in hymnology while studying under Professor Hugh
McElrath at The Southern Baptist Theological Seminary at
Louisville, Kentucky. As of October 1982 she was Minister

of Music at the First Presbyterian Church at Chillicothe, Ohio. Her hymn was awarded first prize at the Presbyterian Men's Convention in Atlanta, Georgia. Suggested tune is MIT FREUDEN ZART 87-87-887 and her hymn was published in the October 1982 edition of The Hymn, A Journal of Congregational Song, by The Hymn Society of America.

CHESTER, HENRIETTA MARY GOFF (1834-1927)
"Unto Thee by glory given. "

Translator and versifier. She was the daughter of George Goff of Lausanne, Switzerland, although her ancestors had settled in Ireland at the time of Cromwell. In 1856 she married Harry Chester, an Assistant Secretary of the Committee Council of Education in London, England. Her husband died in 1868. She published Meg's Primroses and A History of Russia, while her translations of hymns from the Latin and from German appeared in The Hymnary. She died on June 18, 1927 at age 93.

CHRISTIANSEN, AVIS MARGUERITE BURGESON (b. 1895)
"Up Calvary's mountain one dreadful morn. "

Born at Chicago, Illinois on October 11, 1895, she began writing poetry in childhood. Her first two hymns were published in Tabernacle Praises (1915). She was married to Ernest C. Christiansen, who worked for the Moody Institute of Chicago for almost forty years. They were members of the Moody Memorial Church of Chicago, and her hymn appeared in the Baptist Hymnal (1975). Other hymns she wrote appeared in Hymns for the Living Church (1974). "Avis Christiansen is still living and does still write poetry. " [Letter dated 6/17/82 from E. Rankin, Secretary, Moody Memorial Church, Chicago.]

CLAPHAM, EMMA (1830-1899)
"Guide of my steps along life's way. "

Born at Hanover Square, Leeds, England on October 18, 1830, she was raised a Congregationalist. Her hymn, "Lord, we meet to pray and praise, " the one above, and other hymns appeared in Leeds Sunday School Hymn Book (1858). She died on February 4, 1899.

CLAPP, ELIZA THAYER (1811-1888)
"All before us lies the way. "

She resided at Dorchester (Boston), Massachusetts and contributed poems and hymns to Ralph Waldo Emerson's magazine The Dial (1841). Her hymn appeared in Hedge and
Huntington's Unitarian Hymns for the Church of Christ (1853).
"According to the death notice which appeared in the February 27, 1888 Boston Evening Transcript, Eliza Thayer Clapp
died at Dorchester, February 25, 1888 in her 77th year.
She is referred to as 'Miss, ' so I assume she was unmarried. " [Letter received from Patricia Nonamaker, Reference
Librarian, Boston Public Library.]

CLARE, SISTER MARY F. (1829-1899)
"Hark the angels bright are singing. "

Born Margaret Anna Cusack, she was the only daughter of
Samuel Cusack, M. D. , of Dublin, Ireland. She was a nun
at Kenmare, but left the Roman Catholic Church and lectured on Protestantism. Her hymns appeared in Mrs. Brock's
Children's Hymn Book (1881); the Congregational Book of
Praise for Children (1881); and Horder's Hymn Lover (1888).
She died at Leamington, England on June 7, 1899. Her
hymn above is a translation of a Crostian hymn and appeared
in the Evangelical Reformed Hymnal.

CLARK, AMY ASHMORE (1882-1954)
"With love He cleanses every sin. "

Born at Toronto, Ontario, Canada on May 6, 1882, she was
advertising director of the Junior League Magazine for ten
years. She died in New York City on January 9, 1954.

CLARKSON, EDITH MARGARET (b. 1915)
"So I send you to labor unrewarded,
To serve unpaid, unloved, unsought, unknown. "

"So I send you, by grace made strong to triumph
O'er hosts of hell, o'er darkness, death and sin. "

Composer and hymnist, she was born in Melville, Saskatchewan, Canada on June 8, 1915. Presbyterian. She taught in
public schools in Toronto, Ontario, from 1942. A member

of the Knox Presbyterian Church, Toronto, Ontario, she also served on the board of the Church Renewal Foundation and was active working for the Inter Varsity Christian Fellowship. She wrote Let's Listen to Music (1944); The Creative Classroom (1958); The Wondrous Cross (1966); God's Hedge (1968); and Grace Grows Best in Winter (1972). She also wrote books of verse, Clear Shining After Rain (1962); Rivers Among the Rocks (1968); and Conversations with a Barred Owl (1975). Her hymns appeared in the American Service Hymnal (1968); the Baptist Hymnal (1975); and Hymns for the Family of God (1976). Three other hymns she wrote appeared in Hymns for the Living Church (1974). As of February 1983 she was living in Willowdale, Ontario, Canada.

CLAYTON, EDITH (1897-1968)
"Father, we come, with youth and vigor pressing. "

She was born in Orange, New Jersey and was educated at Columbia University School of Journalism in New York City. She also wrote the "Fisherman's Night Hymn" (1941) and a Litany of Youth and Post-War Litany (1942). As a cofounder of the Young People's League of the Episcopal diocese of New York, she edited a news sheet and wrote a number of litanies, hymns, and songs and was an active member of the Altar Guild of the Church of the Epiphany in New York City. Her hymn appeared in The Hymnal of the Protestant Episcopal Church in the USA (1940). "She married Frank L. Johnson and moved to Newtown, Connecticut. When our parish was on a very slender budget, she had the owner of a local iron works make the most graceful candle stands and other chancel items after her designs, from bits of scrap iron she had found in his piles! She made crèche figures for us out of a stone caster's rejects. [Information from Hugh McCandless, retired rector of the Church of the Epiphany.] She died at Newton, CT in 1968. [Letter from Lysbeth Platt, Newton, Connecticut.]

CLEGHORN, SARAH NORCLIFFE (1876-1959)
"Thanks to Saint Matthew, who had been. "

Daughter of Sarah Chestnut Hawley and John Dalton Cleghorn, she was born at Norfolk, Virginia on February 4, 1876. The family lived in Madison, Wisconsin (1877-82) where her father tried farming, but he was no farmer, then in Minneapolis, Minnesota. When Sarah was nine years old, her

mother died, and she went to live with two maiden aunts in
Manchester, Vermont. She published several books, moved
to Philadelphia in 1943 and died there on April 4, 1959.
Her hymn, called "Comrade Jesus," appears in Masterpieces
of Religious Verse (Harper, 1948) and in The World's Great
Religious Poetry (Macmillan, 1934). While on a visit to
South Carolina, she saw small children working in a cotton
factory which stood on the edge of a golf course, and wrote
her famous poem which appeared in the New York Tribune
on January 23, 1915:

> The golf links lie so near the mill
> That almost every day,
> The laboring children can look out
> And see the men at play.

Today it is difficult for us to realize that children, little
boys and girls aged seven and eight, worked in textile mills.
As a result of her poem, Congress passed a Child-Labor
law in 1916 which was declared unconstitutional by the nine
old men of the Supreme Court, holding that property rights
(as with slavery), took precedence over human rights, and
by prohibiting children from working, you were denying the
wealthy from making profits and acquiring more property.
So Congress passed another law in 1919 which was again
declared unconstitutional by the Supreme Court in 1922, and
finally passed the Federal Fair Labor Standards Act of 1938
which was never challenged. But this act allows children of
seven and eight, children of migrant farmers, to pick crops.
Maybe someday a lady driving by in her automobile may spot
this and write a poem about it.

CLEPHANE, ANNA JANE DOUGLAS MACLEAN (1795-1860)
      "Toiling in the path of duty."

The daughter of General W. D. M. Clephane, she was a
member of the Free Church of Scotland (Presbyterian). Her
hymn appeared in Thring's Collection (1882).

CLEPHANE, ELIZABETH CECILIA CURTIS DOUGLAS (1830-
1869)
      "Beneath the cross of Jesus
      I fain would take my stand."

Third daughter of Andrew Clephane, Sheriff of Fife and Kinross, she was born at Edinburgh, Scotland on June 18, 1830 and later resided at Melrose, Roxburghshire, Scotland, where she gained the name "Sunbeam" for her work with the poor. Her hymns were published in William Arnett's Family Treasury (1872-74). She died at Bridgend House, near Melrose, on February 19, 1869. Her hymn appeared in the American Service Hymnal (1968); Broadman (1973); Christian Worship (1955); Episcopal (1940); Hymns for the Family of God (1976); Methodist (1966); Presbyterian USA (1955) hymnals and The Pilgrim Hymnal (1958).

CLYDE, HELEN DIANA (b. 1889)
"And did you see Him little star, long, long ago?"

Born at Dunedin, New Zealand on May 27, 1889, she was educated at Otago Girls High School. In 1907 she was appointed to the Wellington Education Department Head Office in Wellington, New Zealand where she served until her retirement in 1945. She has been a member of the St. John's Presbyterian Church since 1907. Two of her books of verse for children, A Pocketful of Rhymes and Up the Stairs were published in England. Her hymn above, a children's Christmas hymn, was published in Songs for Worship (1969) by the Joint Board of Christian Education of Australia and New Zealand. Her hymn, "Go ye into all the world" was published in Bible Hymns by The Hymn Society of America (1966). On May 27, 1982 she celebrated her 93rd birthday. [Information from David M. Steedman of Wellington, New Zealand, Presbyterian Minister of St. John's.]

COATES, DOROTHY MC GRIFF LOVE
"How much more of life's Burden can we bear?"

Noted black gospel singer, hymnist, and songwriter, she was born in Birmingham, Alabama and later married a Mr. Love. After her divorce from Mr. Love, she married a Mr. Coates. There were five recordings of the above hymn in Phonolog Reports (1978) of Los Angeles, California, four recordings of her hymn, "Lord, you've been good to me," three of "There's always somebody talking about me ... I've got Jesus and that's enough," and two of "He may not come when you want Him, But He's right on time" and two recordings listed for "I won't let go of my faith."

COBBE, FRANCES POWER (1822-1904)
"God draws a cloud over each gleaming morn. "

Great-granddaughter of Charles Cobbe, Archbishop of Dublin,
she was born in County Dublin, Ireland on December 4, 1822.
Her lines first appeared in her Italics: Brief Notes on Poli-
tics, People and Places in Italy in 1864, then in Horder's
Congregational Hymns in 1884. She wrote numerous books.
In her book, The Duties of Women, published in Boston,
Massachusetts in 1881, she wrote: "So immense are the
claims on a mother, physical claims on her bodily and brain
vigor, and moral claims on her heart and thoughts, that she
cannot, I believe, meet them all and find any large margin
beyond for other cares and work. " She was a personal
friend of Theodore Parker, reformer, Unitarian pastor and
anti-slavery lecturer and was with him during the last days
of his life in Florence, Italy (1860).

COCCIA, MARIA ROSA (1759-1833)
Dixit Dominus

Composer, born at Rome, Italy on 4 January 1759, she wrote
a Magnificat for four voices and organ, dated 2 October 1774,
and was examined by four professors of the Roman Accademia di Santa Cecilia, and later was admitted as a member
of the Accademia Filarmonica of Bologna, according to reports of the time, a most unusual honor for a woman. She
also wrote a cantata for four voices (1783), and died at
Rome in November 1833.

COCKBURN-CAMPBELL, MARGARET see LADY CAMP-
BELL

CODNER, ELIZABETH HARRIS (1824-1919)
"Lord, I hear of showers of blessing. "

Born at Dartmouth, Devon, England in 1824, she was married to the Rev. Daniel Codner, curate of Peterborough.
She published The Missionary Ship, The Bible in the Kitchen,
and her hymns appeared in her book, Among the Brambles
and Other Lessons from Life. She was editor of Women's
Work in the Great Harvest Field, a monthly magazine published by the Mildmay Protestant Mission of North London
under the direction of the Rev. W. and Mrs. Pennefather.

She died at Croydon, Surrey, England on March 28, 1919.
Her hymn appeared in the Methodist Hymnal (1911) and more
recently in Hymns for the Living Church (1974).

COGHILL, ANNIE LOUISA WALKER (1836-1907)
"Work for the night is coming. "

Daughter of Robert Walker, a civil engineer, she was born
at Kiddermore, Staffordshire, England. About 1853 they
moved to Canada where her father was employed in the con-
struction of the Canadian Grand Trunk Railway and other pro-
jects. Her hymn was published in a Canadian newspaper in
1854 and her poems were published in Leaves from the Back-
woods (Montreal, 1861). During their years in Canada, Annie
and her two older sisters conducted a private school for
girls. She returned to England about 1863 and obtained a
position as a governess. In 1883 she married Harry Coghill
and they made their home in Hastings where he was a successful merchant. Besides her books of poems, she also
wrote six novels and a book of children's plays. Her hymn
appeared in Ira D. Sankey's Sacred Songs and Solos and
again in her book, Oak and Maple (1890). She died at Bath,
England in 1907. More recently her hymn appeared in the
American Service (1968) and Baptist hymnals (1973).

COLERIDGE, MARY ELIZABETH (1861-1907)
"Bid me, remember, O my gracious Lord. "

Daughter of Mary Anne Jameson and Arthur D. Coleridge, a
great grand niece of the poet Samuel Taylor Coleridge, she
was born at London, England on September 23, 1861. Her
poems were published in her books Fancy's Following (1896),
The King With Two Faces (1897; 10th edition, 1908), and
she wrote numerous short stories and novels. She died, unmarried, at Harrogate on August 25, 1907. Her hymn appeared in A Treasury of Poems for Worship and Devotion
(Harper, 1959).

COLLIER, MARY ANN (1810-1866)
"The sun that lights yon broad blue sky. "

Daughter of the Reverend William Collier, a Baptist minister, she was born at Charlestown (now Boston), Massachusetts
on December 23, 1810. Her hymn appeared in The Psalmist

edited by Baron Stow and Samuel F. Smith (1843). She died at Alexandria, Virginia on December 25, 1866.

COLLINS, MARY FRANCES COVINGTON (b. 1830)
     "Jesus, gracious one, calleth now to thee. "

Born in Middleborough, Massachusetts on May 22, 1830, she was married on May 22, 1850 to the Reverend Samuel A. Collins, Jr. , a Baptist minister. [Information received from Ruth E. Caswell, Town Clerk, Middleboro, Massachusetts.] Mrs. Collins' hymn appeared in Ira D. Sankey's Sacred Songs and Solos (1881). We have been unable to determine her place and date of death.

COLQUHOUN, FRANCES SARA FULLER-MAITLAND (1809-1877)
     "Oft in danger, oft in woe,
     Onward Christians, onward go. "

The fourth daughter of Ebenezer Fuller-Maitland of Stanstead Hall and Park Place, Henley-on-Thames, she was born at Shinfield Park, near Reading, England on June 20, 1809. Her hymn, "Much in sorrow, oft in woe, " first appeared in Collyer's Hymns, etc. (1821), but at age 14 Frances rewrote the hymn adding new lines for verses three and four, and adding verses five and six. Her mother, Mrs. Methia Fuller-Maitland, issued a compilation of hymns in 1827, Hymns for Private Devotion Selected and Original, published by Hatchards, London, which included Frances' hymn and also two hymns by her sister, Esther Herschell. On January 29, 1834 she married John Colquhoun, a sportswriter, son of Sir James Colquhoun, Bart. In her mother's collection, she also contributed "Launched upon the stormy ocean" and another hymn in the 1863 edition. Her hymn also appeared in E. Bickersteth's Christian Psalmody (1833) and in Hall's Mitre Hymn Book (1836). She published her poems, Rhymes and Chimes in 1876 and died on May 27, 1877. More recently her hymn appeared in The Hymnal of the Protestant Episcopal Church in the USA (1940).

CONDER, JOAN ELIZABETH THOMAS (1785-1877)
     "The hours of evening close. "

     "Not Thy garment's hem alone"

She was the granddaughter of the sculptor, L. F. Roubiliac, and she was born on April 6, 1785. She married Josiah Condor, of London, England, editor of the Eclectic Review. Her hymns appeared in the Congregational Hymn Book (1836). Conder's Hymns of Praise, Prayer and Devout Meditation (1856), etc. She died on January 22, 1877.

COOK, ELIZA (1817-1899)
    "Father above, I pray to Thee. "

She was born in Southwark, England on December 24, 1817 and her hymn originally appeared in her book of Poems (1853), then was published in Martineau's Hymns, etc. (1873). She died at Wimbleton, England on September 24, 1889.

COOKE, MARY ANN WOODBRIDGE HAWLEY (b. 1817)
    "In some way or another, The Lord will provide. "

The daughter of Mary Ann Seymour and the Reverend John Woodbridge, she was born on February 25, 1817. On August 4, 1840 she married Captain Aaron Hawley of Bridgeport, Connecticut. He died in 1847. Then on July 20, 1853, she married the Reverend Parsons Cooke, D. D. , pastor of the First Congregational Church of Lynn, Massachusetts. For a time he was editor of the Puritan Recorder in Boston. She had one son and two daughters by her first husband, and one son, Parsons Cooke of Sterling, Illinois by her second husband. [Information from Patricia Nonamaker of the Boston Public Library.] Her hymn appeared in Ira D. Sankey's Sacred Songs and Solos (1878), and is often ascribed in error to Martha E. D. Walker Cook (1806-1874), wife of Lieutenant William Cook, whom she married in 1824. There was one recording of her hymn listed in Phonolog Reports (1978). We have been unable to locate her place and date of death.

COOPER, ROSE MARIE (b. 1937)
    "Great is the Lord. "

A composer, she was born at Cairo, Illinois on February 21, 1937 and was educated at Oklahoma Baptist University (B. M.) at Shawnee, Oklahoma and at Teachers College, Columbia University (M. A.), New York City.

COOTE, MAUD OSWELL (1852-1935)
"The strain of joy and gladness. "

She was British and a member of the Church of England.
Her hymn was written for use in St. Andrew's Church, Frank-
ton, Salop, England and appeared in Church Hymns (1871)
with another hymn she wrote.

COPENHAVER, LAURA LOU SCHERER (1868-1940)
"Herald of Christ, who bear the king's commands. "

Daughter of Katherine Killinger and John Jacob Scherer, a
Lutheran Minister and founder of Marion College, a woman's
school in Marion, Virginia, she was born there on August
29, 1868 and educated in her father's school. On August 26,
1895 she married Bascom Eugene Copenhaver, a schoolteacher, and later Smyth County Superintendent of Schools.
For some 30 years she taught English Literature at Marion
College, founded Rosemont Industries--a mountain craft in-
dustry--and devoted herself to local missionary work for the
United Lutheran Church of America. They had several children. She died at Marion on December 18, 1940. [Informa-
tion from Nancy Raab-Cook of the Smyth-Bland Regional Library, Marion, Virginia.] Her hymn appeared in Christian
Worship (1953); Presbyterian Hymnal-USA (1955); The Methodist Hymnal (1966); and Hymns for the Living Church (1974).

CORELLI, MARIE (1864-1924)
"In our hearts celestial voices softly say. "

While still an infant, she was adopted by poet Charles Mackay
(1814-1889) of Perth, Scotland. Later she resided at Stratford-
on-Avon, England. She wrote A Romance of Two Worlds
(1886); Barabbas (1893); The Master Christian (1900); The
Treasures of Heaven (1906); and other books. Her hymn appeared in Hymns and Choral Songs (Manchester, 1904); the
Sunday School Hymnary (1905); and more recently in the
hymnals of the United Church of Canada; Presbyterian Church
of Canada and Seventh-Day Adventists hymnals.

CORNISH, KATHARINE DEACON (1849-1936)
"Within the Church's sacred fold. "

Daughter of the Rev. Sidney W. Cornish, Vicar of Ottery St.

Mary, Devon, England, from 1841 to 1874, she was born
there on December 31, 1849. He was also master of the
King's School there from 1824 to 1863. She died at Ottery
St. Mary in the same house where she was born, on September 24, 1936. Her hymn appeared in Hymns Ancient and
Modern (1875).

CORUM, BETTY JO (1927-1970)
"Peace in our time, O Lord, for this we pray. "

Born at Knoxville, Tennessee on February 11, 1927, she was
educated at Carson-Newman College, Jefferson City, Tennessee (B. A.) and Southwestern Baptist Theological Seminary
(M. R. E.). After serving as director of the Junior-Intermediate Training Union for the Tennessee Baptist Convention
(1954-60), she then served as editor of Intermediate Training
Union materials for the Baptist Sunday School Board (1960-65)
and director of editorial services of the Woman's Missionary
Union of the Southern Baptist Convention (1965-70). She published a book of verse, A Corner of Today and was co-author
of a youth musical, Hello World, produced at the Mission 70
Conference in Atlanta, Georgia in December 1969. Her
hymn appeared in the Baptist (1975) and Broadman (1977)
hymnals.

CORY, JULIA BULKEY CADY (1882-1963)
"We praise thee, O God, our Redeemer, Creator. "

Daughter of J. Cleveland Cady, a noted New York City architect, she was born there on November 9, 1882 and became
a member of the Brick Presbyterian Church. Her father
was superintendent of the Sunday School in the Church of the
Covenant, which was affiliated with the Brick Presbyterian
Church. On March 28, 1911 she married Robert H. Cory
and they resided in Englewood, New Jersey. She was a
translator and versifier, and her hymn was written at the
request of Archer Gibson, the church organist, in 1904.
More recently her hymn appeared in the Baptist (1975);
Broadman; Family of God; Joyfully Sing; Lutheran (1941);
Presbyterian (1955) hymnals and in The Pilgrim Hymnal
(1958). She died at Englewood, New Jersey on May 1, 1963.

COTTERILL, JANE BOAK (1790-1825)
"O Thou, who hast at Thy command. "

Daughter of the Reverend John Boak, in 1811 she was married to the Reverend Joseph Cotterill, sometime rector of Blakeney, Norfolk, England. They were the parents of the hymnist, Mary Cotterill Bourdillon and the Rt. Rev. Henry Cotterill, Bishop of Edinburgh, Scotland. Her hymn "O, from the world's vile slavery" appeared in the Appendix to Thomas Cotterill's Selection (1815) and later revised to "From this enslaving world's control" and appeared as such in Kennedy's Hymnologia Christiana (1863). The hymn above was published in Cotterill's Selection (1815); Montgomery's Christian Psalmist (1825); and more recently in the Methodist Hymnal (1911).

COUSIN, ANNE ROSS CUNDELL (1824-1906)
"The sands of time are sinking,
the dawn of heaven breaks."

The daughter of David Ross Cundell, a physician of Leith, England who served as a surgeon at the Battle of Waterloo, she was born at Hull, York, England on April 27, 1824 and was raised in Leith. She grew up in the Church of England, but later became a Presbyterian, and married the Rev. William Cousin, a Scottish Free Church minister who served in Duns, then later in Chelsea, Irvine, and Melrose. They had four sons and two daughters. Her hymn appeared in Christian Treasury (1857). Her poems and hymns were published in Immanuel's Land and Other Poems (1876). She was called a "Scottish Christina Rossetti." She died at Edinburgh, Scotland on December 6, 1906. More recently her hymn appeared in The Song Book of The Salvation Army (1953).

COWPER, FRANCES MARIA MADAN (1727-1797)
"My span of life will soon be done."

Daughter of hymnist Judith Cowper Madan, she was a sister of Dr. Spencer Madan, Bishop of Peterborough (England) and born in England. She was a member of the Church of England (Episcopal) and was married to her cousin, Major Cowper, who was also a cousin of Cowper, the poet. Her hymns were published as Original Poems on Various Occasions. By a Lady. Revised by William Cowper, Esq. of the Inner Temple (1792). More recently her hymn appeared in the Methodist Hymnal (1925).

COX, EDITH MAY CAMPBELL (b. 1899)
"God has filled the earth with beauty. "

Born at Knoxville, Tennessee on May 10, 1899, she is the
author of two books of poetry and the texts of many of the
150 hymns and songs for which her husband composed the
music. "I was married for many years to Dr. Emerson C.
Cox, who predeceased me ... in 1978. He was a minister
(Presbyterian pastor for 15 years) and an excellent musician
(church and concert organist). Much of the music has been
used in a number of churches in many places, but only a
very few have been published.... My husband also wrote
quite a lot of instrumental music, some wedding songs and
others. " [Letter dated April 24, 1982 from Mrs. Cox from
Paonia, Colorado.] Mrs. Cox resides in the beautiful North
Fork Valley of the Gunnison River on the western slope of
the Rocky Mountains. The hymn appeared in The Stewardship
of the Environment (Ecology), published by The Hymn Society
of America (1973).

COX, FRANCES ELIZABETH (1812-1897)
"Sing praise to God who reigns above,
The God of all creation. "

"Jesus lives! thy terrors now,
Can no longer death, appall us. "

Translator and versifier, daughter of G. V. Cox, M. A. , she
was born at Oxford, England on May 10, 1812. Her translations were printed in Sacred Hymns from the German,
Pickering, London in 1841, with a second edition, Hymns from
the German in 1864. She had become friendly with Baron
Bunsen who often suggested to her German hymns which he
felt were worthy of translation. She died at Headington,
England on September 23, 1897. Her hymns have appeared
in The New Broadman Hymnal (1977); Episcopal (1940);
Hymns for the Family of God (1976); Lutheran Hymnal (1941);
Methodist Hymnal (1966); Presbyterian USA (1955); and The
Pilgrim Hymnal (1958).

CRAIK, DINAH MARIA MULOCK (1826-1887)
"God rest ye merry gentlemen, let nothing you dis-
may. "

Daughter of the Rev. Thomas and Dinah Mulock, she was

born at Stoke-upon-Trent, Staffordshire, England on April 20, 1826. She went to London about 1846 and wrote The Ogilvies (1849) and numerous other books and short stories. In 1864 she married George L. Craik, partner in the house of Macmillan and Co., and a nephew of the historian of literature of the same name. They lived at Shortlands, near Bromley, England until her death. She died on October 12, 1887. Her hymn appeared in Golden Numbers (Doubleday Doran, 1902) and other books, and is a variation of the old Christmas Carol by an unknown hymnist.

CRAWFORD, EMILY MAY GRIMES (1868-1927)
"Speak, Lord, in the stillness. "

Born at Lambeth, Surrey, England on May 10, 1864, she went as a missionary in 1893 to Pondoland in South Africa. Another hymn she wrote, "The Master Comes, He Calls for thee, " appeared in the Church Missionary Hymn Book (1899). In 1904 she married Dr. T. W. W. Crawford, an Anglican missionary of the Church Missionary Society at Kikuyu, British East Africa. She died at Folkstone, Kent, England on July 9, 1927. Her hymn above appeared in Hymns for the Living Church (1974) and Hymns for the Family of God (1976).

CREWDSON, JANE FOX (1809-1863)
"There is no sorrow, Lord, too slight
To bring in prayer to Thee. "

Daughter of George Fox, she was born at Perraw, Cornwall, England in October 1809 and married Thomas Crewdson in 1836. She published Aunt Jane's Verses for Children (1851), Lays of the Reformation and Other Poems (1860), in which her hymn appeared, and A Little While and Other Poems. She died at Summerlands, near Manchester, England on September 14, 1863. Her hymn appeared in Christian Worship --A Hymnal (1953); the Presbyterian Hymnal (1933); and Songs of Praise (London: Oxford University Press, 1931).

CROPPER, MARGARET BEATRICE (1886-1980)
"The glory of our King was seen. "

Daughter of Charles James Cropper, she was born at Kendel, Westmoreland, England on August 29, 1886. She contributed hymns to Hosanna and to the G. F. S. Jubilee Hymnbook (1923-

25) and to Hymns and Songs for the Church Kindergarten, which she edited for the National Society for the Promotion of Christian Knowledge. She wrote several books of poems, Flame touches Flame, Sparks Among the Stubble, and Collected Poems (1958). She also wrote religious dramas, Christ Crucified and Three Roses. She died at Woodlands, Kendal, Westmoreland, England on September 27, 1980. More recently her hymn appeared in The Hymn Book (1973) of the Anglican and United Church of Canada. Another hymn, "O Christ, whom we may love and know," also appeared in the Girls' Friendly Society Jubilee Hymn Book (London, 1923-25) and more recently in the Lutheran Hymnal (1958).

CROSBY, FANNY (1820-1915)
　　"Blessed assurance, Jesus is mine!"

　　"Jesus, keep me near the cross."

　　"Pass me not, O gentle savior."

　　"All the way my Savior leads me."

Frances Jane Crosby was born at South East, Putnam County, New York on March 24, 1820. She lost her eyesight at age six weeks and was blind for ninety-five years. At the New York Institute for the Blind she was a pupil of composer George F. Root and wrote lyrics for some of his popular songs in addition to writing over 4,000 hymns. She was a Methodist and was married to a blind musician, Alexander van Alystyne. She died at Bridgeport, Connecticut on February 12, 1915. The popularity of her hymns is shown by the fact that Phonolog Reports (1978) of Los Angeles, California lists 32 different recordings of "Blessed Assurance," 21 of "Jesus keep me near the cross," 18 of "Pass me not, O gentle Savior," 8 of "All the way my Savior leads me," 8 of "I am thine, O Lord, I have heard Thy Voice," etc. and by the fact that many of her hymns have appeared in Baptist (1973); Methodist (1966); and Presbyterian hymnals (1955) now currently in use.

CROSS, ADA CAMBRIDGE (1844-1926)
　　"Light of the world, O shine on us."

Daughter of Henry Cambridge, she was born at St. Germains, Norfolkshire, England on November 21, 1844 and married

George F. Cross in 1869, curate in England and in Australia. They resided in Coleraine, Victoria, Australia after 1870. Her husband, with E. J. Bevan and C. Beadle, discovered and patented viscose in 1892. She published Hymns on the Litany (1865), Hymns on the Holy Communion (1866), etc. She also wrote mystery stories, A Marked Man (1891), The Three Miss Kings (1891), The Hand in the Dark (1913) and other novels. Her hymn "The dawn of God's dear sabbath" appeared in Songs of Praise (Anglican, 1931).

CROWELL, GRACE NOLL (1877-1969)
"Because I have been given much, I too must give."

Daughter of Sarah Southern and Adam Noll, she was born at Inland, Iowa on October 31, 1877 and educated in public schools. On September 4, 1901 she married Norman H. Crowell and they had three sons. A prolific writer of verse, she had over 3,500 poems published in addition to over 25 books including White Fire (1925), Flames in the Wind (1930), Songs of Hope (1938), Songs of Faith (1939), The Lifted Lamp (1942), Some Brighter Dawn (1943), and Songs for Comfort (1947). A member of the Methodist Church, she was a resident of Texas for many years and was chosen by the Golden Rule Foundation as the American Mother of 1938. The honorary degree of Litt. D. was conferred upon her by Baylor University, Waco, Texas. She died at Dallas, Texas on March 31, 1969. Her hymns appeared in the Baptist (1975) and Broadman (1977) hymnals.

CRUCIGER, ELISABETHE VON MESERITZ (c. 1506-1535)
"Herr Christ, der einig Getts Sohn."
"The only Son from heaven."
"O Thou, of God and Father."

Her family was of Polish nobility who had sought refuge in Wittenberg, Germany. In May or June 1524, she married Caspar Crueiger (or Creutzigerin), a student of Martin Luther at Wittenberg University; she became a friend of Katherine Luther, wife of Martin Luther. In 1525 he became Rector of St. John's School and preacher in St. Stephen's Church at Magdeburg. At Luther's wish, he became a professor of Theology at Wittenburg in 1528. Her hymn appeared in Eyn Enchiridion (Erfurt, 1524) and in Geistliche Lieder (Wittenburg, 1531). Also in translation, as above, in A. T. Russell's Psalms and Hymns (1851) and Catherine Winkworth's

Gesang-Buch for England (1863) and the Ohio Lutheran Hymnal (1880). More recently her hymn appeared in the Evangelical Lutheran and Concordia (Lutheran, 1932) hymnals. She died at Wittenburg in May, 1535.

CUMMINS, EVELYN ATWATER (1891-1971)
    "I know not where the road will lead
    I follow day by day. "

The daughter of Caroline Swift and Edward Storrs Atwater, she was born at Poughkeepsie, New York on May 17, 1891. "Mrs. Cummins attended Quincy School, the Putnam Hall School for Girls, Poughkeepsie, the National Cathedral School, Washington, D. C. , and the Masters School, Dobbs Ferry, New York. On September 8, 1915 she was married to Dr. Alexander G. Cummins, a former rector of Christ Episcopal Church and the first chaplain of the Poughkeepsie Police Benevolent Association, who died in 1946. ... She served for six years on the staff of the Living Church, an Episcopal weekly, and had been associate editor of The Chronicle for more than 15 years. ... She was a public safety commissioner in Poughkeepsie when the city had a commission, and was an associate member of the State Association of Chiefs of Police. [From an obituary courtesy of Kevin J. Gallagher of the Adriance Memorial Library, Poughkeepsie, New York.] Her hymn appeared in the Hymnal of the Protestant Episcopal Church in the USA (1940). She died at Poughkeepsie, New York on August 30, 1971.

CUNINGGIM, MAUD MERRIMON (1874-1965)
    "O living Christ, chief cornerstone
    Of God's temple thou. "

Daughter of United States Senator Augustus S. Merrimon, she was born at Raleigh, North Carolina on March 7, 1874. She received a diploma from Peace Institute in Raleigh (1892), and later sang in The White House in Washington, D. C. for President and Mrs. Grover Cleveland. She married the president of Scarritt College in Nashville, Tennessee and received two degrees there (B. A. , 1926; M. A. , 1930). She wrote her hymn for ceremonies at Scarritt College. Her hymn appeared in The Methodist Hymnal (1966).

CURRIE, NANCY FORD (b. 1938)
    Tune--WHILE ANGELS SANG

Composer. In 1959 she composed the music for the Christmas Carol, "While angels sang in praises glorified" by Gene
Claghorn, the author of this book. At the time Mrs. Currie's
husband was a student at Yale University, New Haven, Connecticut. It was first sung by Barbara Burger (later Mrs.
Ossorio) at the Manger Service at the First Congregational
Church, Old Greenwich, Connecticut, Christmas Eve, 1959
under the direction of Gerry Mack, Choir Director and Richard Rosan, organist. It was sung again on Christmas Eve
1960 at the church by Nancy Rosan (later Mrs. Richard O.
Roblin, Jr.). At the Christmas Eve services in 1962 and
1965 it was sung by Louise "Bonnie" Hatch (later Mrs. John
Harrison). The original title used was "Come to Him" later
changed to "While Angels Sang" (taken from the first lines).

CURTIS, CHRISTINE TURNER (1890-1961)
      "As the heart with eager learning."

Daughter of Annie Turner and Fred Curtis, she was born at
Norwell, Massachusetts and graduated from Wellesley College, Wellesley, Massachusetts in 1913. She was employed
in the advertising departments of Macmillan Co. and F. A.
Stokes Co., both in New York, then did editorial work for
Ginn & Co. in Boston. She returned to live in North Abington and was a member of the Congregational Church there
and a trustee of the North Abington Public Library. She
published a novel, Amarilis (1927) and a book of poems for
children Nip and Tuck (1931). Her hymn is a metrical version of part of Psalm 42 and appeared in the Evangelical and
Reformed Church Hymnal (1941). She died on June 12, 1961.

CUTHBERT, ELIZABETH HOWARD (1800-1857)
      Tune--HOWARD

A composer, she was born at Dublin, Ireland. Her tune is
used for the hymn on "Love to Christ" by Philip Doddridge
and appeared in the Methodist Hymnal (1911). It was also
used with the hymn "O thou my soul, bless God the Lord,"
taken from Psalm 103 and appeared in the Presbyterian
Hymnbook (1955).

DANA, MARY S. B. see MARY SHINDLER

DANIELS, MABEL WHEELER (1878-1971)
Sacred chorus a capella--The Christ Child

Composer, she was born at Swampscott, Massachusetts on
November 27, 1878 and educated at Radcliffe College (B. A. ,
1900), Cambridge, Massachusetts and was educated privately.
She was director of the Radcliffe Glee Club (1911-13) and
musical director at Simmons College, Boston (1913-18). She
received an Hon. Mus. Doc. from Boston University (1939).
She wrote An American Girl in Munich (Boston, 1905), and
died at Cambridge, Massachusetts on March 10, 1971.

DAVIS, HAZEL (b. 1900)
"Life has come from God the Father. "

Born in Fairfax County, Virginia on August 25, 1900, she
earned degrees at Madison College, Columbia University, and
at the University of Chicago. She served as a researcher
for the National Educational Association, and an active member of the First Methodist Church in Hampton, Virginia,
where she was chairman of the Commission on Stewardship.
Her hymn appeared in The Stewardship of the Environment
(The Hymn Society of America, 1973).

DAVIS, HAZEL (b. 1907)
Tune--THROUGH GOD

Composer, hymnist and songwriter, she was born at Bucklin,
Kansas on February 14, 1907 and educated at Kansas State
Teachers' College. She taught school for five years. Her
hymns and songs were often written in collaboration with Lyon
Percy Wilbur, Jr. She also wrote "America, America, Re-
turn to God. "

DAVIS, KATHERINE KENNICOTT (1892-1980)
Tunes--MASSACHUSETTS, SURETTE, and WACHU-
SETT

Composer and hymnist, she was born at St. Joseph, Missouri on June 25, 1892 and was educated at Wellesley College (B. A. , 1914), Wellesley, Massachusetts where she later
taught. After studying composition with Stuart Mason at the
New England Conservatory of Music in Boston, she studied with

Nadia Boulanger in Paris and studied choral music with Thomas Whitney Surette at his Concord Summer School of Music in Concord, Massachusetts. Later she taught voice and piano in Philadelphia until 1930, when she devoted her full time to composing and arranging. She was a member of the Congregational Church, then a Christian Scientist, then an Episcopalian. Her hymn, "Let all things now living." was published in the United Methodist Book of Hymns (1966); The Covenant Hymnal (1973); Baptist Hymnal (1975); and the Lutheran Book of Worship (1978). The three tunes above were included in the Methodist Hymnal (1964). She died at Concord, Massachusetts on April 20, 1980. She is best known as the composer of "The Little Drummer Boy," that perennial Christmas favorite.

DAVISON, FANNIE ESTELLE CHURCH (1851-1887)
    "Pure in heart, O God Help me to be."

Daughter of Philo and Sarah Ann Linsted Church, she was born at Cuyahoga Falls, Ohio. When she was only ten years old her father was killed in an accident, and later her mother married Henry Christian Warner who owned a hotel in Carthage, Missouri, and the family moved there. Fannie was married to Asa Lee Davison, a court reporter, and they lived in Chicago, Illinois and later in Madison, Wisconsin. They had two daughters. Her hymns were published in Joy and Gladness (Cincinnati: Fillmore Bros., 1881) and The Voice of Joy (1882). She also wrote the libretto for J. H. Rosecrans' cantata Faith, Hope and Love (1886). She died in Chicago, Illinois on March 10, 1887 and was buried in Carthage, Missouri. Her hymn appeared in the Baptist (1975); Broadman (1977); and Christian Worship (1953) hymnals.

DAYE, ELIZABETH (1733-1829)
    "I'll bless Jehovah's glorious name."

She was the daughter of the Rev. James Daye of Lancaster, England. Her poems were published in Liverpool in 1798, and her hymns appeared in the Monthly Repository. The above hymn appeared in Kippis' A Collection of Hymns and Psalms for Public and Private Worship (1795).

DAYTON, MARY ALICE (d. 1940)
"Eternal Mind the Potter is
And thought the eternal clay. "

She studied with Mary Baker Eddy in Boston, Massachusetts
in 1889, then was a resident of Quincy, Illinois. She joined
the Church of Christ, Scientist on October 5, 1892 and moved
to Boston in 1893. Her hymn, "The Potter and the Clay"
was prompted by Jeremiah 18:1-6 and appeared in the Christian Science Journal in September 1890. She was a Christian
Science practitioner from 1892 to 1939, then retired to live
in Concord, New Hampshire. She died on February 2, 1940.
Her hymn appeared in the Christian Science Hymnal (1937).

DEACON, MARY CONNOR (b. 1907)
"I will lift up my eyes. "

Organist, hymnist, and composer, she was born in Johnson
City, Tennessee on February 22, 1907 and was educated at
International College and East Tennessee State University in
Johnson City. She taught piano and theory at the Royal Conservatory in Toronto, Ontario, Canada, and was a church organist (1936-42). The hymn above had four recordings listed
in Phonolog Reports, with one listing for a second hymn,
"Hear my prayers. " As of March 1982 she was enjoying
her retirement.

DE ARMOND, LIZZIE DOUGLAS FOULKE (1846-1936)
"When tempted to wander away from the Lord. "

"I grieved my Lord from day to day. "

Born at Philadelphia, Pennsylvania, she was graduated from
West Chester State Teachers' College in West Chester, Pennsylvania and was married to Andrew Goodrich de Armond.
They had two sons and two daughters. While attending a revival meeting held by evangelist Billy Sunday in Philadelphia,
she wrote her hymn "If your heart keeps right" which became very popular and "Good night, good morning, " which
also became popular. She was a charter member of the
Swarthmore Presbyterian Church and died at Swarthmore,
Pennsylvania at the home of her daughter, Linda de Armond
on October 27, 1936. Some time after her mother's death,
Miss de Armond moved to Clearwater, Florida. The two
hymns above appeared in the Baptist Hymnal (1973) and four

other hymns were published in Rodeheaver's Gospel Solos
and Duets No. 3. An interesting footnote is the plea made
by Dr. Leonard Ellinwood in The Hymn for January 1982:

> The Dictionary of American Hymnology would like
> to be able to cite the location of holograph copies
> of hymns by significant American authors. Many
> of Fanny Crosby's are at Hope Publishing Company,
> but where are those of Alfred Barratt, George Ben-
> nard, Katherine Lee Bates, Ada Blenkhorn, Lizzie
> deArmond, Lydia Sigourney, Ida Reed Smith, and
> several thousands others?... We do not wish to
> make copies of any manuscripts, but it would be a
> valuable addition to our records if we could cite
> the current location of the holographs of many
> American hymns.

DECK, MARY ANN SANDERSON GIBSON (1813-1903)
   "There is a city bright. "

Born at Hull, England, she was married in 1845 to the Rev.
John Deck, vicar at St. Stephen's at Hull. It was a large
working-class parish of 13, 000 inhabitants. Her husband
was the brother of James G. Deck, a minister of the Plymouth Brethren in New Zealand. At age seventy she lost
her eyesight, and went to live with her daughter, Mrs. O. F.
Walton, at Wolverhampton. She became totally blind, and
learned to read Braille. Her hymn appeared in The Church
Hymnary (1898) and in other British hymnals. More recently her hymn appeared in Songs of Praise (Anglican, 1931).

DE FLEURY, MARIA (1753-1794)
   "Ye angels who stand 'round the throne'. "

She resided at Cripplegate, London, England and was a close
friend of Dr. John Ryland (1753-1815). She wrote several
books, and also "Thou soft flowing Kedron, by thy silver
stream. " Her hymns appeared in her Divine Poems and Essays on Various Subjects (1791); also in Joseph Middleton's
Hymns (1793); Dr. Collyer's Collection (1812); Bickersieth's
Christian Psalmody (1833) and in Spurgeon's Our Own Hymn
Book (1866). More recently her hymn appeared in the Presbyterian US (1901) and Moravian hymnals.

DELAND, MARGARET WADE CAMPBELL (1857-1945)
"Blow golden trumpets sweet and clear. "

Daughter of Margaretta Wade and Sample Campbell, she was born near Allegheny (Pittsburgh), Pennsylvania on February 23, 1857. Her mother died at Margaret's birth, and the child was raised by aunts and uncles in Manchester, Pennsylvania. She was educated at Pelham Priory, a boarding school in Pelham, New York and at Cooper Union in New York City, where she studied art and design. On May 12, 1880 she married Lorin Fuller DeLand in Fairfield, Pennsylvania and they resided in Boston, Massachusetts. She was a Presbyterian and he was a Unitarian, so they compromised by both joining the Trinity (Episcopal) Church in Boston. She published her poems in the Old Garden (1886) and numerous other books. Her hymn appeared in Christ in Poetry (Association Press, 1952) and other books. She died at Boston, Massachusetts on January 13, 1945.

DEMAREST, MARY AUGUSTA LEE (1838-1888)
"Like a bairn to his mither, a wee birdie to its nest,
I wud fain be ganging noo unto my Saviour's brest...
An' He carries them Himsel' to His ain countree. "

"I am frae from my hame an' I'm weary aften whiles. "

She was born in Croton Falls, New York. "My Ain Countree" was written in 1864 with music by Mrs. Ione T. Hanna of Denver, Colorado, and harmonized by Hubert P. Main in 1873. She resided with her husband in Passaic, New Jersey and later moved to Pasadena, California. She died in Los Angeles. Her hymn appeared in Sankey's Sacred Songs and Solos (1881).

DENNIS, ETHEL WASGATT (d. 1961)
"A grateful heart a garden is. "

She joined the Church of Christ, Scientist on June 5, 1914 and her hymn appeared in the Christian Science Hymnal (1937). She died on April 7, 1961.

DENT, CAROLINE (1815-1901)
"Jesus, Saviour! Thou dost know. "

A sister of Elizabeth Ryland Dent Trestrail, she was born at Milton, near Northampton, England on August 14, 1815 and was a Baptist. Her hymns appeared in the Baptist Psalms and Hymns (1858) and in the Baptist Hymnal (1879).

DEUTSCH, BABETTE (1895-1982)
"In the bright bay of your morning, O God. "

Born in New York City, she was educated at Barnard College (B. A. , 1917), Columbia (Litt. D. , 1946) and lectured at Columbia University in New York (1944-71). She married Avrahm Varmolinsky and they resided in New York City. She wrote books of verse--Banners (1919), Epistle to Prometheus (1931), Collected Poems (1919-1962)--and also novels and juvenile books. Her hymn is a translation of a hymn by Claire Goll and appeared in A Treasury of Jewish Poetry (Crown Publishers, 1957), and also in Sourcebook of Poetry (Zondervan, 1968).

DICKINSON, HELEN ADELL (1875-1957)
"In Joseph's lovely garden. "

Born at Port Elmsley, Ontario, Canada on December 5, 1875, she was educated at Queens University, Toronto (M. A.) and at Heidelberg University (Ph. D.) in Germany. She married choir director and organist Clarence Dickinson, and he composed the music for her hymns and anthems. They were co-founders of the School of Sacred Music at Union Theological Seminary in New York City. She published German Masters of Art, A Treasury of Worship, etc. Helen and her husband were elected Fellows of The Hymn Society of America (1946). She died at Tucson, Arizona on September 25, 1957.

DICKINSON, MARY LOWE (1839-1914)
"We should fill our lives with the sweetest things
If we had but a day. "

Born in Fitchburg, Massachusetts, she became assistant editor of the magazine Lend a Hand, edited by Edward Everett Hale. She married John B. Dickinson, and became professor of Belles Lettres at Denver University in Colorado and President of the National Council of King's Daughters. She published two books of poems. She contributed articles to Youth's Companion, St. Nicholas Magazine, and the Silver

Link. She was a Methodist and died in June 1914. [Information from Catherine T. Engel, Reference Librarian, Colorado Historical Society, Denver.]

DITTENHAVER, SARAH L. (1901-1973)
    "Light of the lonely Pilgrim's heart. "

Composer, hymnist, and pianist, she was born at Paulding, Ohio on December 16, 1901 and was educated at the Cosmopolitan Conservatory in Chicago and at Oberlin (Mus. B.). She taught at the Smead School for Girls in Toledo, Ohio (1924-27), then later taught piano in Ashville, North Carolina. She composed the music for the above hymn by Edward Denny (1796-1889). She died on February 4, 1973.

DIXON, HELEN CADBURY ALEXANDER (1877-1969)
    "Anywhere with Jesus I can safely go. "

The daughter of Richard Cadbury, a British industrialist and philanthropist, she was born at Birmingham, England in 1877 and was educated in Germany, studying German and music. She was a member of the Society of Friends (Quakers). In 1904 she married Charles M. Alexander, a singer with evangelist R. A. Torrey. Helen and her husband traveled in England with evangelist J. Wilber Chapman, an American Presbyterian evangelist preacher. With May Whittle Moody, Mr. Alexander was co-editor of the Northfield Hymnal No. 3. Mrs. Dixon's hymn appeared in The New Christian Hymnal; Orthodox Presbyterian; Brethren; Mennonite; and Seventh-Day Adventist (1940) hymnals. Her hymn was written with Jessie B. Pounds. In 1924 she married Amsji C. Dixon. She died in Birmingham, England on March 1, 1969.

DOBER, ANNA SCHINDLER (1713-1739)
    "Du heiliges Kind. "
    "Holy Lamb, who Thee receive. "

    "Süsser Heilanddeiner Guado. "
    "Far greater than one thought or could suppose. "

She was born at Kunewald, near Fulnek, Moravia (now Czechoslovakia) on April 9, 1713 and went to Herrnhut, Saxony, Germany in 1725. On July 13, 1737 she became the wife of L. J. Dober, General Elder of the Moravian Church. She

assisted him in the conversion of Jews in Amsterdam to the
Moravian Church. The first hymn, above, appeared in the
Herrnhut Gesang-Buch (1735) and the second in the Appendix
to it. The first one was translated by John Wesley in Hymns
and Sacred Poems (1740) and the second appeared in translation in the Moravian Hymn Book (1754). The Moravian Collection of 1778 contained 18 of her hymns. Later her hymns
appeared in Montgomery's Christian Psalmist (1825); Elliott's
Psalms and Hymns (1855); Methodist Episcopal Hymns (1849);
and the Baptist Service of Song (1871) in America. She died
at Marienborn, near Büdingen, Hesse-Darmstadt on December 12, 1739.

DOBREE, HENRIETTA OCTAVIA DE LISLE (1831-1894)
    "Again the morning shines so bright. "

    "Lord we come to ask Thy blessing. "

She was a member of the Church of England, married a Mr.
Dobree, and later joined the Roman Catholic Church. Her
hymns appeared in Mrs. Brock's Children's Hymn Book
(1881). She died at Kensington, London, England on November 26, 1894.

DOOLITTLE, HILDA (1886-1961)
    "Whenever you are bent with care...
    An earnest prayer draw near to God. "

Daughter of Helen Wolle and Charles L. Doolittle, she was
born at Bethlehem, Pennsylvania on September 10, 1886 and
educated at Bryn Mawr College in Bryn Mawr, Pennsylvania
(1905-07). She married Richard Arlington in 1913 (and divorced in 1938). She wrote poems under the penname "H. D. "
and wrote Sea Garden (1916), Collected Poems (1925), Selected Poems (1957) and Helen in Egypt (1961) and numerous
other books. She resided in Zurich, Switzerland and died on
September 27, 1961. Two of her hymns (including the one
above) appeared in the Baptist Hymnal (1973).

DORR, JULIA CAROLINE RIPLEY (1825-1913)
    "How can I cease to pray for thee? Somewhere
    In God's great universe thou art today. "

She was born in Charleston, South Carolina on February 13,

1825 and was raised in Rutland, Vermont. In 1847 she married Seneca M. Dorr. She wrote novels and books of verse, and died in Rutland on January 18, 1913. Her hymn appeared in Songs of Praise (1931).

DOUDNEY, SARAH (1841-1926)
"The Master hath come, and He calls us to follow. "

"Saviour, now the day is ending. "

She was the daughter of George E. Doudney and was born at Portsea, England on January 15, 1841, but was raised in the small village of Cobham in Hampshire. Her Psalms of Life was published by Houlston in 1871, and many of her hymns appeared in the Sunday School Union Songs of Gladness in 1871; others appeared in Mrs. Brock's Children's Hymn Book in 1881. But there is an interesting story to tell about Sarah. When she was only fifteen, she wrote the following poem:

> "Learn to make the most of life, lose no happy day,
> Time will never bring thee back, chances swept
> away!
> Leave no tender word unsaid, love while love shall
> last;
> The mill cannot grind with the water that is past. "

The poem swept America 1858-59, and was so popular that Sarah became a world celebrity. The first hymn above appeared in the Southern Baptist Hymnal (1956) and the second hymn in the Lutheran; Evangelical Lutheran; United Church of Canada (1930); Presbyterian Church of Canada; and the Army and Navy (1942) hymnals. She died at Headington, England on December 15, 1926.

DOUGLAS, FRANCES JANE HOW (1829-1899)
"For all they love and goodness, so bountiful and free. "

She was born at Shrewsbury, England, and was the sister of Bishop William W. How of East London, under the title of Bishop of Bedford (1879) and Bishop of Wakefield (1888). Her hymn appeared in her April Verses (1848), and was revised by her brother for the Society for Promoting Christian Knowledge Church Hymns of 1871. More recently her hymn appeared in the Hymnal of the Church of Scotland (1927). She died December 11, 1899.

DRANE, AUGUSTA THEODOSIA (1823-1894)
"Thou who hero-like hast striven. "

Also known as Mother Frances Raphael, O. S. D. , she was
born at Bromley, Middlesex, England and entered the Order
of St. Dominic in 1853. She became Mother Superior of the
Dominican Nuns of the Third Order. In 1876 she published
her Songs in the Night, with an enlarged edition in 1887.
Her hymn above was published in the Crown of Jesus (1862);
Parochial Hymn Book (1880); St. Dominic's Hymn Book (1901);
and others. Other hymns she wrote appeared in the Dominican Hymn Book (1881); A. E. Tozer's Catholic Hymns (1887);
and in other hymn books. She died at St. Dominic's Convent,
Stone, Saffordshire, England on April 29, 1894.

DRURY, MIRIAM LEYRER (b. 1900)
"O thou whose favor hallows all occasions. "

Composer and hymnist, daughter of Otto and Edith Leyrer,
she was born at Santa Ana, California on January 27, 1900.
She married Clifford M. Drury, and while he was studying
for his Ph. D. in Edinburgh, Scotland, she took work in music at the University. She began writing songs for little
children when he was pastor of the First Presbyterian Church
in Moscow, Idaho (1928-38) and while there she received her
B. A. degree at the University of Idaho. "Thirty-three of
her pieces--music, words, or both--appeared in When a Little Child Went to Sing, issued by the Presbyterian Board of
Christian Education in 1935. She also had some songs included in the Board's songbook for the Primary and Junior
Departments. Several of her anthems have been printed.
Two of her hymns (words only) were printed in the Worship
Book (1970) of the Presbyterian Church. She is not well now
and has not been doing any writing. " [March 1982 letter
from her husband, Dr. Drury, from Pasadena, California.]
Her hymn "Bless thou thy chosen sons" appeared in Hymns
on the Ministry published by The Hymn Society of America
(1966), "Within the church's hallowed walls" in the Society's
booklet The Mission of the Church and the hymn above appeared in Marriage and Family Life Hymns published by The
Society (1961) and in Hymns for Christian Worship (1970).

DUCLAUX, MADAME see A. MARY F. ROBINSON

DUFF, MILDRED (1860-1932)
"The heart that once has Jesus known. "

Born in England, she lived in North Walsham and joined The
Salvation Army in 1886. She was sent to Sweden, then returned to England to serve on the International Training Garrison in London. She worked in the slums of London, and
then became editor of All the World, and later editor of The
Young Soldier, The Warrior and The International Company
Orders. Ms. Duff wrote a number of books, and upon her
retirement from army service, resided in North Walsham
where she died on December 8, 1932. Her hymn above appeared in The War Cry (September 28, 1889) and The Song
Book of the Salvation Army (1930; 1953).

DUNCAN, MARY LUNDIE (1814-1840)
"Jesus, tender Shepherd, hear me,
Bless thy little lamb tonight;
Through the darkness be thou near me,
Keep me safe till morning light. "

The daughter of the Rev. Robert Lundie, Parish Minister of
Kelso on the Tweed (River) near Melrose, Scotland, she was
born there on April 26, 1814. Her younger sister Jane,
married the famous Scotch hymnist Dr. Horatio Bonar. On
July 11, 1836, Mary married the Rev. William Wallace Duncan, Presbyterian Minister in the obscure village of Cleish,
Kinross-shire, Scotland. She wrote her hymns for her two
children between July and December 1839, when she suffered
a severe chill, and died, apparently of pneumonia, on January 5, 1840. Her mother published her hymns in a Memoir
in 1841, and the above hymn appeared shortly thereafter in
numerous hymnals, and became a bedside prayer for children in Scotland and England. The hymn appeared in The
Hymnal of the Protestant Episcopal Church in the USA (1940),
and certainly should be included in other American hymnals.
It was published in the English Baptist Hymn Book (1962),
and in The Song Book of The Salvation Army (1953).

DUNGAN, OLIVE (b. 1903)
"Be still and know that I am God. "

Composer, pianist, and teacher, she was born at Pittsburgh,
Pennsylvania on July 19, 1903 and was educated at the Pittsburgh Institute of Musical Art; Miami Conservatory; University

of Miami; and the University of Alabama. She made her piano debut at age seven with the Pittsburgh Festival Orchestra and entertained in hospitals during World War II. She taught piano in Miami, Florida. She composed the music for hymns by Florine Ashby and Ada Morley. As of March 1982 she was enjoying her retirement.

DUNN, CATHERINE HANNAH (1815-1863)
    "Children rejoice, for God is come to earth. "

Translator and versifier, born in England, she published 32 Hymns from the German (1857; 2nd edition, 1861) and with her sister, Ann, Hours of Devotion (London, 1857).

DUNSTERVILLE, PATTY CAROLINE SELLON (1831-1887)
    "The day is done, O God the Son. "

The daughter of a Captain of the Royal Navy, she was born in England on July 10, 1831 and married Colonel Lionel D'Arcy Dunsterville. A member of the Church of England, her hymn was published in Thring's Collection (1882).

DUTTON, ANNE (c. 1698-1765)
    "The Soul's joy in God as its Portion. "

She was born in Northampton, England, and in 1720 married the Rev. Benjamin Dutton, a Baptist minister of Great Gransden, Hunts. In 1743, upon returning from a trip to America, he was drowned in a shipwreck off the English coast. She turned to writing theological treatises. She published Sixty-one Hymns on Several Subjects in 1734, which were reprinted in 1833.

EAKIN, VERA (1890-1977)
    "Oh come, let us sing unto the Lord. "

Composer, hymnist, pianist, and organist, she was born at Emlenton, Pennsylvania on August 6, 1890 and was educated at Slippery Rock Teachers' College in Slippery Rock, Pennsylvania and at the New England Conservatory of Music in Boston, Massachusetts. She composed music for the original hymn which had appeared in the Scottish Psalter (1650). She died on June 4, 1977.

EDDY, MARY BAKER (1821-1910)
"Blest Christmas morn, though murky clouds. "

"Brood o'er us with Thy shelt-ring wing. "

She was born in Bow, New Hampshire on July 16, 1821 and
had three brothers and two sisters.   She became a member
of the Congregational Church in 1838, then married George
W. Glover in 1843, who died the next year.   In 1853 she
married Daniel Patterson, an itinerant dentist, but they
were divorced in 1873.   Then she met Asa Gilbert Eddy, a
traveling sewing-machine salesman, and they were married
on New Year's Day, 1877.   He died in 1882.   She founded
the Church of Christ, Scientist, Boston.   Mark Baker Eddy
died in Chestnut Hill, Massachusetts on December 3, 1910.
Six of her hymns appeared in the Christian Science Hymnal
(1937).

EDGAR, MARY SUSANNE (1889-1973)
"God, who touchest earth with beauty,
Make my heart anew. "

She was born in Sundridge, Ontario, Canada on May 23, 1889
and educated at Havergal College and the University of Toronto.   She also was graduated from the National Training School
of the Y. W. C. A. in New York City and worked for the
Y. W. C. A. in Canada, with a special interest in camping,
having founded Camp Glen Bernard for Girls in northern Ontario in 1922.   In 1925 she retired to live in Toronto and
was a member of the Anglican Church.   She died at Toronto
on September 17, 1973.   Her poems were published in Wood-
fire and Candlelight (1945), and A Christmas Wreath of Verse
(1965); her book of essays was titled Under Open Skies (1955).
Her hymn appeared in The Brethren Hymnal (1951); The Hymn
Book (Presbyterian, Reformed; 1955); The Book of Hymns
(United Methodist; 1964-66); Christian Worship (1953); The
Covenant Hymnal (1973); and The Hymn Book (Anglican and
United Church of Canada; 1973).

EDWARDES, MRS. ANNIE (1832-1896)
"He must reign who won the right. "

She was a Moravian, lived in England, and wrote many novels, The Morals of May Fair (London, 1858); Creeds (1859);
The Ordeal for Wives (1864); Leah, A Woman of Fashion

(London, 1875; a novel in three volumes); Blue Stocking (London, 1877); The Playwright's Daughter (London, 1886); etc.

EDWARDS, ALICE PURDUE (1878-1958)
   "Saviour, my all I'm bringing to Thee. "

Composer, hymnist, pianist, she was born at Battersea, London, England in October 1878 and was converted to Christianity as a child of twelve at a Salvation Army meeting in Notting Hill, and later became a soldier of the corps.   She studied theory, harmony, and the pianoforte with a London musician, and then also the mandolin and advanced musical lessons with an Italian professor.   She would play the piano while a soldier at Notting Hill as an accompanist to Lt. Colonel Slater's musical parties.   She once wrote that the inspiration for the song was her act of surrender to God's will.   At first her soul rebelled against what she felt to be God's unreasonable demands.   But after serious prayer, her heart was put to rest.   Alice entered the Training Home to become an officer in December 1896.   Then in 1899 she married Major Robert Edwards, who had been a Household Trooper in the Salvation Army.   Later he served in the Public Relations Department.   He died in 1945 and she died on October 22, 1958.   Her hymn appeared in The Musical Salvationist (July 1893) and in The Song Book of the Salvation Army (1899; 1953).   She also composed the music for her hymns.

EDWARDS, LIZZIE pen name of FANNY CROSBY

EDWARDS, MATILDA BARBARA BETHAM (1836-1919)
   "God made my life a little light. "

The daughter of Edward Edwards and a cousin of Amelia B. Edwards, the Egyptologist, Matilda was born at Westerfield, near Ipswich, Suffolk, England on March 4, 1836.   She wrote a number of books.   Her hymns were published in Good Words (1873) and in the Congregational Church Hymnal (1887). More recently her hymn appeared in the English Baptist Hymn Book (1962).   She died at Suffolk, England on January 4, 1919.

ELIZABETH I, QUEEN OF ENGLAND   see   ENGLAND and
   IRELAND, ELIZABETH I

ELLIOTT, CHARLOTTE (1789-1871)
"Just as I am, without one plea. "

"O Holy Savior, friend unseen. "

"My God, my Father, while I stray. "

She was born at Clapham, London, England on March 17,
1789 and never married. She became an invalid about 1820
and devoted her time to writing verses and corresponding
with the evangelish César Malan of Geneva (for 40 years).
She was editor of the Christian Remembrance Pocket-book
(1834-1859), and wrote some 150 hymns. Her Hymns for
the Week (1839) sold 40, 000 copies. Her hymns were also
published in The Invalid's Hymn Book (1836); her brother
Henry's Psalms and Hymns for Public, Private and Social
Worship (1835-48); and Thoughts in Verse and Sacred Subjects
(1869). She died at Brighton, East Sussex, England on September 22, 1871. More recently her hymns appeared in The
American Service Hymnal (1968); Baptist (1973); Broadman
(1977); Christian Worship (1953); Christian Science (1937);
Episcopal (1940); Family of God (1976); Lutheran (1941); Methodist (1966); Presbyterian USA (1955); The Pilgrim Hymnal
(United Church of Christ, 1958); and others.

ELLIOTT, EMILY ELIZABETH STEELE (1836-1897)
"Thou didst leave Thy throne and Thy kingly crown,
When Thou camest to earth for me. "

Daughter of the Rev. E. B. Elliott and a niece of hymnist
Charlotte Elliott, she was born at Brighton, England on July
22, 1836. Anglican, Low, she edited the Church Missionary
Juvenile Instructor for six years, contributed to Additional
Hymns (1866) for use in St. Mark's Church in Brighton, and
48 of her hymns were published in Under the Pillow, a book
with tunes for people hospitalized and those in infirmaries,
or sick at home. In addition, 70 of her hymns were published in Chimes of Consecration (1873) and 71 hymns in
Chimes for Daily Service (1880). She died at Mildmay Park,
London, England on August 3, 1897. Her hymn appeared in
the American (1968); Baptist (1973); Christian (1953); Episcopal (1940); Family of God (1976); Presbyterian (1955) hymnals,
and The Pilgrim Hymnal (1958).

ELLIOTT, JULIA ANNE MARSHALL (1809-1841)

"Father, who the light this day
Out of darkness didst create. "

Daughter of John Marshall of Hallsteads, Ullswater, England,
she was born about 1809. On a visit to Brighton, England,
she met the Rev. Henry Venn Elliott, a brother of the hymnist Charlotte Elliott, and on October 31, 1833 she married
the Rev. Elliott. Eleven of her hymns appeared in her husband's collection, Psalms and Hymns (1835; 1839). Shortly
after the birth of her fifth child, she passed away on November 3, 1841. Her hymn appeared in The Lutheran Hymnal
(1941).

ELLIOTT, RUTH (b. 1887)
"Glorious is thy name, Most Holy. "

Born at Hannibal, Missouri on October 8, 1887, she was
educated at Dorchester High School, Boston, Massachusetts
and at Wellesley College (B. A.). She taught four years at
the Northfield Seminary in Massachusetts and at the Plainfield High School in Plainfield, New Jersey. She served with
the Board of Foreign Missions of the United Presbyterian
Church in New York City (1921-54). "In 1929 I became an
active member of the Madison Avenue Presbyterian Church,
New York City. After retirement I became a resident of the
Presbyterian Home, New York City, thence to Amsterdam
House, where I presently reside. " [January 1982 letter to
this author.] Her hymn appeared in the Broadman Hymnal
(1977); Hymns for the Family of God (1976); and the Southern
Baptist Hymnal (1975).

ELLIS, SARAH STICKNEY (1812-1872)
"Shepherd of Israel! hear my prayer. "

Her hymn appeared in Dr. James Martineau's Unitarian
Hymns of Praise and Prayer in 1873. She was born in London, England and married William Ellis (1794-1872). She
wrote Women of England (1838), Daughters of England (1842)
and other books. She died at Hoddesdon, Hertfordshire,
England on June 16, 1872.

ELY, EFFIE SMITH (1879-1968)
"Lord of all power and goodness. "

Born at Church Hills, Hawkins County, Tennessee on September 10, 1879, she was educated at Sullins College, Bristol, Tennessee and at Peabody Normal College in Nashville, Tennessee. She married the Rev. Joseph B. Ely, a Methodist minister, and the two of them worked in rural parishes in the vicinity of Morristown, Tennessee. Her hymn appeared in New Rural Hymns (The Hymn Society of America 1955). She died on August 27, 1968.

ENGLAND and IRELAND, ELIZABETH I, QUEEN OF (1533-1603)
    "Christ was the Word who spake it. "

Daughter of King Henry VIII, she was born at Greenwich Palace on September 7, 1533. She studied Greek and Latin classics and became proficient in French, Italian, and Spanish. While her sister, Mary, was Queen of England, Elizabeth was a virtual prisoner at the Old Palace of Hatfield in the County of Hertford, England. While still a princess, she translated and versified the psalms of Queen Marguerite of Navarre in 1547, which were published in 1843-45. Elizabeth became queen on the death of Mary on November 17, 1558. She died on March 24, 1603. The above hymn, credited to Queen Elizabeth I, appeared in The Worship Book of the United Presbyterian Church (1972).

ESLING, CATHERINE HARBISON WATERMAN (1812-1897)
    "Come unto me, when shadows darkly gather. "

Born in Philadelphia, Pennsylvania on April 12, 1812, her poems and hymns were published under her maiden name. In 1840 she married Captain George J. Esling of the Merchant Marine, and they resided in Rio de Janeiro, Brazil, until his death in 1844 when she returned to Philadelphia. Her hymns appeared in Christian Keepsake (1839) and later were collected and published as The Broken Bracelet and Other Poems (1850). She was a member of the Protestant Episcopal Church and died in Philadelphia. Her hymn above appeared in the Methodist Hymnal (1911); the Evangelical Lutheran; Augustana Lutheran; Reformed; Brethren; and Seventh-Day Adventist (1940) hymnals.

FAGAN, FRANCES (d. 1878)
    "Mine be the tongue that always shrinks. "

Fanny Fagan was a Sunday School teacher in Dr. W. M. Furness's Church in Philadelphia, and also wrote "The still voice that speaks within." Her hymns appeared in Hymns for the Sunday School of the First Congregational Unitarian Church (Philadelphia, 1866). Her poems were published after her death, In Memorium: A selection from the poems of Fanny Fagan (Philadelphia, 1878). She also wrote Something New for My Little Friends, and died in 1878. [Linda Feit, The Free Library of Philadelphia, Pennsylvania.]

FAIRCLOTH, ALTA COOK (b. 1911)
    Tune--DUNWOODY

Composer and hymnist, she was born at Valley Mills, Texas on November 8, 1911, and was educated at Louisiana College (B. A.), Pineville, Louisiana. She taught at public schools in Memphis, Tennessee and was the supervisor of music at the Louisiana Baptist Children's Home in Monroe, Louisiana (1942-1951). During this time she was also choir director and pianist of the College Place Baptist Church, and accompanied and directed an opera club music chorus. She joined the Baptist Sunday School Board in 1951 in the Church Music Department as an assistant editor and continued working there until her retirement in 1976. Her tune above appeared in the Baptist Hymnal (1975).

FARJEON, ELEANOR (1881-1965)
    "Lord, thou who gavest me all I have."

Daughter of Benjamin Farjeon, a popular novelist, and sister of composer Harry Farjeon (1878-1948), she was born at Westminster, London, England on 13 February 1881. She wrote Nursery Rhymes of London Town and Singing Games from Arcady. She also wrote the libretto for her brother's opera Floretta produced at the Royal Academy of Music in London (1899), the libretto for Mackenzie's Eve of St. John, Martin Shaw's Philomel and Shaw's choral works, Ithacaus. The hymn above appeared in Songs of Praise (1931) with the tune NEED by her brother. At age 70 she became a Roman Catholic. She died at Hempstead, London on 5 June 1965. Her hymn "Morning has broken like the first morning" appeared in the New Broadman Hymnal (1977); Hymns for the Family of God (1976); the Pilgrim Hymnal (1958); and the Presbyterian Hymnbook (1955).

FARNINGHAM, MARIANNE pen name of MARY ANN HEARN

FAUSSETT, ALESSIE BOND (1841-1902)
"Be with us all for ever more."

Daughter of the Rev. William Bond, Rector of Ballee, County
Down, Ireland, she was born there on January 8, 1841. In
1875 she married the Rev. Henry Faussett, Incumbent of
Edenderry, Omagh, County of Tyronne, Ireland. Her hymn
was published in her book Thoughts for Holy Words (1867)
and with another hymn in the Irish Church Hymnal (1873).
She also wrote The Triumph of Faith (1870) and The Cairns
of Ions and Other Poems (1873). She died on September 30,
1902. She contributed several hymns to Lyra Hibernia (2nd
edition, 1879) and to the Church Hymnal (Dublin, 1881).

FELKIN, ELLEN THORNEYCROFT FOWLER (1860-1929)
"Now the year is crowned with blessing."

She was the granddaughter of the Rev. Joseph Fowler, Wesleyan Minister, and the daughter of Sir Henry H. Fowler,
Bart., and was born at Wolverhampton, Staffordshire, England on April 9, 1860. In 1903 she married A. L. Felkin,
Senior Assistant Master of Eltham College in England. Her
hymn was published in The Methodist Hymn Book (1904).
She wrote Songs and Sonnets (1888); Verses, Grave and Gay
(1891); Verses, Wise or Otherwise (1895); and several novels.
She died at Bournemouth, Hampshire, England on June 22,
1929.

FERGUSON, JESSIE MARGARET MacDOUGALL (1895-1964)
"Gentle Jesus, hear our prayer."

Born at Essex, England, she was graduated from the Selly
Oak Colleges, Birmingham, with a diploma in Religious Education. After graduation she became a field worker on the
staff of the Youth Department of the United Free Church of
Scotland, then was a Sunday School Organizer with the Sabbath School Society of the Presbyterian Church in Ireland
(1927-34). Later she worked for the Religious Education
Press and then became Woman's Secretary for the British and
Foreign Bible Society in 1960. She published The School Assembly (1943), Services of Worship for Schools, and the Pupils' Service Book. She was a well-known lecturer and demonstrator of Scripture teaching in schools.

FERGUSON, MANIE PAYNE (b. 1850)
"Joys are flowing like a river. "

Born in Carlow, Ireland, she married T. P. Ferguson,
evangelist, who was committed to a Wesleyan "holiness"
theological position. They established a number of Peniel
missions on the west coast of England and in other parts of
the world. Her hymns were published in Echoes from Beu-
lah. The above hymn appeared in Hymns for the Living
Church (1974). She was living in Los Angeles, California
in 1913.

FINDLATER, SARAH LAURIE BORTHWICK (1823-1907)
"Rejoice, rejoice, believers. "

Translator and versifier, daughter of James Borthwick, Manager of the North British Insurance Office in Edinburgh,
Scotland, she was born there on November 26, 1823 and was
the sister of hymnist Jane Borthwick. She married the Reverend Eric John Findlater of Lockearnhead, Pertshire, Scotland. He died on May 2, 1886. With her sister, Jane, she
translated hymns from the German which were published in
Hymns from the Land of Luther (1854-62). Sarah translated
31 of the 122 hymns in the book. She died at Torquay,
Devonshire, England on December 25, 1907. Her hymns appeared in Christian Worship (1953); Episcopal (1940); Lutheran (1941); and Presbyterian (1955) hymnals.

FLINT, ANNIE JOHNSON (1866-1932)
"He giveth more grace when the burdens grow greater. "

Daughter of Eldon Johnson, she was born at Vineland, New
Jersey on December 24, 1866. Three later later, upon the
birth of a sister, Annie's mother died at age 23 and the two
girls were adopted by a family named Flint. Later the family moved to Camden, New Jersey, where Annie attended
high school and one year of normal school. After Mrs.
Flint had a stroke, Annie taught school for three years until she, herself, was stricken with crippling arthritis and
was sent to the Clifton Springs Sanitarium. Her lovely hands
were twisted and almost completely paralyzed, and Annie had
to learn to write again. Her poems were accepted by greet-
ing card manufacturers, published in various magazines, and
in several books, starting with By the Way--Travelogues of
Cheer. When the Sunday School Times printed an article

about her in 1926, describing her condition, she received
three thousand letters of support and praise. Her hymn was
first published by the Lillenas Publishing Company (1941)
and appeared in the Broadman Hymnal (1977). She died on
September 8, 1932.

FLOWER, ELIZABETH "ELIZA" (1803-1846)
    Anthem--Adoration

Composer, daughter of Benjamin Flower, she was born at
Harlow, England on April 19, 1803 and was the elder sister
of hymnist Sarah Flower Adams. Her musical compositions
were published in Fourteen Musical Illustrations of the Waverly Novels (1831); Songs of the Seasons, "Now we pray for
our country" (1842); Hymns and Anthems, the words Chiefly
from the Holy Scriptures, etc. in 5 parts; Adoration (1841);
Aspiration, Belief, Heaven Upon Earth (1846); and Life after
Death, which were composed for the congregation of South
Place Chapel, Finsburg. She also composed music for her
sister's hymns "Darkness clouded Calvary" and "Nearer, my
God, to Thee." Sixty-three of her hymn tunes were published in W. J. Fox's Hymns and Anthems (1840-41). She
died of tuberculosis at London, England on December 12,
1846 and was buried at Harlow.

FLOWERDEW, ALICE (1759-1830)
    "Father of mercies, God of love. "

She married Daniel Flowerdew, a government employee in
Jamaica, the West Indies. After he died in 1801 she operated a Ladies' Boarding School at Islington, England, and was
a member of the Baptist church. Her Poems on Moral and
Religious Subjects was published in 1803, and the 1811 edition included her hymn, the original line being "Fountain of
mercy, God of Love. " Later she lived at Bury St. Edmunds
and at Ipswich, England, where she died on September 23,
1830. Her hymn appeared in Hymns Ancient and Modern
(1904) and in Songs of Praise (Anglican, 1931).

FOLLEN, ELIZA LEE CABOT (1787-1860)
    "God, Thou art good, each perfumed flower. "

Daughter of Samuel Cabot, she was born at Boston, Massachusetts on August 15, 1787. Her hymns were published in

the Christian Disciple (1818), Sabbath Recreations (1829) and the above hymn in Hymns for Children, Boston (1825). On September 15, 1828 she married Professor Charles Follen. A well-known Unitarian writer, she was editor of The Children's Friend (1843-50) and wrote A Well-Spent Hour (1827); The Skeptic (1835); Poems (1839); To Mothers in Free States: Anti-Slavery Hymns and Songs (1855). Her husband died on the ship Lexington when it burned and sank in Long Island Sound, New York State, on January 13, 1840. She died at Brookline, Massachusetts on January 26, 1860.

FOLTZ, MILDRED HARNER (b. 1910)
"Before thee, Lord, we join our hearts."

Born in Pennsylvania, she was graduated from Pennsylvania College for Women (Chatham College). She started writing poetry early, and one of her poems was published in Best College Verse in 1931 by Harper and Brothers. She married Ralph A. Foltz, and was a member of the secretarian staff of the First Dallas Christian Church in Dallas, Texas. A member of the Dallas Pen Women, four of her sonnets were included in the 1958 Bethany Guide. Her hymn was published in Marriage and Family Life Hymns by The Hymn Society of America (1961) and also in Christian Worship--A Hymnal (1970).

FORESTER, FANNY pen name of EMILY C. JUDSON

FORSYTH, CHRISTINA (1825-1859)
"O Holy Spirit, now descend on me."

Sixth daughter of Jane Hamilton and Thomas Forsyth, she was born at Liverpool, England. Of delicate constitution, she never married. She was the sister of the Rev. John Hamilton Forsyth, Douglas Forsyth, Esq., C. B. and William Forsyth, Esq., Q. C. member for Cambridge. She published her Hymns by C. F. (London, 1861) and four of her hymns were published in Lyra Britannica (1867). She died at Hastings, England on March 16, 1859.

FORSYTH, JOSEPHINE (1889-1940)
Setting for the Lord's Prayer

A composer, she was born at Cleveland, Ohio on July 5, 1889 and married to R. A. Meyers on April 29, 1928. She wrote the setting to the Lord's Prayer for her wedding and it was sung at Easter sunrise ceremonies at the Hollywood Bowl in California for many years. She died at Cleveland on May 24, 1940.

FORTESCUE, ELEANOR, LADY (1798-1874)
    "At eve appears the morning star. "

The fifth daughter of Hugh Fortescue, first Earl of Fortescue, she was baptized on April 2, 1798 and was raised in the Church of England. As a translator and versifier she published thirty Hymns mostly taken from the German (Exeter and Barnstaple, 1843). She died on August 12, 1874.

FOSTER, FAY (1886-1960)
    "The place where I worship. "

Pianist, hymnist, and composer, she was born at Leavenworth, Texas on November 8, 1886. She was head of the voice department at the Ogontz School in Rydall, Pennsylvania for ten years. She died at Bayport, New York on April 17, 1960. One recording of her hymn is listed in Phonolog Reports of Los Angeles, California. She also composed music for hymns by Florence Tarr.

FOX, ELEANOR FRANCES (b. 1875)
    "God of all pity and all power. "

The daughter of the Rev. H. E. Fox, she was born in London, England on February 24, 1875 and was raised in the Church of England. She wrote several hymns for the Church Missionary Society which appeared in the Church Missionary Hymn Book (1899).

FOX, FRANCES A. (d. 1915)
    "In Thee, O Spirit true and tender. "

She joined the Church of Christ, Scientist, on July 3, 1897. Her hymn first appeared in The Christian Science Journal in October 1888, then in the Christian Science Hymnal (1937). She died in June 1915.

FOX, RUTH MAY (1853-1958)
   "Firm as the mountains around us."

Daughter of James and Mary Ann May, she was born in West-
bury, Wiltshire, England on November 16, 1853. When Ruth
was only sixteen months old, her mother died, and in 1856
her father went to America, leaving Ruth with a widow who
also had a daughter. James sent for the widow and the two
girls in October of that year, and upon their arrival in Philadelphia he married the widow. In July 1867 they started for
Salt Lake City, traveling nine days by rail to reach North
Platte, Nebraska. Here they joined Brother Gentry who had
a wagon, and Brother May agreed to drive all the way for
his share of the wagon. He became a carder in Brigham
Young's factory, and later started his own carding business.
On May 8, 1873 Ruth was married to Jesse W. Fox and bore
him twelve children: six sons and six daughters. She served
forty years as a member of the General Board of the Young
Women's Mutual Improvement Association (M. I. A.), and
served as its president (1929-37). She retired in October
1937 at age 84, and died at the age of 104 years. Her hymn
appeared in Hymns (1948), The Church of Jesus Christ of
Latter-day Saints.

FRANCES, GRACE J. pen name of FANNY CROSBY

FREEMAN, CAROLYN R. (b. 1895)
   "Never fear tho' shadows around your path may fall."

Composer, hymnist, pianist, and songwriter, and the daughter of Fred A. and Lenora G. Freeman, she was born at
Taylor Center, New York on October 22, 1895. About 1902
they sold their farm and moved to Taylor, New York, where
they operated a large general store. Upon her father's death,
the family moved to Cortland, New York. She was an active
Methodist.

        She wrote her high school graduation song (1912),
        and later became a staff writer for the Teacher's
        Magazine. She established the Freeman Music
        Company in Cortland to publish her own songs and
        the music of others. She published Very Best
        Christmas Helps (1938) which included recitations,
        dialogues, tableaus, etc.; Very Best Easter Enter-
        tainment (1939) for primary children and tiny tots;

The Coming of the Christ-Child (1939), a pageant;
also the words and music of The Heart of America
(1942) and other songs. Her hymn "Back of the
Clouds" was recorded on the record "I Believe, "
Chapel Records (Mountain View, California) and appeared in Rodeheaver's Gospel Solos and Duets No.
3. She is now crippled with arthritis but can still
play the piano, which was moved into the nursing
home where she is residing in Cortland. [Letter
from her sister, Mrs. Freda M. Miner of Cortland, New York, June 8, 1982.]

FREER, FRANCES (1801-1901)
"Present with the two or three. "

She was born on March 16, 1801 and her hymn first appeared
in the Catholic and Apostolic Church Hymns for the Use of
the Churches in 1871, and later in other collections. More
recently her hymn appeared in the Church of Scotland and
Anglican (London, 1965) hymn books. She died in June 1901
at the age of 100 years.

FRYXELL, REGINA CHRISTINA HOLMEN (b. 1899)
Arrangement of Tune--SKARA

Composer, arranger, pianist, and organist, she was born at
Morganville, Kansas on November 24, 1899 and educated at
Augustana College (B. A. & B. Mus. 1922) in Rock Island,
Illinois and taught there (1922-25). She studied at Juilliard
in New York City (1925-27) and with Leo Sowerby, Dr. Luther
D. Reed and others. In 1928 she married Fritiof M. Fryxell,
who later was Professor of Geology at Augustana College.
She taught organ at Knox College (1956-58) in Galesburg,
Illinois, then at Black Hawk College in Moline, Illinois. She
composed numerous solos and anthems. Her music appeared
in the Lutheran Service Book and Hymnal (1958). In April
1982 she was living in Rock Island, Illinois. [Information
from Augustana College.]

FULLER, ESTHER MARY (1907-1969)
Unison Anthems for Children

Composer, conductor, organist, and pianist, she was born at
Amboy, Indiana on November 7, 1907 and was educated at

Taylor University (B. M.) in Upland, Indiana; Fletcher College (B. M.), and the University of Michigan. She taught music in public schools for 15 years and was church organist, choir director, and Director of Music for the Paoli Methodist Church in Paoli, Pennsylvania. Lucy Lewis wrote the words for her music, and she also collaborated with Doris Paul. Her words include A Child's Book of Anthems; Chapel Bells; We Bow Our Heads; Altar of Christmas; Little Children Sing. She was married to Roy Fuller. She died on March 28, 1969.

FULLER, SARAH MARGARET (1810-1850)
   "Jesus, a child, His course began. "

She was born in Cambridgeport, Massachusetts on May 23, 1810, the first of nine children. She became the editor of the Dial, Emerson's transcendentalist quarterly (1840-42), then worked for Horace Greely's New York Tribune. She went to Italy in 1847, and in 1849 married the Marchese d'Ossoli. Later they sailed from Livorno aboard the Elizabeth, but when just a few hours' sail from New York City, a severe storn broke up the ship, and Margaret, her husband, and child drowned, on July 19, 1850.

FULLER-MAITLAND, FRANCES SARA see FRANCES S.
   COLOQUHOUN

FULLERTON, LADY GEORGIANA CHARLOTTE (1812-1885)
   "I'll never forsake thee, I never will be. "

   "Mary, mother! Shield us through life. "

The daughter of the first Earl Granville, she was born at Tixall Hall, Staffordshire, England on September 23, 1812. In 1833 she married A. G. Fullerton of Ballintoy Castle, Antrim, North Ireland and was received into the Church of Rome in 1846. She was a popular novelist, wrote Ellen Middleton (1844) and other books. Her translations and orig- inal hymns appeared in the Holy Family Hymns (1860); Parochi- al Hymn Book (1880); Tozer's Catholic Hymns (1898); and other hymnals. She died at Bournemouth on January 19, 1885.

FYLEMAN, ROSE AMY (1877-1957)
   "Lift your hidden faces,
   Ye who wept and prayed. "

She was born at Basford, near Nottingham, England on March 6, 1877. Her parents were free-thinking Jews from Jever in Oldenburg. She studied singing in Paris and was graduated from the Royal Academy of Music in London. She changed her name from Feilmann to Fyleman in 1914. She wrote a number of plays and books of verse, never married, and died in London on August 1, 1957. Her hymn appeared in Songs of Praise (1931).

GABBOTT, MABEL JONES (b. 1910)
"In humility, our Savior, Grant thy Spirit here, we pray. "

She was born in Malad, Idaho, on October 23, 1910. In 1937 she spent two years as a missionary in the Northwest, where she met her husband-to-be, John Donald Gabbott. They were married on June 30, 1941, and had five children. In 1945 she was invited to submit lyrics for a new hymnbook, and three of her hymns were selected. The above hymn appeared in Hymns (1948) of the Church of Jesus Christ of Latter-day Saints. She received her B. S. in Education at the University of Idaho and taught school for five years before her marriage. She had many stories, poems, and articles published; A Woman's Way (poems), Mothers in Miniature (poems and essays); Heroes of the Book of Mormon; among others. As of May 1982 she was living in Bountiful, Utah. [Information from Mrs. Gabbott in a letter dated May 3, 1982.]

GAITHER, GLORIA (b. 1942)
"God sent his Son, they called him Jesus. "

Born at Battle Creek, Michigan on March 4, 1942, she was educated at Anderson College (B. A.; M. A.), Anderson, Indiana, majoring in English, French, and Sociology. During her college days she met William J. Gaither of Alexandria, Indiana whom she married. They both taught at the Alexandria High School. He founded the Gaither Music Company, which publishes his compositions and other musical works. Gloria and her husband, Bill, together with his brother Dan, formed the Gaither Trio, famous gospel singing group. Her hymns appeared in the Baptist (1975); Broadman (1977); and Family of God (1976) hymnals. Her hymn "There's something about that name" listed nineteen recordings for the song by Phonolog Reports of Los Angeles (1978). Her husband composed the music for her hymns.

GARNETT, ADA (1866-1931)
"I have a home that is fairer than day. "

Born at London, Ontario, Canada, she wrote her hymn when
she was sixteen years old for the farewell party for Hattie
Yerex who was leaving the Lindsay (Ontario) Corps to become an officer in the Salvation Army. She based the words
on a song her music teacher had taught her, "Home in the
valley, far from the sea. " Ada also took officer training,
and served as Captain at Coaticook, Quebec in 1886 when her
hymn was first published in the Canadian War Cry (November 6, 1886). In 1893 she married John Nisbett and they
had six children. He died in 1914. She wrote a total of 36
songs and hymns which were published anonymously in the
Canadian War Cry. The song was sung at the funeral of
Mrs. Nisbett's mother. Her hymn was included in The Song
Book of the Salvation Army (1899; 1953).

GARRIOTT, JEAN E. (b. 1918)
"World around us, sky above us. "

Born in St. Louis, Missouri on September 1, 1918, she was
educated at the Conservatory of Music, Millikin University,
Decatur, Illinois. She married the Rev. Christopher T. Garriott, who served as minister of the St. Paul Community
Church of Homewood, Illinois. She has conducted music
clinics in Massachusetts, Colorado, and Ohio for the International Convention of Community Churches and was well-
known in the Chicago area for her hymn programs given as
piano talks. The mother of four sons, she took an active interest in the life of the church and later resided in Chevy
Chase, Maryland. Her hymn above appeared in Hymns for
the 70's (Hymn Society of America, 1970) and another hymn,
"Entrusted with an earthly home, " in The Stewardship of the
Environment (Hymn Society, 1973).

GATES, ELLEN M. HUNTINGTON (1835-1920)
"O, the clanging bells of time. "

"Come home, come home, you are weary at heart. "

The youngest sister of Collis P. Huntington, she was born at
Torrington, Connecticut and married Isaac E. Gates. In
1860, on a snowy afternoon, she wrote on her slate the lines
"If you cannot on the ocean ... " and the hymn became a

favorite of the singing evangelist Philip Phillips (1834-1895) who sang the hymn at a meeting of the Christian Commission in the Hall of Representatives in Washington, D. C. on February 28, 1865 when President Lincoln was present. Her hymn was entitled "Your Mission." Lincoln was so overcome with emotion that he sent a note to the Chairman, Secretary of State William H. Seward: "Near the end let us have 'Your Mission' repeated by Mr. Phillips. Don't say I called for it. A. Lincoln.'" Mr. Phillips, in his book Singing Pilgrim (1866) included a photocopy of Lincoln's note on page 97. The first hymn listed above appeared in the Christian Science Hymnal (1937) and the second hymn was published in Ira D. Sankey's Sacred Songs and Solos (1881) and there are two recordings listed in Phonolog Reports (1978). Her hymn, "I will sing you a song" appeared in The Hymnbook (Presbyterian, 1955). She lived in Elizabeth, New Jersey for a number of years and died in New York City.

GATES, MARY CORNELIA BISHOP (1842-1905)
"Send thou, O Lord, to every place."

Born in Rochester, New York on February 14, 1842, she was married in 1873 to Dr. Merrill E. Gates, Secretary to the U. S. Indian Commissioners, who afterwards was president of Rutgers University at New Brunswick, New Jersey and still later president of Amherst College at Amherst, Massachusetts. (She should not be confused with Ann Cornelia Bishop Gates, whose maiden name was Rochester, and she was the daughter of the city's founder. In 1851 she married William S. Bishop, and he died in 1863, leaving no children. In 1867 she married Seth M. Gates, but she died leaving no issue.) [Information from Lawrence Naukam, Local History Division, Rochester Public Library, Rochester, New York.] For many years Mary Gates served on the Women's Board of Foreign Missions of the Reformed Church of America. She was a frequent contributor to The Youth's Companion and to The Atlantic Monthly, and her hymn appeared in Sursum Corda (1898). She died on December 17, 1905. More recently her hymn appeared in the Presbyterian Hymnal (1933) and the Evangelical and Reformed Church Hymnal (1941).

GAULTNEY, BARBARA FOWLER (1935-1974)
"In the lightning flash across the sky."

Born in Atlanta, Georgia on July 14, 1935, she attended the
University of Georgia in Atlanta and was a member of the
First Baptist Church of Forest Park, Georgia, a suburb of
Atlanta. She died at Riverdale, Georgia on January 21,
1974. Her hymn appeared in the Baptist (1975) and Broad-
man (1977) hymnals.

GAY, ANNABETH McCLELLAND (b. 1925)
    Tune: SHEPHERDS' PIPES

A composer and daughter of a Presbyterian minister in Ottawa, Illinois, she was born there and was graduated from
Knox College (B. M. E. , 1947) in Galesburg, Illinois and attended the School of Sacred Music of Union Theological Seminary in New York City (M. S. M. , 1949), where she met the
Rev. William Gay who gained his B. D. at the Seminary.
They were married in 1949, and he served Congregational
Churches in Jefferson, Ohio, three rural churches in Brown
county, then at Pleasant Hill, Ohio from 1958. She served
as leader of the Ohio Women's Fellowship of Congregational
Christian Churches in hymn-singing. The tune, with the
hymn "The Lord is rich and merciful, " appeared in The Pilgrim Hymnal (1958).

GERSTMAN, BLANCHE (b. 1910)
    Christmas cantata--Die Boodskap aan Maria

Composer and teacher, she was born at Cape Town, South
Africa on 2 April 1910 and studied piano with Colin Taylor
and composition with W. H. Bell at the South African College
of Music at Capetown, graduating in 1930. She taught harmony and counterpoint at the college for many years and also
was the principal double bass player in the Municipal Orchestra. She also composed music for "The Lord's Prayer" for
women's voices, unaccompanied. The words for her Christmas cantata were written by N. P. van Wyk Louw, W. E. G.
Louw and Elizabeth Eybers.

GIBBS, ADA ROSE (1865-1905)
    Tune--CHANNELS

A composer, she was born in England and was married to
William J. Gibbs, who was superintendent of the Central Hall
(Methodist), at Bromley, Kent. She was an active member in

the Keswick Convention movement, and was the mother of one of the directors of Marshall, Morgan and Scott, Ltd., London. She published Twenty-four Gems of Sacred Song (1900) and her tune was used with the hymn "How I praise Thee, precious Savior" which appeared in Hymns for the Living Church (1974).

GILBERT, ANN TAYLOR (1782-1866)
> "Great God, and wilt Thou condescend
> To be my Father and my Friend?"

The daughter of Isaac and hymnist Ann Martin Taylor, originally of Ongar, Essex, she was born at Islington, England on January 30, 1782 and was raised at Lavenham in Suffolk. With her sister, Jane Taylor, she published Hymns for Infant Minds (1810). On December 24, 1813 she married the Reverend Joseph Gilbert. He died in 1852. One of her poems, "For a Very Little Child," is worth repeating:

> Oh, that it were my chief delight
> To do the things I ought!
> Then let me try with all my might
> To mind what I am taught.

Ann and her husband lived in Nottingham, England where she died on December 20, 1866. Her hymn above was published in the Baptist Hymnal (1973).

GILBERT, ROSA MULHOLLAND, LADY (d. 1921)
> "Give me, O Lord, a heart of grace."

The daughter of J. S. Mulholland of Belfast, North Ireland, she was married to Sir John T. Gilbert. Her hymn was published in her Vagrant Verses (1886) and later in Horder's Worship Song (1905) and in other hymnals. More recently her hymn appeared in The American Student Hymnal and the Student Hymnary (1937).

GILMAN, CAROLINE HOWARD (1794-1888)
> "Sweet hour of holy, thoughtful prayer,
> Thy peace and calm may we improve."

Born at Boston, Massachusetts on October 8, 1794, she was the fifth of six children. On December 14, 1819 she married the Reverend Samuel Gilman, author of the ode "Fair Harvard." They moved to Charleston, South Carolina, where he became the minister of a Unitarian Church there. In March 1862 her house in Charleston was shelled during the Civil War, and she moved to Greenville, South Carolina. She died in Washington, D. C. on September 15, 1888 but was buried in Charleston next to her husband. Her hymn appeared in the Christian Science Hymnal (1937).

GIPPS, RUTH (b. 1921)
    Choral work--The Temptation of Christ

Composer, oboist, and pianist, she was born at Bexhill-on-the-Sea, Sussex, England on 20 February 1921 and studied at the Bexhill School of Music where her mother, Mrs. Bryan Gipps was principal. Later she studied composition with R. O. Morris, Gordon Jacob and Vaughan Williams and piano with Arthur Alexander and Kendall Taylor at the Royal College of Music in London (1937-43). Her choral work for soprano, tenor, chorus, and small orchestra was based on the gospel according to St. Matthew. In 1942 she married Robert Bake, first clarinettist in the City of Birmingham Orchestra, where she became second oboist and English horn player in 1944. She received her Doctor of Music degree from Durham University in 1948.

GLASER, VICTORIA (b. 1918)
    Arrangement--Cradle Song of the Shepherds

Composer, arranger, conductor, and teacher, she was born at Amherst, Massachusetts on September 11, 1918 and was educated at Radcliffe College (B. A.; M. A.), Cambridge, Massachusetts and studied privately with Walter Piston and others. She was a music instructor at Wellesley College (1943-45), Choral Director and Chairman of Theory Department at Dana Hall School (1944-59) and at the New England Conservatory in Boston from 1957. Her works include arrangements for the Twelve Days of Christmas, and To Mary We Sing Praises.

GLEN, IRMA (b. 1908)
    "This I know...."

Composer and hymnist, she was born at Chicago, Illinois on

August 3, 1908 and was educated at the American Conservatory in Chicago, Sherwood Music School in Illinois, Golden State University, and Institute of Religious Science, Los Angeles (Mus. D.). She was Minister of Music at the Beverly Hills Church of Religious Science in Beverly Hills, California (1946) and ordained (1955). Later she was a minister in Palm Springs, California and La Jolla, California. As of March 1982 she was enjoying her retirement.

GLENN, MARGARET M. see MARGARET M. G. MATTERS

GLOVER, ELLEN J. (d. 1966)
"In speechless prayer and reverence. "

She joined the Church of Christ, Scientist on November 6, 1936 and her hymn appeared in the Christian Science Hymnal (1937). She died on June 24, 1966.

GLYDE, ELIZABETH (1815-1845)
"Be with me in the valley. "

Daughter of Jonathan L. Glyde, a merchant in Exeter, England, she was born on September 28, 1815. She had been in ill health, and went to see a doctor in Malvern, but he gave her no chance of recovery, and she returned to Exeter. Her poem was read at her funeral services by the Rev. John Bristow at the Castle Street Chapel in Exeter. Later her hymn was published in the Christian Remembrancer (1859) and in Shepp's Songs of Grace and Glory (1880). She died at Exeter, England on February 15, 1845.

GODWIN, ELIZABETH AYTON ETHERIDGE (1817-1889)
"My Saviour, 'mid life's varied scene. "

The daughter of William Ellis Etheridge, she was born at Thorpe Hamlet, Norfolk, England on July 4, 1817. In 1849 she was married to C. Godwin. She published Songs for the Weary; The School of Sorrow and Other Poems (London, 1873); Songs Amidst Daily Life (London, 1878). She died at Stoke Bishop, England.

GOODENOUGH, LUCY M. (d. 1958)
"Thou living light of pentecostal glory. "

She joined the Church of Christ, Scientist on June 3, 1910 and her hymn appeared in the Christian Science Sentinel on June 22, 1929 and in the Christian Science Hymnal (1937). She died on March 14, 1958.

GOODMAN, LILLIAN ROSEDALE (1887-1972)
"My Shepherd is the Lord. "

Composer and hymnist, she was born at Mitchell, South Dakota on May 30, 1887 and educated at Columbia University in New York City, Juilliard, Boguslawski College (hon. Mus. D.) and then taught there. She was vocal coach at Desilu Workshop in Hollywood, California (1958) and wrote hymns with her husband, Mark Goodman. She died on January 23, 1972.

GOREH, ELLEN LAKSHMI (1853-1937)
"In the Secret of His presence. "

Daughter of the Rev. Nehemiah Goreh, a Brahmin of the highest class, and a Christian convert, she was born at Benares, India on September 11, 1853. After her mother's death, she was adopted by a Mr. Smailes, but unfortunately he lost all his property in the Mutiny of 1857, so she was taken to England by the Rev. W. T. Storrs, where she was educated. But in 1830 she returned to India to do missionary work at Allahabad. Her hymns were published in From India's Coral Strand; Hymns of the Christian Faith (1883). More recently her hymn appeared in the American Lutheran Hymnal (1930).

GOULD, HANNAH FLAGG (1789-1865)
"O Thou who hast spread out the skies. "

"Who, when darkness gathered o'er us. "

She was born in Lancaster, Vermont on September 3, 1789 and when still a child, the family moved to Newburyport, Massachusetts. Her poem and hymns were published in her Poems in 1832, 1835 and 1841. She never married, and died at Newburyport on September 5, 1865.

GOWER, JEAN MILNE (1867-1957)
"Father, loving Father, hear Thy children's call. "

Born in England, she married John Henry Gower (1855-1922) of Rugby, England. He was graduated from Oxford University (1876), received his D. Mus. there (1883), then emigrated to Denver, Colorado where he became organist and choirmaster of the Cathedral of St. John in the Wilderness. He composed the music for her hymns. She died in November 1957 at Great Barrington, Massachusetts [Information from Joanne E. Classen of the Denver Public Library.] Two of Jean Gower's hymns appeared in Christian Worship (1953). Here is an interesting anecdote about the church:

> Trumpets blared a fanfare and heavy wooden carved doors swung open as Britain's Princess Anne entered Denver's St. John's Church in the Wilderness for a Sunday service. Nearly 600 people stood as the princess' procession made its way down through the gothic Episcopal cathedral.... The princess took communion as 20 robed children sang "Fairest Lord Jesus." Princess Anne has been in Colorado for six days. [News dispatch 23 June 1982.]

GRAHAM, SARAH (1854-1889)
  "On the cross of Calvary."

Born in Canada, she wrote songs and one day while attending a meeting of The Salvation Army Lindsay Corps, Ontario, Canada, a duet was singing one of her songs. She joined the corps, and was engaged to be married when her fiancé was stricken with "galloping consumption" (tuberculosis) and died. She never fully recovered from the shock, and wrote a song, "Life's morn will soon be waning." Her hymn above appeared in The Musical Salvationist (July 1886) and in The Song Book of The Salvation Army (1889; 1953).

GRANDVAL, MARIE FELICIE CLEMENCE DE REISET (1830-1907)
  Oratorio--St. Agnes

A composer, she was born at Saint-Remy-des-Monte, Sarthe, France on January 21, 1830 and studied composition with Saint-Saëns and von Flotow. Her oratorio was performed in Paris on April 13, 1876. She also wrote six operas and died at Paris, France on January 15, 1907.

GRANT, EDNA FAY (1905-1981)
"Walk softly in Springtime, to hear the grass sing. "

Born at Rockland, Ontario, Canada on October 26, 1905,
near Ottawa, she was raised in British Columbia. She became Field Secretary for the Women's Christian Temperance
Union in Toronto, Ontario, which position she served for
many years. A diabetic condition robbed her of her eyesight, but her marvelous memory served her well for almost
thirty years. She took a course on Poetry Enjoyment from
the Hadley School for the Blind in Winnetka, Illinois, cared
for six groups of children every week, and directed a camp
during the summer months. Her hymn appeared in Hymns
for Children published by The Hymn Society of America
(1965) and in the Canadian Baptist and United Church hym-
narys. She died at Toronto, Ontario, Canada on September
15, 1981. [Information from Miss Verna Wice of Toronto,
Canada.]

GRAY, JANE LEWERS (1796-1871)
"Am I called? and can it be?"

Daughter of William Lewers, she was born at Castle Blayney,
county Monagham, Ireland on August 2, 1796 and married
the Rev. John Gray, D. D. , a Presbyterian Minister. In
1820 they emigrated to America where Dr. Gray became a
pastor in Easton, Pennsylvania in 1822. The above hymn
appeared in the Reformed Church Psalms and Hymns (1834)
and in other hymnals. Six of her hymns appeared in the
Presbyterian Church Devotional Hymns (1842).

GREENAWAY, ADA RUNDALL (1861-1937)
"O word of pity, for our pardon pleading. "

The daughter of General Thomas Greenaway, she was born
at Trirandrum, India on October 12, 1861 and brought to
England as a child. The family resided at Guilford, where
she published her book of verses, A Book of Posies, and a
book for children, The Story of a Father's Love. Seven of
her hymns appeared in the Rev. E. Handley's Children's
Supplement (1897). The above hymn, together with four
others, was published in Hymns Ancient and Modern (1904;
1950), as well as in The Pilgrim Hymnal (1958). She died
at St Kintas Home, Woking, England on May 15, 1937.

GREENSTREET, ANNIE LOUISE ASHLEY (1835-1915)
"A little talk with Jesus. "

Daughter of William Ashley, a schoolmaster in Sheffield,
England, she was born on February 17, 1835. Her hymn
appeared in A. L. Ashley's Heart Yearning after Home published by T. W. Hall, Sheffield, in 1871. On March 7, 1876
she married W. T. Greenstreet of Sheffield.

GREENWELL, DORA (1821-1882)
"I am not skilled to understand, What God hath willed.
What God hath planned. "

Born Dorothy Greenwell at Greenwell Ford, Lanchester, Dur-
ham, England on December 6, 1821, she later resided at the
Ovingham Rectory in Northumberland (1848) and the Golborne
Rectory in Lancashire and in Durham (1854). She published
fifteen books of verse and hymns, the most notable being
The Patience of Hope (1860); Carmina Crucis (1869); and
Songs of Salvation (1873). She died at Clifton, near Bristol,
England on March 29, 1882. Her hymn appeared in the
Baptist (1975); Broadman (1977); and Family of God hymnals
(1976).

GRIFFITHS, ANN (1776-1805)

She was born in Wales in 1776, and resided at Dolwar Fechan,
Montgomeryshire, Wales. Her hymns were published posthu-
mously in Hymnau ofawl i Dduw ar Oen (Hymns of Praise to
God and the Lamb) in 1806 and 1808. Many of her hymns
were translated into English and appeared in H. Elvet Lewis'
Sweet Singers of Wales in 1889.

GRIMES, E. MAY see EMILY M. G. CRAWFORD

GRIMES, KATHARINE ATHERTON (b. 1877)
"We are heralds of the Master. "

Her hymns appeared in the Baptist Hymnal (1973), Rodeheaver's Gospel Solos and Duets No. 3 and in Hymns for the
Living Church (1974).

GRÜNBECK, ESTHER MAGDALENE AUGUSTA NAVEROFSKY (1717-1796)
"Dem blut'gen Lamme. "
"To the Lamb stain'd with Blood. "

She was born at Gotha in East Germany on October 21, 1717 of a Polish-Jewish family who had been converted to Christianity. In 1734 she married Michael Grünbeck, a sculptor in Gotha, and in 1738 they joined the Moravian Church. After his death in 1742 she entered the Widow's Choir. But then in 1746 she married David Kirchhof, a baptized Jew, and they spent some time in Prussia and Poland doing mission work. The above hymn appeared in the Supplement to the 8th Appendix of the Herrnhut Gesang-Buch (1739) and translated in the Moravian Hymn Book (1742). Other translations of her hymns appeared,, such as "Unto the Lamb of God" in the Moravian Hymn Book (1789); "To Christ, the Lamb of God" in J. A. Latrobe's Collection (1841); a cento beginning with stanza 2, "To Thee I wholly give" in Lady Huntington's Collection (1780); and others. Eight of her hymns appeared in the Historische Nachricht to the Brüder Gesang Buch (Hymn Book) of 1778 in the 1851 edition. More recently her hymn appeared in the Moravian hymnals (1876; 1908). After her second husband died, she became leader of the Widow's Choir at Zeist, near Utrecht, The Netherlands, and died there on October 13, 1796.

GUINEY, LOUISE IMOGEN (1861-1920)
"The little cares that fretted. "

Daughter of a Civil War General, she was born at Boston, Massachusetts on January 7, 1861 and was Roman Catholic. In 1894 she was appointed Postmaster of Auburndale, Massachusetts, but the anti-Irish and anti-Roman Catholic feeling was so strong there that she was forced to resign. She worked for a time in the Boston Public Library, then in 1901 emigrated to England. Her poems were published in Songs of the Street (1884); A Roadside Harp (1893); and Happy Endings (1909). Her hymn appeared in The Student Hymnary (1937). She also wrote biographies and essays. She died at Chipping Camden, England on November 2, 1920.

GURNEY, DOROTHY FRACES BLOMFIELD (1858-1932)
"O perfect Love, all human thought transcending,
Lowly we kneel in prayer before thy throne. "

She was born at 3 Finsbury Circus, London on October 4, 1858, the eldest daughter of the Rev. F. G. Blomfield, Rector of St. Andrews' Undershaft, London, and granddaughter of the Dr. Blomfield, Bishop of London. Her hymn was written for her sister's marriage in 1883, and later set as an anthem by J. Barnby for the marriage of the Duke of Fife with the Princess Louise of Wales on July 27, 1889. It was included in the Supplement to Hymns Ancient and Modern (1889) and in the Hymnal Companion (1890). She married Gerald Gurney in 1897, and they were received into the Roman Catholic Church in 1919. She published two volumes of her poetry. She died at Kensington, England on June 15, 1932. Her hymn (above) appeared in the Broadman (1977); Episcopal (1940); Hymns for the Family of God (1976); Lutheran (1941); Methodist (1966); Presbyterian (1955); and The Pilgrim Hymnal (1958).

GUYON, JEANNE MARIE BOUVIER (1648-1717)
    "My Lord, how full of sweet content. "

Daughter of Claude Bouvier, Lord Proprietor of La Motte Vergonville, she was born at Montargis, Department Loiret, France on April 13, 1648 and educated there. When she was only sixteen years old she was given by her parents in marriage to Jacques Guyon, who was 22 years her senior, and in weak health, but a very wealthy man. She bore him three children, and he died in 1676. After his death she embraced Quietism, founded by Molinos of Spain, and practiced by Quakers. She became an evangelist for the movement, later becoming the leader in France and Switzerland. In 1686 she went to Paris, where she was arrested for her beliefs and preaching, and imprisoned for eight months in the Convent of St. Marie in the Faulbourg St. Antoine. At this point, Madame de Maintenon became interested in her case. Françoise D'Aubigne, who became the Marquise de Maintenon (1635-1719) had been governess to the children of King Louis XIV of France, and she once made the statement, recorded in history:

> We shall have all eternity to engage in contemplation; this life is made for work.

After Queen Marie Theresa died, the king married Mme. de Maintenon in 1684. After she heard the plight of Madame Guyon, she had the king order her release from confinement. But Madame Guyon continued preaching, and Madame de Main-

tenon's College of Ladies at Cyr came under her spell. Molinos was condemned in 1685, and her beliefs were also condemned by the Roman Catholic Church. A commission led
by Boussuet banned her from Paris, and ordered her to remain quiet. But in 1795 she returned to Paris and continued
preaching. She was a strong believer in the witness of the
Spirit, perfect faith, and perfect love. So in December 1695
she was imprisoned at Vincennes, and in the following year
removed to Vaugirard, then in 1698 she was imprisoned in
the Bastille in Paris, and not released until 1702. During
her seven years in prison she wrote forty books. Some 37
of her poems and hymns were translated by William Cowper,
the poet, in 1782 and published by William Bull in 1801.
After her release from prison she lived with her daughter,
the Marquise de Vaux, at Blois, France. Famous people
from all over the world visited her, persons of all rank paid
her homage, and she is considered one of the great religious
personages of all time. One of her hymns, translated by
Cowper, follows:

> No bliss I seek, but to fulfill
> In life, in death, Thy lovely will;
> No succor in my woes I want,
> Except that Thou are pleased to grant. "

Although persecuted by the Roman Catholic Church for her
beliefs, she attended mass daily and died in full communion
with the Church of Rome. She died at Diziers, France on
June 9, 1717. Various of her hymns appeared in Hatfield's
Church Hymn Book (New York, 1872); the Andover Sabbath
Hymn Book (1858); Songs for the Sanctuary (1865); Spurgeon's
Our Own Hymn Book (1866). The hymn above, more recent-
ly, in the Methodist Hymnal (1911) and in Songs of Praise
(Anglican, 1931).

HACKETT, ROSEMARY B. (d. 1950)
    "Loving Father, we Thy children. "

She joined the Church of Christ, Scientist on November 5,
1901 and her hymn appeared in the Christian Science Hymnal
(1937). She died on January 6, 1950.

HAIGH, EMILY WADDINGTON (1857-1933)
    "In sunny days. "

Born in England, she was the daughter of a Methodist min-

ister, and her hymn appeared in the Methodist School Hymn
Book and then in the Methodist Hymn Book (1962).

HALE, MARY WHITWELL (1810-1862)
    "Whatever dims thy sense of truth,
    Or stains thy purity."

Daughter of Eliphalet Hale, she was born in Boston, Massachusetts on January 29, 1810. She was a teacher in Boston,
Taunton, and Keene, New Hampshire. Her hymns appeared
in her Poems (1840), the Unitarian Christian Hymns for Public and Private Worship, commonly known as the Cheshire
Collection (1844) and Putnam's Singers and Songs of the Liberal Faith (1874). She died on November 17, 1862. Her
hymn appeared in the Christian Science Hymnal (1937).

HALE, SARAH JOSEPHA BUELL (1788-1879)
    "Our Father in heaven, we hallow Thy name."

Daughter of Captain Gordon Buell, a Revolutionary soldier,
she was born in Newport, New Hampshire on October 24,
1788 and in 1813 she married David Hale, a lawyer in Newport. But he died in 1822, leaving her with five small children to raise. She published a novel in 1827, was editor of
the Rev. J. L. Blake's Ladies' Magazine in Boston (1828-
1837). Her Poems for Our Children (1830) included her famous poem, "Mary had a little lamb." She was editor of
Louis A. Godey's Ladies Magazine (1837-1877) in Philadelphia,
Pennsylvania. She published 36 volumes of her works. She
retired as editor of Ladies' Magazine in December 1877 in
her 90th year, and died in Philadelphia, Pennsylvania on
April 30, 1879. She was a member of the Protestant Episcopal Church and her hymn appeared in Manson and Greene's
Church Psalmody in 1831. But there is an interesting story
to tell about Sarah Hale. When George Washington was President, he declared a Thanksgiving Day, but then the holiday
was forgotten and neglected for many, many years. But Sarah Hale didn't forget. From 1833, for some 30 years, she
wrote to every President of the United States asking them to
declare Thanksgiving a holiday, and she wrote to many Gov-
ernors, and to leading Senators and Representatives to intro-
duce bills to declare Thanksgiving a holiday, to no avail.
Her letters either landed in the wastepaper baskets, or were
ignored. Until one day in 1863, during the dark days of the
Civil War, her letter, by mistake, or by the will of God, was

placed on the desk of President Lincoln, who then declared
Thanksgiving Day a holiday that year, and in doing so gave
credit to Sarah J. Hale of Boston and Philadelphia. We may
consider Sarah Hale one of our great Americans, who has
also been long forgotten, for not only her hymns, and for
"Mary had a little lamb, " but also for our Thanksgiving Day.
More recently her hymn appeared in the Mennonite, Southern
Baptist (1956) and American Baptist (1958) hymnals.

HALL, ELVINA MABLE REYNOLDS (1820-1889)
    "I hear the Savior say
    Thy strength indeed is small. "

The daughter of Captain David Reynolds, she was born at
Alexandria, Virginia on June 4, 1820 and later resided in
Baltimore, Maryland where she was a member of the Monument Street Methodist Church for over forty years. She
was married first to Richard Hall, and after his death married the Rev. Thomas Myers of the Baltimore Conference of
the Methodist Church in 1885. She wrote her hymn on the
fly-leaf of the New Luke of Zion while in the church choir.
It first appeared in Ira D. Sankey's Sacred Songs and Solos
(1878). She died at Ocean Grove, New Jersey on July 18,
1889. More recently her hymn appeared in the American
Service (1968); Baptist (1975); Broadman (1977); Christian
Worship (1953); and Family of God (1976) hymnals.

HALL, JANE E. pen name of J. Edward Hall (1845-1917) of
    Brattleboro, Vermont.

HALL, LOUISA JANE PARK (1802-1892)
    "Never, my heart, wilt thou grow old. "

Born at Newburyport, Massachusetts on February 7, 1802,
she was raised in Boston where her father became a teacher
at a young ladies' school. Her poems were published in the
Literary Gazette (Boston, 1823). She wrote Miriam (1830),
Joanna of Naples, Life of Elizabeth Carter (1830) and Dra-
matic Fragment. In 1840 she married the Reverend Edward
B. Hall, Unitarian Minister of Providence, Rhode Island.
After his death in 1866 she returned to Boston. She died
at Cambridge, Massachusetts on September 8, 1892.

HAMBLEN, SUZY (b. 1913)
"There's a place in God's heart."

Born in Gage, Oklahoma on May 9, 1913, she married Stuart
Hamblem (b. 1908), a singer. They have written a number
of songs together. There are two recordings of the above
hymn listed in Phonolog Reports, and one recording of another hymn of theirs, "Help thy unbelief." As of May 1982
she was still active.

HAMMOND, MARY JANE (1878-1964)
Tune--SPIRITUS VITAE

A composer, she was born in England and died at the Hilling-
don Nursing Home on Hillside Road in St. Albans, Herts,
England on January 23, 1964. Her tune with the hymn "O
Breath of Life" appeared in Hymns for the Living Church
(1974).

HANAFORD, PHOEBE A. COFFIN (1829-1921)
"Cast thy bread upon the waters."

The daughter of Captain George W. Coffin, and a descendant
of Tristram Coffin, an early settler of Nantucket Island,
Massachusetts, she was born there on May 6, 1829. After
being tutored by an Episcopal clergyman in Latin and higher
mathematics, she began teaching school at age sixteen and
married a Mr. Hanaford when she was twenty. In 1862 she
wrote "The Empty Sleeve" about a Civil War amputee case,
and her poem was set to music by the Rev. John W. Dadum
and published by George W. Bagby in The Southern Literary
Messenger. In 1868 she was ordained as a Universalist minister and was pastor of the Universalist Church in Hingham,
Massachusetts. She was the first woman ordained as a minister in New England, the first woman who ever offered an
ordaining prayer, the first woman to exchange pulpits with
her own son, both being settled pastors, the first woman to
officiate at the marriage of her own daughter, the first woman
to serve as chaplain of the Connecticut Legislature, which she
did in 1870 and 1872, the first woman-minister to give the
charge to a man-minister, the Rev. W. G. Haskell of Marblehead, Massachusetts, and the first woman to attend a Masonic
Festival, and to respond, by invitation, to a toast. In 1870
she was installed as pastor at New Haven, Connecticut, was
pastor of a church in New Jersey, then returned to New Haven

in 1883. Her hymn appeared in Laudes Domini (1884) and
other hymnals. She died at Rochester, New York.

HANKEY, ARABELLA KATHERINE (1834-1911)
"I love to tell the story, Of unseen things above,
Of Jesus and His glory, Of Jesus and His love. "

"Tell me the old, old story ... "

"Advent tells us Christ is near;
Christmas tells us Christ is here. "

She was born at Clapham, England, the daughter of a banker.
She was a member of the "Clapham Sect, " which followed
the leadership of William Wilberforce, an evangelical society.
Miss Hankey led Sunday School classes. "I love to tell the
story" comes from part one of "The Story Wanted" in her
book of the life of Jesus, written in 1866, called The Old,
Old Story. "Tell me the Old, Old Story" comes from part
two of her book, called "The Story Told. " Part three was
called "The Story Welcomed. " At age eighteen she started
Bible classes for working girls in London. She also wrote
books on Bible Class Teachings and on Confirmation. She
traveled to South Africa to look after and bring home an invalid brother. Conditions were still primitive in that area
and transportation was by bullock-cart only. She became
interested in mission work in Africa, and spent her last
years visiting the sick in hospitals in London. At the time
of her death, at Westminster, England, May 9, 1911, five
of her old Sunday School members, of over fifty years before, attended her funeral services. [Information from R.
Jayne Craven, The Public Library of Cincinnati and Hamilton
County, Cincinnati, Ohio.] Her hymn appeared in Philip
Bliss' Gospel Songs, Cincinnati (1874), and has been translated into German, Italian, Spanish, Welsh and other lan-
gusges. It was set to music by William G. Fischer in 1869,
and first appeared in a pamphlet issued by the Methodist
Episcopal Book Room, Philadelphia (1869). Modern hymnals
which include this hymn are the American Service Hymnal
(1968); The Baptist Standard Hymnal (1973); The New Broadman Hymnal (1977); Christian Worship (1953); Christian Science Hymnal (1937); Hymns for the Family of God (1976);
Joyfully Sing (1968); The Methodist Hymnal (1966); The Hymn-
book (Presbyterian, 1955); Pilgrim Hymnal (1958); and others.
"Advent tells us Christ is near" is in the Hymnal of the
Protestant Episcopal Church in the USA (1940).

HANNA, IONE T. MUNGER (1837-1924)
Tune--MY AIN COUNTREE

Composer, eldest of the eight children of Martha S. Whitney
and Lyman Munger, a druggist in Penn Yan, New York, she
was born there. Later the family moved to Galva, Illinois.
She married John Rowland Hanna, a banker, and they moved
to Denver, Colorado in 1871. She was a member of the
First Congregational Church in Denver, and wrote the music
for Mary Demarest's hymn, which appeared in Sankey's
Sacred Songs and Solos (1881) and later in the Methodist
Hymnal. She was elected to the Denver School Board in
1893 and was the first woman to hold such office. She was
a member of the Daughters of the American Revolution. She
died in Los Angeles, California on August 6, 1924 and funeral services were held in the First Congregational Church in
Denver. [Information from Catherine T. Engel, Reference
Librarian, Colorado Historical Society, Denver, Colorado
80203.]

HARDCASTLE, CARRIE HITT (b. 1894)
"The earth is thine in beauty, Lord. "

Born in rural Davidson County, near Nashville, Tennessee,
she was educated there and has spent her life in Tennessee.
She married a Mr. Hardcastle and was the mother of five
children, two of whom became ministers. An active member
of Walker's Methodist Church in Goodlettsville, Tennessee,
she wrote poetry, hymns and contributed meditations to the
Upper Room devotional magazine. She also wrote "O holy
day, of peace and benediction" which was published in Lord's
Day Hymns by The Hymn Society of America (1968), the
above hymn published by the Society in The Stewardship of
the Environment (Ecology) in 1973, and "Dear God of all
creation" published in 1975.

HARKNESS, GEORGIA EMMA (1891-1974)
"Hope of the world, thou Christ
of great compassion. "

Born in Harkness, New York on April 21, 1891, she was
educated at Cornell University (B. A. , 1912), Boston University (M. A. , 1920; Ph. D. , 1923) and taught at Elmira College
after 1923. She was graduated from Union Theological Seminary in 1936 and became a Methodist minister, then taught

at Mount Holyoke College in South Hadley, Massachusetts
(1937-39), at the Garrett Biblical Institute (1939-50), and at
the Pacific School of Religion at Berkeley, California (1950-
61). She published twenty-eight books, mostly on religion,
wrote several hymns, and died at her home in Claremont,
California on August 21, 1974. Her hymn appeared in the
Baptist Hymnal (1975); Broadman (1977); The Mennonite Hymnal (1969); Hymnal and Liturgies of the Moravian Church
(1969); Methodist (1966); Service Book & Hymnal Lutheran
(1958); Presbyterian (1955); and The Pilgrim Hymnal (1958).

HARRISON, SUSANNA (1752-1784)
    "Begone, my worldly cares away. "

    "O happy souls that love the Lord. "

A resident of Ipswich, England, her father died when she
was young and her mother had to support a large family. At
age 16 Susanna went to work as a domestic servant, and became invalided at age 20 of a complicated disease which baf-
fled all medical skill (probably infantile paralysis). In 1780
her friends published 133 of her hymns in Songs in the Night.
She died on August 3, 1784.

HARTICH, ALICE (1888-1967)
    "Each year the Spring puts on her gown. "

The daughter of Joseph Buxton and Alice Doughty Hartich,
she was born in Brooklyn, New York City on April 26, 1888
and was educated at the Brooklyn Training School for Teachers, Adelphi College (B.S., 1927) and at New York University (M.A., 1940). She taught in elementary schools in
Brooklyn and was also a principal there (1910-55) and wrote
books of verse, Gift of Light (1949), Pure White Flame
(1964), and short stories for children. She was a member
of the Flatbush-Tompkins Congregational Church in Brooklyn.
Her hymn appeared in Hymns for Children published by The
Hymn Society of America (1965). She died on April 8, 1967.
[Information from the Flatbush-Tompkins Congregational
Church, Brooklyn, and from New York University Alumni
Office, New York City.]

HASLOCH, MARY (1816-1892)
    "Christian, work for Jesus. "

The daughter of the Rev. John Hasloch, Congregational Minister at Kentish Town, London, England, she was born on July 2, 1816. Her hymn appeared in the Congregational Church Hymnal in 1887 and other publications. More recently her hymn appeared in the Church of Scotland (1927) and Presbyterian Church of Canada (1930) hymnals. She died on March 11, 1892.

HASTINGS, LADY FLORA (1806-1839)
    "O Thou, Who for our fallen race. "

Daughter of the Marquess of Hastings, she was born at Edinburgh, Scotland on February 11, 1806. Her sister, the Marchioness of Bute in 1841 published her Poems by the Lady Flora Hastings, Edited by her Sister. Her hymn appeared in W. F. Stevenson's Hymns for the Church and Home in 1873. She died on July 5, 1839.

HAUSMANN, JULIE KATARINA VON (1825-1901)
    "So nimm denn meine Haende"
    "Take thou my hand, O Father and lead me. "

The daughter of a Gymnasium (preparatory school) teacher in Riga, Latvia (now part of Soviet Russia), she was born there, but raised at Mitau, Kurland, Latvia where her father had moved to become a government councilor. Under Russian law at that time his position raised him to the status of a nobleman, so the German "von" was added to his name. She was one of six daughters and served as a governess in various homes, then cared for her aged father until his death in 1864. She lived in Biarritz, France with an older sister who was an organist at the English church there (1866-70), then made her home with another sister in St. Petersburg (now Leningrad). Later she lived with other relatives in Estonia. She published Hausbrot, a devotional book, and her poems and hymns in Maiblumen, Lieder einer Stillen im Lande. She died near Wösso, Estonia. Her hymn appeared in the Evangelical and Reformed Church Hymnal (1941) and in Hymns for the Living Church (1974).

HAVERGAL, FRANCES RIDLEY (1836-1879)
    Tune--HERMAS--"Golden harps are sounding. "

Composer and hymnist, the youngest child of William Henry

Havergal, she was born at Astley, Worcestershire, England on December 14, 1836 and never married. In 1852-53 she studied in Dusseldorf, Germany. In 1880 she published Life Chords, Coming to the King (1886) and other books. In 1878 she moved from her home in Leamington to Oystermouth, Glamorganshire, Wales. She wrote many popular hymns, such as

> Take my life, and let it be
> Consecrated, Lord to Thee.
>
> Truehearted, wholehearted, faithful and loyal,
> King of our lives, by Thy grace we will be.

She once wrote to a friend. "It does seem wonderful that God should so use and bless my hymns, and yet it really does seem as if the seal of his own blessing were set upon them, for so many testimonies have reached me. Writing is praying for me." She died at Caswell Bay near Swansea, Wales on June 3, 1879. Her hymns appear in the Broadman (1977); Christian Science (1937); Episcopal (1940); Lutheran (1941); Methodist (1966); Presbyterian (1955) hymnals and the Pilgrim Hymnal (1958).

HAWKINS, HESTER PERRIAM LEWIS (1846-1926)
   "To thee, the giver of all good. "

She married Joshua Hawkins of Bedford, England. Seven of her hymns, including the one above, were published in her books, The Home and Empire Hymn Book and The Home Hymn Book, A Manual of Sacred Song for the Family Circle (London: Novello & Co., 1885). Julian in his Dictionary of Hymnology wrote: "For home use we know of no book of equal comprehensiveness and merit." More recently her hymn, "Heavenly Father, Thou hast brought us" appeared in The Song Book of the Salvation Army (1953).

HAWKS, ANNIE SHERWOOD (1835-1918)
   "I need Thee every hour. "

She was born at Hoosick, New York on May 25, 1835. In 1859 she married Charles Hial Hawks (1833-1888) and they resided in Brooklyn, New York. Two of her children died as infants. [Information from Mrs. Charles Rudd, First Baptist Church, Hoosick, New York.] She was a member of the

Hanson Place Baptist Church when Robert Lowry was the
pastor there. Although she wrote more than 400 hymns, the
one above has been the most popular. It first appeared in
a small collection prepared by Robert Lowry and William H.
Doane for the National Baptist Sunday School Association
which met in Cincinnati, Ohio in November 1872. She died
in Bennington, Vermont on January 3, 1918. Phonolog Reports of Los Angeles, California lists seventeen (17) different recordings of her hymn as of 1978, and her hymn appeared in The American Service Hymnal (1968); Baptist (1973);
Broadman (1977); Episcopal (1940); Hymns for the Family of
God (1976); The Pilgrim Hymnal (1958); and others.

HAWTHORNE, ALICE pen-name of Septimus Winner (1827-
1902) of Philadelphia, Pennsylvania.

HAY, VIOLET SPILLER (d. 1969)
"All glory be to God most high. "

Born Violet Spiller, she married Commander, the Honorable
Gerald Hay in Cape Town, South Africa. She joined the
Church of Christ, Scientist on November 7, 1899 and was a
Christian Science practitioner and teacher (1902-1969). She
also served as Chairman of the Christian Science Hymnal
Committee (1928-32) and was a committee member through
1955. She published a book of solos and a book of poems,
and died on July 18, 1969. Her hymn appeared in the Christian Science Hymnal (1937), together with five additional
hymns she wrote.

HAYCRAFT, MARGARET SCOTT MAC RITCHIE (1853-1936)
"Thou art my Shepherd, Caring for all my need. "

Born at Newport Pagnell, Bucks, England, she later resided
at Bournemouth and married a Mr. Haycraft. Her hymn appeared in William B. Bradbury's New Golden Shower (1866)
and in Clarion (1867). Other hymns of hers appeared in the
Christian Endeavour Hymnal (1896); Hymns and Choral Songs
(Manchester, 1904); Sunday School Hymnary (1905); and the
Junior Hymnal (1906). Her hymn was written with Elsie Thal-
heimer. It also appeared in the New Hymnal for American
Youth (1930) and the New Christian Hymnal (1929). She died
on June 29, 1936.

HAYN, HENRIETTA LUISE VON (1724-1782)
"Weil ich Jesu Schäflein bin. "
"I am Jesus' little lamb. "

Daughter of Georg Heinrich von Hayn, master of the hounds
to the Duke of Nassau, she was born at Idstein, Nassau,
near Frankfort-am-Main, Germany on May 22, 1724. In 1742
she was received into the Moravian community at Herrnhaag,
later at Grosshennersdorf, then after 1751 at Herrnhut. She
taught at a girl's school there, and after 1766 cared for the
invalid sisters of the community. Her hymn first appeared
in the Brüder Gesang Buch (1778). She wrote some 40 hymns,
some in the Moravian Hymn Book (1789); Lyra Germania
(1858); Methodist Sunday School Hymn Book (1883); etc. She
died at Herrnhut on August 27, 1782. Various translations
of her hymn above appeared in The New Broadman Hymnal
(1977) and The Lutheran Hymnal (1941).

HEAD, ELIZABETH "BESSIE" ANN PORTER (1850-1936)
"O breath of Life, come sweeping thro' us. "

Born in Norfolk, England on January 1, 1850, she married
Albert Alfred Head, an insurance broker with the firm of
Henry Head Company of London, England. She was a member of the Church of England. Her husband was Chairman
of the Keswick Convention for several years, and her hymns
appeared in the Keswick Hymn Book (1937). She died at
Wimbledon, Surrey, England on June 28, 1936. More recently her hymns appeared in the Broadman (1977), Family
of God (1976); Great Hymns of Faith (1972); and Hymns for
the Living Church (1974).

HEADLAM, MARGARET ANN (1817-1897)
"Holy is the seed-time, when the buried grain. "

Daughter of the Venerable John Headlam, Archdeacon of
Richmond, England, she was born on January 4, 1817. Her
hymn was written for a Harvest Festival in the parish of
Whorlton in Durham and published in the Supplement to Potts'
Hymns and also in the Society for Promoting Christian Knowl-
edge Church Hymns (1871). She died on July 13, 1897.

HEARN, MARY ANN (1834-1909)
"Just as I am, thine own to be,
Friend of the young, who lovest me. "

Raised a Baptist, she was born at Farningham, Kent, England on December 17, 1834 and wrote verses under the pseudonym "Marianne Farningham." She taught school from 1852 to
1866, wrote for the Christian World from 1857 until her death
and was editor of the Sunday School Times from 1865. Her
collected works, based upon her contributions to the Christian
World, were published in 20 volumes. She never married,
and died at Barmouth, Merionethshire, Wales on March 16,
1909. Her hymns appeared in her Songs of Sunshine (1878);
G. Barrett's Book of Praise for Children (1881); Sankey's
Sacred Songs and Solos; Broadman (1977); Christian Worship
(1953); Joyfully Sing (1968); Methodist (1966); Presbyterian
(1955); and Baptist (1956) hymnals, and in The Song Book of
the Salvation Army (1953).

HEATH, ELIZA (1830-1905)
    "Praise the Lord, sing 'Hallelujah'. "

Her hymn appeared in the Irvingite Hymns for the Use of
Churches (1864; 1871) and in the Scottish Church Hymnary
(1898). She died at No. 4, The Cloisters, Gordon Square,
London, England on December 29, 1905.

HEMANS, FELICIA DORTHEA BROWNE (1793-1835)
    "Come to the land of peace,
    From shadows come away. "

She was born in Liverpool, England on September 25, 1793
and was raised at Gwrych, near Abergele, North Wales. In
1812 she married Captain Alfred Hemans, who had served in
the King's own 4th Foot Regiment in Spain. They had five
sons, but he went out to sea and never returned. She published numerous books, but is best known for her poem:

    The boy stood on the burning deck,
    Whence all but he had fled;
    The flame that lit the battle's wreck,
    Shone round him o'er the dead.

The boy was Giacomo Casabianca, son of the captain of the
Orient at the battle of the Nile in August 1798, who stayed
aboard to assist his dying father as the crew fled the ship.
The poem was included in her book of Poems in 1826. She
died in Dublin, Ireland on May 16, 1835. She wrote or compiled numerous books, including Hymns for Childhood (1827),

Scenes and Hymns of Life (1834), etc. Her hymn above first appeared in The Works of Mrs. Hemans (1839), later in Dr. Martineau's Hymns, etc. (1873), and two of her hymns appeared in J. Curtis' Union Collection (1827). More recently her hymn appeared in the Christian Science Hymnal (1937).

HENSEL, LUISE (1798-1876)
      "Müde bin ich, geh' zur Ruh. "
      "Now that o'er each weary head. "
      "Weary now I go to rest. "

Daughter of J. J. L. Hensel, Lutheran pastor at Linum, near Fehrbellin, Brandenburg, Germany, she was born there on March 30, 1798. She was raised a Lutheran, but was drawn toward the Roman Catholic faith, and joined that Communion on December 7, 1818. Her best hymns were written before she was 23 years old and appeared in F. Föster's Singerfahrt (1818); in Diepenbrook's Geistlicher Blumenstrauss (Sulzbach, 1829); H. W. Dulken's Gold Harp (1864); C. H. Bateman's Children's Hymns (1872); and in the Ohio Lutheran Hymnal (1880). Her hymn also appeared in the Eastern Mennonite Hymnal (1902). In 1874 she entered the Union of Daughters of Christian Love at Paderborn and died there on December 18, 1876.

HERNAMAN, CLAUDIA FRANCES IBOTSON (1838-1898)
      "Lord, who throughout these forty days,
      For us did fast and pray. "

The daughter of W. H. Ibotson, Vicar of Edwinstowe, Motts, England, she was born at Addlestone, Surrey, on October 19, 1838. In September of 1858 she married one of Her Majesty's Inspector of Schools, the Rev. J. W. D. Hernaman. She wrote mostly hymns for children, a total of some 150, and also translated hymns from the Latin. The above hymn appeared in her book The Child's Book of Praise (1873) together with eight other hymns. She also published Hymns for the Children of the Church (1878); Story of the Resurrection (1879); The Altar Hymnal (editor; 1884); Hymns for the Little Ones in Sunday Schools (1884); Lyra Consolationis, from the Poets of the 17th, 18th and 19th centuries (1890). She died at Brussels, Belgium on October 10, 1898. More recently her hymn appeared in the Episcopal (1940); and Presbyterian (1955) hymnals and The Pilgrim Hymnal (1958).

HERSCHELL, ESTHER FULLER-MAITLAND (1803-1882)
"Whence these sorrows, Saviour say?"

The sister of hymnist Frances Sara Colquhoun and the daughter of Ebenezer Fuller-Maitland of Henley-on-Thames, England, she married the Rev. Ridley Herschell. Her hymns appeared in her mother, Mrs. Bethia Fuller-Maitland's Appendix to Hymns for Private Devotion--Selected and Original (London: Richards, 1827) and in later hymnals.

HESSE-DARMSTADT, ANNA SOPHIA, COUNTESS OF (1638-1683)
"Rede, liebster Jesu, rede."
"Speak, O Lord, Thy servant heareth."

The daughter of the Landgrave Georg II of Hesse-Darmstadt (West Germany), she was born at Marburg on December 17, 1638. In 1657 she was elected "Pröpstin" of the Lutheran Fürstentocher-Stift at Quedlinburg and became abbess there in 1680. Her hymns appeared in her Der treue Seelenfreund, etc. Jena (1658). She died on December 13, 1683. More recently her hymn appeared in The Lutheran Hymnal (1941).

HEUSSER, META SCHWEIZER (1797-1876)
"Herz, du hast viel geweinet."
"Long hast thou wept and sorrowed."

Daughter of Diethelm Schweizer, pastor of the Reformed Church at Hirzel, near Zurich, Switzerland, she was born there on April 6, 1797 and in 1821 was married to Dr. Johann Jacob Heusser at Hirzel. The hymn above was published in Albert Knapp's Christoterpe (1841); [Translation in Hymns from the Land of Luther in 1862 by Jane Borthwick.] Other hymns appeared in Lieder einer Verborgenen (Leipzig, 1858); and later in Schaff's Christ in Song (1870); W. F. Stevenson's Hymns for the Church and Home (1873); and other hymnals. More recently her hymn appeared in the Evangelical Lutheran (1913) and Augustana Lutheran (1925) hymnals. She died at Hirzel on January 2, 1876.

HEWITT, ELIZA EDMUNDS STITES (1851-1920)
"More about Jesus would I know."

The daughter of Captain James S. and Zeruiah Edmunds Stites

and a first cousin of hymnist Edgar Page Stites, she was
born in Philadelphia, Pennsylvania on June 28, 1851 and was
graduated from the Girl's Normal School as valedictorian of
her class.   She taught in public schools for a number of
years and was superintendent of the Sunday School of the
Northern Home for Friendless Children and an active member
of the Olivet Presbyterian Church in Philadelphia.   She married a Mr. Hewitt.   Later she moved to another section of
the city and served as superintendent of the Primary department of the Calvin Presbyterian Church.   Her hymns were
published by John R. Sweney and William J. Kirkpatrick.
She died at Philadelphia on April 24, 1920.   More recently
her hymns appeared in the American Service (1968); Baptist
(1975); Broadman (1977); Family of God (1976); and Presbyterian (1955) hymnals.   Two of her hymns appeared in Rodeheaver's Gospel Solos and Duets No. 3 and four of her hymns
in Hymns for the Living Church (1974).

HILL, FRANCES THOMPSON (d. 1979)
     "Let us sing of Easter gladness. "

When she was still a child, Frances was taken to see Mary
Baker Eddy, the founder of Christian Science, and played the
piano for her.   Together they sang a much-loved hymn which
begins, "Shepherd show me how to go, " the words of which
were written by Mrs. Eddy.   She married a Mr. Hill, and
she was an accomplished musician and served for many years
as assistant organist of the Mother Church in Boston, Massachusetts.   She was also a member of the committee for
the last revision of the Christian Science Hymnal (1937) and
two of her hymns appeared in that hymnal.   In addition, she
was a longtime public practitioner of Christian Science.

HINKSON, KATHARINE TYNAN (1861-1931)
     "I would choose to be a doorkeeper
     In the House of the Lord. "

When General Andrew Jackson ran for President of the United
States in 1828, there was much scandal about his marriage to
Rachel Robards in August 1791, when it was revealed that
Robards had not received a divorce until September 1793.
The scandal so distressed Rachel that she suffered a heart
attack and died five days later on December 22, 1828.   And
her dying words were: "I had rather be a doorkeeper in the
house of God than to live in that place (The White House). "

Katharine Tynan was born in Dublin, Ireland on January 23, 1861. She suffered an attack of measles as a child, which affected her eyesight. In 1863 she married Henry A. Hinkson, barrister and novelist. She was a friend of William Butler Yeats, George Russell (AE), Christina Rossetti and others. She died at Wimbledon, England, on April 2, 1931. Her hymn was published in Songs of Praise (1931).

HINSDALE, GRACE WEBSTER HADDOCK (1833-1902)
"A light streams downward from the sky."

Daughter of Professor Charles B. Haddock, D. D., whose mother was a sister of Daniel Webster, she was born at Hanover, New Hampshire on May 17, 1833 and in 1850 she married Theodore Hinsdale, a New York lawyer, who died in 1880. She published Coming to the King, a Book of Daily Devotion for Children (1865) which was published in England as Daily Devotions for Children (1867). The above hymn appeared in this book. She also wrote Thinking Aloud, and wrote under the pseudonym "Fairn." Four of her hymns appeared in Schaff's Christ in Song (New York, 1869). She resided in Brooklyn, New York and was a member of Dr. Richard S. Storrs' congregation. She died on August 31, 1902.

HOATSON, FLORENCE (1881-1964)
"God whose Name is Love,
Happy children we are."

Daughter of the Rev. John Hoatson, a Congregational minister, she was born in Leyton, London, England and educated at Christchurch, New Zealand and at Melbourne, Australia. She taught kindergarten for many years, and was a lecturer and demonstrator to the National Sunday School Union in Cardiff, Wales. She wrote The Palace of Gifts, stories for young children, and The Little White Gate and Lavender's Blue, books of verses for young people. Her hymns were published in Carey Bonner's Child Songs (1908) and more recently in The Hymnal of the Protestant Episcopal Church in the USA (1940) and in Songs of Praise (London: Oxford, 1931). She died on January 28, 1964.

HOFER, MARIE RUEF (1858-1929)
"Come all ye shepherds."

Translator and versifier, and daughter of Marianna Ruef and Andreas Franz Hofer, she was born at Littleport, Iowa on July 18, 1858 and was raised at McGregor, Iowa. After being educated at Mount Carroll (Illinois) Seminary and at the University of Chicago, she taught music in public schools in La Crosse, Wisconsin, in Chicago and in Rochester, Minnesota. Later she taught at the University of California at Berkeley, University of Georgia and the University of Tennessee. She managed the musical programs at the Columbian Exposition in Chicago, Illinois in 1893 and helped direct a chorus of 5,000 children and 5,000 adults. She published Music for the Child World (in 3 volumes), Children's Messiah, The Story of Bethlehem, a nativity play (1912), which was published in Chinese in 1927, also Polite and Social Dances (1917). After directing a pageant in Los Angeles one night in November 1929, she boarded a train for Portland, Oregon where she suffered a severe pulmonary attack and died on board. The body was taken off the train at Bakersville, Oregon. Her hymn appeared in the Evangelical and Reformed Church Hymnal (1941).

HOKANSON, MARGRETHE (1893-1975)
     Choral--O Praise Him

Composer, arranger, conductor, organist, and pianist, she was born at Duluth, Minnesota on December 19, 1893 and was educated at the American Conservatory in Chicago, at the Margaret Morrison School with Joseph Lhevinne and studied privately. She was Dean of the Organ Department at St. Olaf College in Northfield, Minnesota, director of the Northland Choral Group, founded the Nordic Choral Ensemble (1939-43) and was associate professor of music at Allegheny College in Meadville, Pennsylvania (1944-54). She died on April 24, 1975.

HOLBROOK, FLORENCE (c. 1857-1932)
     "Not more of light I ask, O God. "

Daughter of Anne Case and Edmund S. Holbrook, she was born at Peru, Illinois and educated at the University of Chicago (B. A. , 1879-A. M. , 1885). She was a high school principal in Chicago and wrote Elementary Geography (1896), Northland Heros (1906), The Holbrook Reader for Primary Grades (1912) and other books. She resided in Chicago, and died unmarried. Her hymn appeared in Prayer Poems (Abington-Cokesbury, 1942).

HOLMES, AUGUSTA (1847-1903)
    Psalm--In exita

A composer, born Mary Anne Holmes of Irish parentage in
Paris, France on 16 December 1847, she studied harmony
and counterpoint with H. Lambert, organist of the cathedral
at Versailles, and later with César Franck (in 1875). In
exita was performed by the Société Philharmonique (1873)
and her "Hymme à la paix" at Florence in May 1890. She
also wrote two or three symphonies and operas. She died
at Paris on 28 January 1903.

HOMER, CHARLOTTE G. pen-name of Charles H. Gabriel
    (1856-1932) of Los Angeles, California.

HOPPE, ANNA BERNADINE DOROTHY (1889-1941)
    "This night a wondrous revelation. "

    "O'er Jerusalem Thou weepest. "

The daughter of Albert and Emily Hoppe, she was born in
Milwaukee, Wisconsin on May 7, 1889. She started writing
hymns when she was 25 years old, and 23 of her hymns appeared in the Augustana Synod Hymnal (1925). She translated many hymns from the German and the Selah hymnal
contains some 30 of her translations. The first hymn listed
above is a translation, and the second is one of her original
hymns. A collection of her hymns was published as Songs
of the Church Year and eight of her hymns were published in
the American Lutheran Hymnal (1930). She died at Milwaukee,
Wisconsin on August 2, 1941. Her hymns above appeared in
The Lutheran Hymnal (1941).

HORNABROOK, MARY WISEMAN (1850-1930)
    Tune--EVEN ME (2)

Composer, she studied under Walter Macfarren, and was the
sister of the Rev. F. L. Wiseman. She was the wife of the
Rev. John Hornabrook. Her hymn tune appeared in the New
People's Hymnary (1922) and in the British Methodist Hymn-
Book (1935).

HORNBLOWER, JANE ROSCOE (1797-1853)
    "My Father, when around me spread. "

Daughter of William Roscoe, attorney and writer, she was born in Liverpool, England, and was the sister of Mary Ann Roscoe Jevons. Jane married Francis Hornblower in 1838. Her Poems by one of the Authors of Poems for Youth and Family Circle was published in 1820. The hymn above appeared in Sacred Offering (1832). She published her Poems in 1843.

HOWARD, BEATRICE THOMAS (b. 1905)
"Christ is my pilot."

Born at Eutaw, Alabama on March 7, 1905, she was a school teacher and principal for twenty years. As of March 1982 she was enjoying her retirement.

HOWE, JULIA WARD (1819-1910)
"Mine eyes have seen the glory of the coming of the
Lord...
Glory! Glory! Hallelujah!"

She was born in New York City on May 27, 1819, and married Dr. Samuel Gridley Howe in 1843 and moved to Boston. Upon visiting the troops at Bailey's Cross Roads, near Fairfax Court House, Virginia, on November 20, 1861, and hearing the soldiers sing "John Brown's Body," she returned to her hotel in Washington, D.C. and that evening wrote her inspiring words, and called her hymn "The Battle Hymn of the Republic." A Unitarian, she died at Middletown, Rhode Island, on October 17, 1910. Her hymn was published in the American Service (1968); Baptist (1973); Broadman (1977); Family of God (1976); Joyfully Sing (1968); Methodist (1966); Songs of Praise (1931); and The Pilgrim Hymnal (1958); together with 46 recordings listed in Phonolog Reports (1978), Los Angeles, California.

HOWITT, MARY BOTHAM (c. 1804-1888)
"Clothe me with Thy saving grace."

Daughter of Samuel Botham, a member of the Society of Friends, she was born at Uttoxeter, Staffordshire, England and married in 1823 to William Howitt. Her hymns appeared in her Hymns and Fireside Verses (London, 1839), her Ballads and Other Poems (1847). The above hymn appeared in Lyra Britannica (1867), and her hymn "Let me suffer; let me

drain" also appeared in that hymnal and in Lays of the Sanctuary (1859). She died on January 30, 1888.

HUBBERT, FRANCES MARTHA (b. 1900)
    "God the Father hears today. "

The seventh child of Martha Srigley and James Hubbert, she
was born at Holly, near Barrie, Ontario, Canada on January
9, 1900 and was educated at Hamilton Normal School (Teachers' College). She taught at Hamilton, Moon River, Nanticoke
and at the Indian Residential School at Sioux Lookout, all in
Ontario. Entering the Church of England Deaconess and Missionary House in Toronto in 1926, she was graduated three
years later. She was a Friendship Worker for the Anglican
Woman's Auxiliary of the Toronto Diocese (1950-65). Her
hymn above appeared in the Hymn Book for Children (1962--
Anglican) and another hymn, "Cradled in a manger" in Hymns
for Children published by The Hymn Society of America
(1965). In 1965 she became a part-time literature secretary
in the National Office of the Women's Christian Temperance
Union. In 1973 she entered the Grove Park Home for Senior
Citizens in Barrie to be near her family. She still resides
in the Home in frail health but is able to go to the dining
room each day in a wheel chair (May 1982). [Letter from
her niece, Mrs. Jean Saunter, Lefroy, Ontario, Canada.]

HUBER, JANE McAFEE PARKER (b. 1926)
    "Creator God, creating still,
    by will and word and deed. "

Born at Tsinan, China on October 24, 1926, she was educated at the Northfield School for Girls, East Northfield,
Massachusetts (1944), Wellesley College, Wellesley, Massachusetts (1944-47) and Hanover College, Hanover, Indiana
(B. A. , 1948). On September 3, 1947 she married William
A. Huber and they had six children. Six of her hymns appeared in Creation Sings, compiled by Ann Lodge for the
United Presbyterian Women (Philadelphia: Geneva Press,
1979) and the hymn above also appeared in the Hymnal of
the Reorganized Church of Jesus Christ of Latter-day Saints
(1981). "Having begun to write hymns only in 1976, now,
early in 1982, I have thirty hymn texts, several of which
have been written as theme hymns for meetings of United
Presbyterian Women. ... Inclusive language and non-militaris-
tic images are high priorities in my writing. Reformed and

liberation theologies are the major theological influence. "
[January 1982 letter from Mrs. Huber from Indianapolis, Indiana, where she resides.]

HULL, AMELIA MATILDA (1825-1882)
"And it is true as I am told. "

Daughter of William Thomas Hull, she was born at Marpool
Hall, Exmouth, England.   Some 22 of her hymns appeared in
Miss H. W. Soltan's Pleasant Hymns for Boys and Girls
(1860), including the hymn above.   She also published Hymns
by A. M. H. (1850), Heart Melodies (1864) and other books.
Other hymns she wrote appeared in The Enlarged London
Hymn Book (1873).   More recently her hymn, "There is life
for a look at the Crucified One, " appeared in The Song Book
of The Salvation Army (1953) and The Hymnbook (Presbyterian, 1955).

HULL, ELEANOR HENRIETTA (1860-1935)
"Be thou my vision, O Lord of my heart. "

This hymn was translated from the ancient Irish into prose
by Mary E. Byrne (1880-1931) and put into verse by Miss
Hull.   Born in Manchester, England on January 15, 1860,
Eleanor was onetime president of the Irish Literary Society
in London and the founder of the Irish Text Society.   Her
hymn above appeared in her book Poem Book of the Gael
(1912).   She died at London, England on January 13, 1935.
More recently her hymn appeared in the Baptist (1975);
Broadman (1977); Christian Worship (1953); Family of God
(1976); Methodist (1966); Presbyterian (1955) hymnals and The
Pilgrim Hymnal (1958).

HYMPHREYS, JENNETT (1829-1917)
"March, my little children. "

Born at London, England on April 17, 1829, she was a member of the Church of England.   Her hymn was read at the
Rosslyn Hill School at Hampstead and appeared in the Inquirer
on April 4, 1885 and later in the Rev. W. A. Oxford's Children Service Hymns and Songs (1889) and in the Sunday School
Hymnary (1905); etc.   She died on February 6, 1917.

HUNGARY and BOHEMIA, MARIA, QUEEN OF (1505-1558)
"Oh God! though sorrow be my fate. "

Sister of Charles V, Holy Roman Emperor, Maria of Austria
was born at Brussels, Belgium on September 17, 1505 and
on January 13, 1522 she was married to Louis Jagiello, King
of Hungary and Bohemia, known as Louis II. In 1526 the
Turkish hordes under Sultan Suleiman the Magnificent invaded
Hungary, and Louis II (1506-1526) prepared for the defense
of his country and his throne, but his army was defeated at
the battle of Mohacs on the Danube on August 29, 1526.
Louis II was drowned while trying to escape, and 20, 000 of
his men were killed. The Turkish army occupied Buda on
September 10, 1526, but quickly left the city with 100, 000
captives. Hungary was partitioned and most of the land an-
nexed by the Ottoman Empire. In the meantime, Queen Maria
fled Buda and wrote her hymn in the belief that God would
give her strength to carry on. Her hymn appeared in the
Library of Poetry and Song Volume II (Doubleday, Doran,
1925) and in numerous other publications. She died at Ci-
gales, near Valladolid on October 18, 1558. [Letter dated
24 November 1982 from Erno Pesti, Head of the Reference
Dept., Municipal Library, Budapest, Magyar (Hungary).]

HUNTINGTON, SELINA SHIRLEY HASTINGS, COUNTESS OF
(1707-1791)
> "When Thou, my righteous Judge, shalt come
> To take Thy ransomed people home,
> Shall I among them stand?"

She was the daughter of the second Earl Ferrers, and was
born on August 24, 1707. She married Theophilus Hastings,
ninth Earl of Huntington on June 3, 1728 and lived in Donington Park in the parish of Castle Donington, in Leicestershire,
England. She often entertained John and Charles Wesley, and
was a member of the first Methodist Society formed in Fet-
ter Lane in 1739. Later she became acquainted with George
Whitefield, and in 1748 opened her house in Park Lane, London, for Whitefield to preach there, and later favored Whitefield over the Wesleys. She died in London on June 17,
1791. The hymns "Come, Thou Fount of every blessing" and
"O when my righteous Judge shall come" have been claimed
for her, but John Julian in the Dictionary of Hymnology doubts
that she wrote them. With her brother-in-law, W. W. Shirley, she compiled nine hymn books, such as A Collection of
Hymns (London, 1764), The Collection of Hymns sung in the

Countess of Huntington's Chapel, Bristol (1765), A Select Collection of Hymns to be universally sung in all the Countess of Huntington's Chapels, Collected by her Ladyship (London, 1780). She spent her income freely, and built some 60 chapels in Sussex, Bath, Bristol, Lincolnshire, etc. Her hymn appeared in the Baptist Standard Hymnal (1973).

HUSSEY, JENNIE EVELYN (1874-1958)
"King of my life, I crown thee now. "

She was born in an old farm home in Henniker, New Hampshire on February 8, 1874, where her family had lived for four generations. At age eight she started writing verses, and her poems were published when she was thirteen. Her first hymns appeared in 1898. Her mother was a Congregationalist, but Jennie joined the Society of Friends at an early age. She suffered from arthritis in her fingers. [Information on Miss Hussey was received from Gertrude Dye, Copyright Department, Word Music, Winona Lake, Indiana 46590.] Her hymn appeared in The New Broadman Hymnal (1977); Hymns for the Family of God (1976); and Rodeheaver's Gospel Solos and Duets No. 3. Her hymn also appeared in the Evangelical United Brethren (1957) and Mennonite (1959) hymnals. She spent the last years of her life in the Home for the Aged in Concord, New Hampshire, where she died.

HUTTON, FRANCES A. (1811-1877)
"In the hour of trial, Jesus, plead for me. "

A versifier, she was born in England and married Prebendary Henry Wollaston Hutton. The original hymn was written by James Montgomery and extensively altered by Mrs. Hutton. Her revised version appeared in her husband's Supplement and Litanies (Lincoln-England); in Church Hymns (1871); Thring's Collection (1882); and more recently in The Pilgrim Hymnal (1958).

HUTTON, LAURA JOSEPHINE (1852-1888)
Tune--ETERNITY

A composer, the sister and fellow worker of the Rev. V. W. Hutton, Vicar of Sneinton, she was born at Spridlington, England on July 17, 1852. When her brother retired, she went to live with him at Lincoln. She wrote tunes for Mrs.

Alexander's Hymns for Children and also published a book of
her own hymn tunes, Twenty Hymns for Little Children (1880).
After her brother's death she returned to Spridlington, where
she died on June 17, 1888. Her hymn tune appeared in
Hymns Ancient and Modern (1904).

HYDE, ABIGAIL BRADLEY (1799-1872)
   "Behold the glorious dawning bright. "

She was born at Stockbridge, Massachusetts on September
28, 1799 and was married to the Rev. Lavius Hyde of Salisbury, Massachusetts on September 28, 1818. She lived at
his various charges--in Salisbury, then at Bolton, Connecticut, Ellington, Connecticut, where she became a friend of
Mrs. Phoebe Brown, at Wayland and Beckett, Massachusetts,
then again at Bolton. In 1822 she met a Rev. Joseph Wolff,
a converted Israelite, and wrote a long poem, "Address to
Mr. Wolff, " which was printed in the New Haven Religious
Intelligencer, from which two hymns were formed, which
were included in the Andover Hymns for the Monthly Concert
(1823), which attracted the attention of Dr. Asahel Nettleton
who included nine of her hymns, including the one above, in
his Village Hymns (1824). His enlarged edition of 1851 included 34 of her hymns, and Nason's Congregational Hymn
Book (1857) also included some of her hymns. Her hymn,
"Dear Saviour, if these lambs should stray, " appeared in
the Moravian Hymnal (1920). She died at Andover, Massachusetts on April 7, 1872.

IMELDA TERESA, SISTER (1861-1916)
   "Mine to rise when Thou dost call me. "

Born Susie Forrest Swift, daughter of a banker in Amenia,
New York, she was graduated from Vassar College, Poughkeepsie, New York (1883) and then taught for a year at Miss
Davis' School in Morristown, New Jersey. In 1884 she went
to England on a vacation with her sister Elizabeth (later Mrs.
Colonel Brengle). In Glasgow, Scotland, they met The Salvation Army, and were born again. The two sisters entered
the training school in the East End of London. Susie became editor of All the World. She returned to a Vassar re-
union in 1892 and joined the Protestant Episcopal Church.
In 1896 she returned permanently to the United States as secretary to Eva Booth and became head of the Auxiliary League
in America. Then Brigadier Swift was converted to Catholi-

cism, and she entered The Dominican Convent in Albany, New York. Her hymn appeared in All the World (April 1887) and in The Song Book of the Salvation Army (1899; 1953). She died at Saint Clara College, Sinsinawa, Wisconsin on Wednesday, April 19, 1916. [Information in 2/25/83 letter from Joanne Shafer, Alumnae and Alumni of Vassar College, Poughkeepsie, New York.]

INGELOW, JEAN (1820-1897)
"And didst thou love the race
    that loved not Thee"
And didst thou take to heaven a human brow?"

She was born in Boston, Lincolnshire, England on March 17, 1820 and lived in Ipswich, and later in London. She wrote novels and poems, and died at Kensington, London, on July 20, 1897. The hymn (above) appeared in her Poems (1863) and in the Congregational Church Hymnal (1887) and in Songs of Praise (1931).

INGLIS, CATHERINE H. MAHON (1815-1893)
"Abide in Me, Most loving counsel this."

Daughter of A. Mahon, she was born at Roscommon, Ireland on June 24, 1815 and in 1844 married Captain Inglis. Her hymns were published in Songs in Sorrow and Songs in Joy (Edinburgh: 2nd edition, 1864) and One Hundred Songs in Sorrow and in Joy (Edinburgh, 1880). She died on September 22, 1893.

INGLIS, MARGARET MAXWELL MURRAY (1774-1843)

She was born at Sanquhar, Dumfriesshire, Scotland and was married, first to a Mr. Finlay, then to Mr. John Inglis. Her poems and hymns were published in her Miscellaneous Poems, Edinburgh (1838), where she died in December 1843.

IRONS, GENEVIEVE MARY (1855-1928)
"Drawn to the Cross, which Thou hast blest,
With healing gifts for souls distrest."

Granddaughter of the Rev. Joseph Irons, a Congregational

minister at Camberwell, and daughter of Dr. W. J. Irons,
she was born at Brompton, England on December 28, 1855
and became a Roman Catholic. She wrote: "I always feel
that the hymn is part of me, it contains expressions and allu-
sions which to my mind are only capable of a Catholic meaning, but I am interested and gratified in knowing that the
hymn speaks to the hearts of many who would probably differ
from me on most points of doctrine." Her hymn was printed
in the Sunday Magazine (1880); in her Corpus Christi (1884);
in the Primary Methodist Hymnal (1887); and more recently
in the Lutheran Hymnal (1941) and the English Baptist Hymn
Book (1962).

IRVINE, JESSIE SEYMOUR (1836-1887)
      Tune-CRIMOND

Daughter of a Presbyterian minister in Dunottar, Aberdeen-
shire, Scotland, she was born there and later lived in
manses at Peterhead and Crimond, Scotland, where she died,
having named her hymn tune after the town. The tune was
first used in the Northern Psalter (1872). Apparently she
gave the tune to David Grant for harmonization. It appeared
in the Baptist Hymn Book (London, 1966) and in Hymns for
the Living Church (1974) with the hymn "The Lord's my shepherd, I shall not want. "

IRWIN, LOIS (b. 1926)
      "He'll make a way. "

Pianist, singer, hymnist, and composer, she was born in
Westmont, Illinois on July 29, 1926. She was a gospel singer
with her husband in evangelistic programs. Her hymn above
is listed with five recordings in Phonolog Reports of Los Angeles, California, with four recordings for "It was Jesus, "
three for "The Healer" and one for "There'll be an answer
Bye and Bye" (1978).

JACKSON, HELEN MARIA FISKE HUNT (1830-1885)
      "Not as I will. "

Daughter of Deborah Vinal and Professor Nathan W. Fiske,
she was born at Amherst, Massachusetts on October 15, 1830
and educated at Abbott Brothers School in New York City.
On October 28, 1852 she married Edward B. Hunt. She wrote

poetry for Nation magazine (first poem in 1865) and articles
for the New York Independent (first prose in 1866). On October 22, 1875 she married William S. Jackson. Her publications were Verses (1870); Bits of Travel (1872); Ramona
(1884); Between Whiles (1887); and other books. She died at
Colorado Springs, Colorado on August 12, 1885. Her hymn
appeared in 1000 Quotable Poems (1937).

JAMES, DOROTHY (b. 1901)
       Choral--The Little Jesus Came to Town

A composer, she was born at Chicago, Illinois on December
1, 1901 and studied at the Chicago Musical College and the
American Conservatory of Music (M. M.). She served on the
staff of the Eastern Michigan State Normal College, Ypsilanti,
Michigan. She also wrote Mary's Lullaby and other works.
As of May 1982 she was living in St. Petersburg, Florida.

JAMES, MARY D. (1810-1883)
       "All for Jesus, all for Jesus!"

Born on August 10, 1810, she was married to a Mr. James.
In 1840 she met Mrs. Phebe Palmer of New York City and
they became close friends. Mrs. James was a regular contributor to Guide to Holiness. She also wrote "My body, soul
and spirit" on July 10, 1869 while at a Round Lake Methodist
camp meeting and the hymn tune was written for it by Phebe
Palmer Knapp. It appeared in Notes to Joy (1869) published
by Mrs. Knapp. Mrs. James published The Soul Winner:
A Sketch of Edmund J. Yard, for Sixty-five Years a Class
Leader and Hospital Visitor in Philadelphia, Pennsylvania
(1883). Her hymn above appeared in the American Service
Hymnal (1968) and in Hymns for the Family of God (1976).

JANOTHA, NATALIA MARIE CECILIA (1856-1932)
       Anthem--Ave Maria

Composer and pianist, born at Warsaw, Poland on 8 June
1856, she was a pupil of Clara Schumann, Princess Czartory-
ska, Rudorff, F. Weber and others. She played at the Prus-
sian Court for William I, and later for Frederick III and for
Kaiser Wilhelm II. She went to London and played for Queen
Victoria, and later for Edward VII and for George V. She
wrote her Ave Maria for Pope Leo XIII. She was known as

the "Kaiser's pianist, " and so was arrested in 1916 and de-
ported. She settled at The Hague, in the Netherlands, where
she died on 9 June 1932.

JANVRIN, ALICE JANE (1846-1908)
"Lord of all the ages of Eternity. "

Daughter of William Janvrin, she was born on the Island of
Jersey, on December 30, 1846, but later lived in London.
Her hymn was included in Dodderidge's Hymns for the Church
and Home (1904). Other hymns she wrote appeared in the
Church Missionary Hymn Book (1899). She died on April 3,
1908.

JARVIS, MARY ROWLES (1853-1929)
"O God of ages, in Whose light. "

Daughter of Samuel Rowles of Gloucester, England, she was
married in 1888 to the Rev. George Jarvis, Congregational
Minister at Stonehouse, Gloucester, and after 1896 at Cole-
ford, Gloucester. Her poems and hymns were published in
1895, and the above hymn in Sunday at Home (1888) and in
the Public School Hymn Book (1903). More recently her
hymn was published in the Anglican Hymn Book (1965). She
died on May 7, 1929.

JERSEY, MARGARET ELIZABETH CHILD-VILLIERS LEIGH,
COUNTESS OF (1849-1945)
"Speak the truth, for that is right. "

Her hymn was published in Hymns and Poems for Little Children (1871). She was born at Stoneleigh Abbey, Warwickshire,
England on October 29, 1849. Her uncle was the first duke
of Westminster. In 1872 she married the seventh Earl of
Jersey. They had two sons and four daughters, but she outlived three of her children. She lived at Middleton Park,
near Bicester, and at Osterley Park, near Isleworth, considered the finest Georgian mansion by the Adams brothers.
She knew the first Duke of Wellington and Prince Albert, con-
sort of Queen Victoria. She died at Middleton Park on May
22, 1945 in her 96th year.

JEVONS, MARY ANN ROSCOE (1795-1845)
"When human hopes and joys depart. "

Daughter of William Roscoe, an attorney and writer, she was born in Liverpool, England and in 1825 married Thomas Jevons. She was the sister of Jane Roscoe Hornblower, hymnist. Her hymn appeared in Poems for Youth, by a Family Circle (London, 1820), which she edited, and which included poems and hymns by her brothers and sister. She also edited the Sacred Offering (1831). Her seven hymns were published in her Sonnets and Other Poems, chiefly Devotional (1845).

JEWETT, SOPHIE (1861-1909)
    "Lord, we praise Thee for our brother Sun. "

Born in Moravia, New York, she was educated at Buffalo University and became an assistant professor of English at Wellesley College in Massachusetts. She was a translator and versifier, and the above line was translated from "Song of the Sun" by St. Francis of Assisi and appeared in her book God's Troubadour.

JILLSON, MARJORIE ANN (b. 1931)
    "Praise the Lord! Praise, O servants of the Lord. "

Born in Detroit, Michigan on October 29, 1931, she was educated at the College of Wooster (B. A.) in Wooster, Ohio and for several years taught at Gallaudet College in Washington, D. C. , a liberal arts college for the deaf. Later she moved back to Michigan and became a member of the Grosse Point Memorial Church (United Presbyterian Church in the U. S. A.). Her hymns were published in her Three Simple Melodies (1972) and Five Hymns (1973) with tunes by Heinz Werner Zimmermann. Her hymn appeared in the Baptist (1975) and Broadman (1977) hymnals.

JOHNSON, JAKOBINA (1883-1977)
    "The fading day adorns the west. "

Translator and versifier, she was born at Husavik, Iceland on October 24, 1883 and was brought to Canada by her parents in 1888. She was educated at a college in Winnipeg, Manitoba. The family later resided in Victoria, British Columbia, then about 1909 went to Seattle, Washington. She was married to a Mr. Johnson and he died in 1949. They had six sons and one daughter. She wrote I Beheld a Swan,

Northern Lights, Life of a Candle and other books. She translated the works of Icelandic poets and dramatists, and received the Order of the Falcon from the King of Denmark.
Her hymn appeared in the Lutheran Service Book and Hymnal
(1958). She died at Seattle, Washington on July 8, 1977.

JOHNSON, KATHERINE SPENCER HARDENBURGH (1835-1907)
  "The whole wide world for Jesus. "

Daughter of John H. Hardenburgh, she was born at Auburn,
New York. On September 6, 1860 she married the Reverend
Herrick Johnson, minister of the Troy (New York) Presbyterian Church (1860-2), 3d Church, Pittsburgh (1862-67), 1st
Church, Philadelphia (1868-74), Professor at Auburn Seminary
(1874-80), 4th Church, Chicago (1880-98). Her hymn "An
earthy temple here we build" was written for the dedication
of a church in Pittsburgh, Pennsylvania in 1866 and appeared
in Hatfield's Church Hymns (New York, 1872) and her hymn
(above) was written for a meeting of the Woman's Foreign
Missionary Society in Baltimore, Maryland on May 9, 1872,
and this hymn appeared in Stryker's Church Song (New York,
1889). After her death, her husband married Margaret B.
Duncan in 1910, and he died in 1913 in Germantown, Philadelphia, Pennsylvania. Her poems and hymns were published
in Comfort (New York: Randolph & Company, 1877) with a
new and enlarged edition (1888). [Information from Linda
Feit, The Free Library of Philadelphia, Pennsylvania.] More
recently her hymn appeared in the English Baptist Hymn Book
(1962).

JOHNSTON, JULIA HARRIETTE (1840-1919)
  "Marvelous grace of our loving Lord. "

Daughter of the Rev. Robert Johnston, she was born at Saline-
ville, Ohio on January 21, 1840. When she was only seven
years old, the family moved to Peoria, Illinois, where her
father served as pastor of the First Presbyterian Church
from 1856 until his death in 1864. Her mother founded the
Presbyterian Missionary Society of Peoria, and Julia served
as the society's president for twenty years. In addition, she
was superintendent of the younger children's department of
the Sunday School for forty-one years. She published School
of the Master (1880); Bright Threads (1897); Indian and Spanish Neighbors (1905); and Fifty Missionary Heroes (1913).
She wrote over 500 hymns, and died in Peoria, on March 6,

1919. Her hymns appeared in the American Service (1968); Baptist (1975); Broadman (1977); Family of God (1976) hymnals and Songs of Praise (1931).

JOLLEY, FLORENCE W. (b. 1917)
    Works: Gloria in Excelcis

Composer, arranger, and teacher, she was born at Kingsburg, California on July 11, 1917 and was educated at Fresno State College (B. A.) in Fresno, California and at the University of Southern California (M. M.) in Los Angeles. She was professor of music at Pierre Junior College in Los Angeles. She also composed an arrangement for All People That on Earth Do Dwell.

JOLLIFFE, FANNIE PEGG (1862-1943)
    "I do not ask Thee, Lord."

She was born in England on September 18, 1862 and was converted to Christianity at a Salvation Army Penitent-form at Leamington, in an old railway car. She received her officer's commission in 1886 and served at garrisons in Northampton, Bath, Oxford, Battersea, and Leamington in special service in charge of revival brigade Lieutenants from the training garrison. After a number of years (in 1891) she was placed in charge of the Sheffield I Corps, where the Sunday evenings were so popular they had to use Albert Hall to accommodate the large crowds. In 1891 she married Commissioner Jolliffe. Her hymn appeared in The Song Book of The Salvation Army (1899; 1953). She died on February 10, 1943 [letter from Gordon Tayler, The Salvation Army, Croyden, England, 20 June 1983].

JONES, EDITH (1849-1929)
    "Father, who art alone,
    Our helper and our stay."

She resided in South Norwood, England and her hymn appeared in The Home Hymn Book: A Manual of Sacred Song for the Family Circle (1885) and more recently in Christian Worship-- A Hymnal (1953; 1970) and in the British Baptist Hymn Book (1962).

JONES, ELIZABETH BROWN (b. 1907)
"Father, in the early morning praise
We offer thanks to Thee. "

She was born in Kansas City, Missouri on September 27,
1907 and was married to Clare Hartley Jones, an attorney,
on June 4, 1929. She served in the editorial division of the
Church School of the Church of the Nazarene in Kansas City
from 1962, and has published numerous books on religion.
Her hymn appeared in Joyfully Sing, A Hymnal for Juniors
(1968). "I telephoned the International Headquarters of the
Church of the Nazarene in Kansas City and they informed me
that Mrs. Jones is alive. " [February 1982 letter from Rose
Bell, Missouri Valley Room, Kansas City Public Library in
Missouri.]

JONES, HARRIET E. RICE (b. 1823)
"Trusting in the blessed Jesus. "

Daughter of Eleazer Rice, she was born on a farm in Onon-
daga County, near Oran, New York on April 18, 1823 and
was married to a son of the Reverend Zenus Jones on July
7, 1884. She was a Methodist and a Prohibitionist. Her
hymns were titled "Redeemed, " "Blue Sea of Galilee, " "At
the Pool of Siloam, " "There is Sweet Rest, " etc. Her hymn
"We have a Rock, a safe" was published in The Hymnbook
(Presbyterian, 1955). We have been unable to locate the
place and date of her death.

JONES, RUTH CAYE (1902-1972)
"In times like these you need a Savior. "

Born in Wilmerding, Pennsylvania, she taught herself to play
the piano and organ. She married Bert Jones, an evangelist
Methodist preacher, and in 1948 they started a weekly family
devotional radio program from their home in Erie, Pennsylvania. They had five children, and three of their sons became ordained ministers. Their program was called "A
Visit with the Joneses. " She died at Erie, Pennsylvania on
August 18, 1972. Their son, the Rev. Bert L. Jones, carried on their radio ministry. Her hymn appeared in the
American Service (1968); Baptist (1975); Broadman (1977);
and Hymns of Glorious Praise (1969) hymnals.

JOSEPH, JANE MARION (1894-1929)
"On this day earth shall ring. "

As a gifted young English musician, she studied under Gustav
Holst. Her hymn is a translation from the Swedish and appeared in the Hymnbook for Colleges and Schools (1956);
Hymns for Christian Worship (1972); United Presbyterian Hymnal (1972); and The Pilgrim Hymnal (1958).

JUDSON, EMILY CHUBBUCK (1817-1854)

She was born at Eaton, New York on August 22, 1817 and in
1846 she married Dr. Adoniram Judson, an American missionary in India, thus becoming his third wife. He had founded the American Baptist Missionary Union in Burma in 1814.
She had a hymn published in the Baptist Missionary Hymn
Book of Burma. He died at sea on April 12, 1850 and was
buried in the deep. She died at Hamilton, New York on
June 1, 1854. She wrote books under the name "Fanny Forester, " and after her arrival in Moulmein, Burma in 1846
with her bridegroom, she wrote to a friend: "Frogs hop
from my sleeves when I put them on, and lizards drop from
the ceiling to the table when we are eating, and the floors
are black with ants. "

JUDSON, SARAH HULL BOARDMAN (1803-1845)
"Proclaim the lofty praise. "

She was born in Alstead, New Hampshire on November 4,
1803 and was the eldest of thirteen children. She was married on July 3, 1825 to George D. Boardman, a Baptist missionary to India, but he died in 1831 and she married Dr.
Adoniran Judson, a prominent missionary to India and hymnist, on April 10, 1834 and became his second wife. Her
hymn appeared in W. Urwick's Dublin Collection (1829). She
died at sea in 1845, just off the island of St. Helena, in the
South Atlantic Ocean.

KENNY, ALICE PATRICIA (b. 1937)
"Creator God, whose glory is Creation. "

Daughter of Prof. Ralph Burch and Marjorie Waite Kenny,
she was born at Schenectady, New York on May 1, 1937 and

educated at Middlebury College in Middlebury, Vermont (B. A.,
1958) and Columbia University (M. A., 1959; Ph. D., 1961).
She was an instructor and assistant professor at Cedar Crest
College, Allentown, Pennsylvania (1961-69), then Chairman
of the Department of Interstudies from 1970. She wrote the
History of the American Family (1967), The Gansevoorts of
Albany: Dutch Patricians in the Upper Hudson Valley (1969)
and other books. Her principal extracurricular activity is
the Bach Choir of Bethlehem, Pennsylvania and she has sung
in the Columbia University Chapel Choir and in the Madison
Avenue Presbyterian Church in Albany, New York, where she
is a member. Her hymn appeared in Hymns for the 70's
(The Hymn Society of America, 1970).

KER SEYMER, VIOLET (c. 1860-1954)
    "In God I find a precious gift. "

Born in Paris, France of wealthy English parents, she received her early education at home with French and English
governesses, and later attended private schools in Paris,
Dresden, and Brussels. The family had a country estate at
Hanford, Dorsetshire, England with a chapel attached to the
main house. Her aunt, Gertrude Ker Seymer, married Ernest Clay and he changed his name to Ernest Clay-Ker-Seymer,
and both families enjoyed summers at their estate. A frequent visitor was Sir Arthur Sullivan, who loved to play the
harmonium in the chapel. He spent weeks at a time with the
Ker Seymers. Once Miss Ker Seymer told in the Christian
Science Mother Church in Boston about a time Sir Arthur was
staying at the estate in Dorsetshire (in 1871), and he composed the tune ST. GERTRUDE, in honor of Gertrude Clay-
Ker-Seymer, for Baring Gould's hymn "Onward Christian
Soldiers. " Violet was a child at the time, and Sir Arthur
rehearsed the children to sing the new hymn for the first
time while he played the harmonium for the maiden performance. [Letter from Joanne E. Wilson, Committee on Publications, First Church of Christ, Scientist, Boston Massachusetts.] Brought up in the Church of England, she began study
of Christian Science in 1900 and on June 10, 1902 joined the
church. She served as a practitioner, teacher, lecturer,
and associate editor of the Christian Science periodicals.
She died on July 2, 1954. Two of her hymns appeared in
the Christian Science Hymnal (1937).

KERGER, ANN (b. 1894)
"Little children come to Jesus. "

She was born in Austria on May 25, 1894 and joined the American Society of Composers, Authors and Publishers in New York City in 1961. As of March 1982 she was still active.

KIDDER, MARY ANN PEPPER (1820-1905)
"Lord, I care not for riches, Neither silver nor gold.
I would make sure of heaven, I would enter the fold. "

"Ere you left your room this morning,
Did you think to pray?"

She was born in Boston, Massachusetts on March 16, 1820. Her hymns appeared in Ira D. Sankey's Sacred Songs and Solos (1878). She was a member of the Methodist Episcopal Church, and resided in New York City for 46 years. When the Civil War ended in 1865, she wrote "Victory at Last": "For many years we've waited to hail the day of peace, When our land shall be united and the war and strife shall cease. " Her poem was set to music by William B. Bradbury (1816-1868). She died at Chelsea, Massachusetts on November 25, 1905. The second hymn listed above appeared in the American Service Hymnal (1968) and the first in Hymns for the Family of God (1976) and Great Hymns of the Faith (1972).

KIMBALL, HARRIET MC EWEN (1834-1917)
"Pour thy blessing, Lord, like showers. "

Born at Portsmouth, New Hampshire on November 2, 1834, she was a member of the Roman Catholic Church and was chief founder of the Cottage Hospital at Portsmouth. She published her Hymns (1866), Swallow Flights of Song (1874), Blessed Company of All Faithful People and Poems (1889) with a revised edition in 1911. Her hymns appeared in Poets of Portsmouth (1864); the Unitarian Hymns of the Spirit (1864); Baynes' Illustrated Book of Sacred Poems (1867); the Pilgrim Hymnal (1904); and the Methodist Hymnal (1911). More recently her hymn was included in the Methodist Hymnal (1925). She died at Portsmouth, New Hampshire on September 3, 1917.

KINGHAM, MILLICENT DOUGLAS (b. 1866)
    Tune--BENSON

Composer and organist, she served as organist for St. Andrew's in Hertford, England. Her tune was first published in leaflet form (Eton, 1894), and with the hymn "God is working his purpose out" in Church Hymns (1903), Hymns Ancient & Modern (1904; 1950). She also served as organist at St. Thomas' Hospital Chapel, London, which post she relinquished in 1926. We have been unable to locate her date of death.

KINNEY, ELIZABETH CLEMENTINE DODGE STEDMAN (1810-1889)
    "Jesus, Saviour, pass not by."

Her hymn appeared in Songs of Christian Praise (New York, 1880). She was born in New York City on December 18, 1810 and married Colonel Edmund M. Stedman in March, 1830, and they had one son. After the Colonel's death, she married William B. Kinney in November 1841, but they had no children. She wrote a novel and a book of poems (1867) and died in Summit, New Jersey on November 19, 1889.

KINSCELLA, HAZEL GERTRUDE (1893-1960)
    Our Prayer

Composer, born at Nora Springs, Iowa on 27 April 1893, she was a pupil of Rafael Joseffy (1912-13) and studied composition with Rossiter Gleason Cole and Howard Brockway. She was educated at the University of Nebraska (Music Bac., 1916; B. F. A., 1928; A. B., 1931), earned her A. M. in Music at Columbia University (1934) and her Ph. D. at the University of Washington (1941), then became Professor of Music at University of Nebraska (1941-47). She wrote a Psalm CL, some settings of Christmas carols, etc. Our Prayer for unaccompanied chorus was composed in 1934. She died at Seattle, Washington on 15 July 1960.

KLEINMEN, BERTHA ELIZA ANDERSON (1877-1971)
    "Come, hail the cause of Zion's growth."

Born in Salt Lake City, Utah on October 31, 1877, she had her first poem published when she was only twelve years old. She married Orson Conrad Kleinman and they had six children, four sons and two daughters, 21 grandchildren and 56 great-grandchildren. Besides writing eleven pageants, including "The Message of the Ages" which was presented in the Tabernacle in Salt Lake City for six weeks (1947), her short stories and poems appeared in the Ladies Home Journal, Arizona Highways, Harper's Bazaar, Musician, and other magazines. She was named "Arizona Woman of the Year" at age 80, and her book Through the Years was a collection of her poems to age 80. She was appointed assistant recorder of the Arizona Temple, Church of Jesus Christ of Latter-day Saints, where she served for 26 years. Her hymn appeared in the church Hymns (1948). She died at Mesa, Arizona on September 14, 1971. [Information from Mrs. Eloise Sirrine, daughter of Bertha Kleinman, from Temple, Arizona.]

KLOTZ, LEORA NYLEE DRETHE (b. 1928)
       "In praise and adoration."

Conductor, composer, hymnist, organist, and singer, she was born at Canton, Ohio on October 17, 1928 and educated at Mt. Union College in Alliance, Ohio (B. M. ; B. P. S. M.) and Western Reserve University (M. A.) in Cleveland, Ohio. She was head of the vocal department of high schools in Louisville, Kentucky and director of an adult church choir.

KNAPP, PHOEBE PALMER (1839-1908)
       Tune--ASSURANCE

A composer and daughter of the Methodist evangelist Walter C. Palmer and hymnist Phoebe Worrall Palmer, she was born in New York City on March 8, 1839. She married Joseph Fairfield Knapp, founder of the Metropolitan Life Insurance Company and they were members of the John Street Methodist Church in New York City. She wrote more than 500 gospel hymns and tunes including the music for her mother's hymns, and two of her tunes remain in common use, both with texts by Fanny Crosby, "Blessed Assurance" and "Open the gates of the Temple." She died at Poland Springs, Maine on July 10, 1908. Her tune appeared in the Methodist Hymnal (1964).

KOCH, MINNA (1845-1924)
       Tune--MINNA

A composer, she was German, and her tune was written to

the original words of the hymn "Star whose light shines o'er me, " which was translated from the German by Bishop Frank Houghton while attending a conference of the China Inland Mission in Germany in 1948. Her tune appeared in the English Baptist Hymn Book (London, 1962).

KROEHLER, LOIS C. (b. 1927)
"Only by thy spirit. "

She was born at St. Louis, Missouri on September 9, 1927 and was graduated from University of Nebraska at Lincoln (1949) and went to Cuba for a two-year work-study scholarship to learn Spanish. "This was followed by ten years as a regular missionary in the Presbyterian Schools in Cuba, until they were nationalized in 1961. Since then I have been working directly with the Cuban Presbyterian Church (Iglesia Presbiteriana-Reformada en Cuba) since 1967, as national director of music and professor of music and related subjects at the Evangelical Theological Seminary in Matanzas. We have published two small hymnals in Spanish, Toda La Iglesia Canta (The Whole Church Sings) in 1968 and Que Se Oiga Musica (Let There Be Music) in 1976. My one English hymn (above) was published in Come Let Us Sing by the Presbyterian Distribution Service (1958) and later in Creation Sings (Philadelphia: Geneva Press, 1979). My Spanish hymns are: "Que la iglesia sea la iglesia" (1963) [Let the church be the church]; "Todos sean uno" (1965) [That all may be one]; "Hoy miramos al pasado" [I make all things new], which appeared in Toda La Iglesia Canta (1968), Presbyterian-Reformed Church in Cuba; "Vida nueva" (1976) [New Life]; "Dios el Lunes" (1971) [God on Monday]; "Siguiendo la Verdad en armor" (1971) [Following the truth in love]; and the following hymns in Cantos de Compromiso (1975): "La mano de Dios" [The hand of God]; "Navidad es solidariad" [Christmas is solidarity]; "Por un camino nuevo y vivo" [Along a new and living road]. The above hymns also appear in Que Se Oiga Musica, published by the Program and Work Agency of the Presbyterian-Reformed Church (1976). " [Letter of April 1982 from Miss Kroehler from Cárdenas, Cuba, where she is presently residing.]

KRUGER, LILLY CANFIELD (b. 1892)
"He lives. "

Born at Portage, Ohio on April 13, 1892 she was educated

at the University of Toledo (B. A.) Ohio and was a public school teacher. As of March 1982 she was enjoying her retirement.

KUHLMAN, KATHRYN (1910-1976)
"He's the Savior of my soul. "

Radio and TV evangelist, faith healer and hymnist, she was the daughter of Emma Walkenhorst and Joe Kuhlman and was born at Concordia, Missouri. She originated daily radio broadcasts in the United States and overseas and weekly TV shows in the United States and Canada (1966-76). She established 22 missions overseas, including Hong Kong, India, Republic of South Africa and Viet Nam. For ten years she preached at the Shrine Auditorium in Los Angeles, California, She wrote I Believe in Miracles (1962); Nothing Is Impossible with God (1974); and several other books. Her gospel song above was recorded by the Shrine Choir of Los Angeles on the album: A Tribute to Kathryn Kuhlman (Manna Records MS-2044 Stereo) at the time of her death on February 20, 1976. [Information from Lou Willadsen of Cocoa Beach, Florida.]

LA GUERRE, ELIZABETH CLAUDE JACQUET DE (1659-1729)
TE DEUM

Composer and harpsichordist, born at Paris, France, the daughter of a harpsichord maker, she made her debut playing at the French Court at age fifteen. Her Opera, Céphale and Procris was the first opera by a woman composer performed at the Académie Royal de Musique (1694). She also composed three books of cantatas. She was married to Marin de la Guerre, organist of the Church of Saint Severin in Paris. Her Te Deum, for full choruses, was performed in 1721 in the Chapel of the Louvre for the Convalescence of His Majesty, Louis XV. She died at Paris on 27 June 1729.

LAMBERT, EDNA ALICE COLES (b. 1915)
"Behold His cross against the sky. "

Born at Gisborne, New Zealand on December 10, 1915, she was educated at Wellington Girls' College and at Victoria University (B. A.), Wellington, New Zealand. On April 7, 1938 she married Alan Murdock Lambert in Wellington, and they had three children and eight grandchildren. Her hymn appeared in Twelve New World Order Hymns published by the Hymn Society of America (1958) and another hymn, "We sing Thy song with thankful heart" was published in Social Welfare Hymns by the Society (1961). As of May 1982 she was living in Wellington, New Zealand was an active member of the Presbyterian Church there.

LANCASTER, MARY ANN ELIZABETH SHOREY (b. 1851)
    "I have a Friend so precious. "

She was born in London, England on January 27, 1851 and later lived at Leyonstone, Essex, England and married a Mr. Lancaster. Her hymns were published in her The Broken Angel and Other Poems (1892) and in the Baptist newspaper and Hymns of Consecration and Faith (1902). She was a member of the Church of England, and wrote under the pseudonym "L. Shorey. " More recently her hymn was included in the Reformed; Seventh-Day Adventist; and Baptist (1958) hymnals. We have been unable to locate the place and date of her death.

LANG, MARGARET RUTHVEN (1867-1972)
    The Heavenly Noël

A composer, she was the daughter of pianist and composer Benjamin J. Lang and was born at Boston, Massachusetts on November 27, 1867. She studied with her father in Boston and later in Munich, also with George W. Chadwick and Edward A. MacDowell. She also wrote In the Manger for mixed choir, a Christmas Cycle for vocal quartet, etc. The above piece was written for solo, women's chorus, piano, and string orchestra. She died at Jamaica Plain, Massachusetts on May 30, 1972, at the grand old age of 105.

LARCOM, LUCY (1824-1893)
    "Draw thou my soul, O Christ, closer to Thine. "

Daughter of a sea captain, she was born at Beverly, Massachusetts on May 5, 1824 and had one brother and eight sisters, the only one to remain single. Her father died when she was a small child, and she worked in the textile mills in Lowell, Massachusetts with her mother and sisters. For a time she was a rural schoolteacher in Looking Glass, Illinois, and graduated from the Monticello Female Seminary in Godfrey, Illinois in 1852. After graduation she returned to Massachusetts and attended the Wheaton Seminary in Norton, Massachusetts where she then taught (1854-1862). She published her hymns and poems in Poems (1869); Wild Roses of Cape Ann (1881); Poetical Works (1885); As It Is in Heaven (1891); At the Beautiful Gate and Other Songs of Faith (1892); and The Unseen Friend (1892). Her poems attracted the attention of John Greenleaf Whittier and they became lifelong friends. She died at Boston on April 17, 1893. More recently her hymns appeared in the Baptist (1975); Broadman (1977); Christian Worship (1953); Methodist (1975); Songs of Praise (1931); Presbyterian (1955); hymnals and The Pilgrim Hymnal (1958).

LARSEN, ELIZABETH "LIBBY" (b. 1950)

Composer, she was born at Wilmington, Delaware on December 24, 1950. She composed operas and choral works.

LATHBURY, MARY ARTEMISIA (1841-1913)
"Break thou the bread of life,
Dear Lord, to me."

"Day is dying in the west,
Heaven is touching earth with rest.
Wait and worship while the night
Sets her evening lamps alight
Through all the sky."

The daughter of a Methodist minister, she was born in Manchester, Ontario County, New York on August 10, 1841. She was the assistant editor of Sunday School Advocate, Classmate, and Picture Lesson Paper and wrote The Child's Story of the Bible (1898). Late in life she was influenced by the teachings of Emanuel Swedenborg and joined the Church of the New Jerusalem in Orange, New Jersey in 1895. Her hymn, "Day is dying in the west," is a classic among hymns, and contains the most beautiful words ever written on the subject of death, and were written in 1877 at the request of the Reverend John H. Vincent for the Chautauqua Conference in New York State. She never married and died in East Orange, New Jersey on October 20, 1913. More recently the first hymn above appeared in the American Service Hymnal (1968);

Baptist (1973); Broadman (1977); Christian Worship (1953); Family of God (1976); Methodist (1966); Presbyterian (1955) hymnals and The Pilgrim Hymnal (1958) and also four recordings were listed in Phonolog Reports, Los Angeles, California (1978) for "Day is dying in the west. "

LAWATSCH, ANNA MARIA DEMUTH (1717-1759)

She was born at Karlsdorf, Moravia (now a region in Czechoslovakia) on November 13, 1707 and came to Pennsylvania with the Moravians. Her hymns appeared in Moravian Hymn Books. She married a Mr. Lawatsch and died in America.

LEATHAM, EDITH RUTTER (1870-1939)
"Thank you for the world so sweet. "

Daughter of William Rutter, an architect, she married G. H. Leatham. She published three volumes of poems and hymns and contributed to various magazines. Her hymn has been used as a grace before meals and appeared in Child Songs (1908) and later in the English Baptist Hymn Book (1962). She died at Durham, England.

LEAVELL, LILIAN YARBOROUGH (1902-1974)
"We lift our hearts in song of praise. "

Born at Jackson, Mississippi on July 20, 1902, she was educated at Judson College in Marion, Alabama and at Mississippi Woman's College, now William Carey College (B. S.) in Hattiesburg, Mississippi. She was married to Roland Q. Leavell, president of the New Orleans Baptist Theological Seminary (1946-58), where she served as director of the Women's Division of the Seminary's Board of Development. She wrote several hymns, was active in the Woman's Missionary Union of her church, and died at New Orleans, Louisiana on December 13, 1974. Her hymn appeared in the Baptist (1975) and Broadman (1977) hymnals.

LEE, ELVIRA LOUISE OSTREHAN (1838-1890)
"Starry hosts are gleaming. "

She was born at the Shepscombe Vicarage in Gloucestershire,

England on November 22, 1838. On June 9, 1859 she married the Rev. Frederick G. Lee, D. D. , who later became
Vicar of All Saints, Lambeth, Surrey in 1867. She published
The Departed and Other Verses (1865). Her hymn appeared
in A. E. Tozer's Catholic Hymns (1887). She died on September 1, 1890.

LEECH, LYDIA SHIVERS (1875-1962)
    Tune--GIVING--"Bring ye all the tithes into the store-
      house. "

Composer, hymnist, and pianist, she was born at Mayville,
New Jersey on July 12, 1873, raised at Cape May Court
House, New Jersey, and was educated at Columbia University
in New York City and Temple University in Philadelphia,
Pennsylvania. She was organist at the Bethany Methodist
Church in Camden, New Jersey and also traveled as a pianist-
companist for singing evangelist services. She wrote about
500 gospel songs. "We often grow weary, and lonely, and
sad" and "This I would ask from day to day" were published
in Rodeheaver's Gospel Solos and Duets No. 3 and "God's
Way" had three recordings listed in Phonolog Reports (1978)
of Los Angeles; there were two recordings for "Someday He'll
make it plain. " Her hymn above appeared in the Baptist Hymnal (1956) and her hymn "I was a sinner, but now I'm free.
He rescued me, " appeared in the Baptist Hymnal (1973). She
died at Long Beach, California on March 4, 1962.

LEEFE, ISABELLA (1831-1902)
    "The clouds of night have rolled away. "

Born at Richmond, Yorks, England on August 18, 1831, she
later became Mother of the House of Charity in Edinburgh,
Scotland. Her hymns appeared in her Cantica Sanctorum
(1880) and in C. W. A. Brooke's Additional Hymns (1903).
She retired to Coatham, Yorks, and died there on March 15,
1902.

LEESON, JANE ELIZABETH (1807-1882)
    "Savior, teach me day by day,
    Thine own lesson to obey. "

Born in London, England, she was an active worker in the
Catholic Apostolic Church, Gordon Square, London. Her

translations from the Latin appeared in the Rev. Henry Formby's Catholic Hymns arranged in order for the Principal Festivals, Feasts of Saints, and other occasions of Devotion
throughout the Year, published by Burns and Lambert (London, 1851). Late in life she became a Roman Catholic. Her
own hymns (including the one above), appeared in her Hymns
and Scenes of Childhood, James Burns (London, 1842);
Hymns for Congregational Singing (1853); the Irvingite Hymns
for the Use of Churches (1864); and more recently in the
Broadman (1977); Christian Worship (1953); Episcopal (1940);
Joyfully Sing (1968); Lutheran (1941); Methodist (1966); Songs
of Praise (1931); and the Presbyterian (1955) hymnals. She
died at Warwickshire, England in 1882. Her hymn, "Christ
the Lord is Risen today: Christians, haste your vows to
pay, " a translation, appeared in St. Basil's Hymnal (1953)
for use in Roman Catholic churches.

LEMMEL, HELEN HOWARTH (1863-1961)
        "O soul, are you weary and troubled?"
        Tune--LEMMEL

A composer and hymnist, born in Wardle, England on November 14, 1863, she was brought to Milwaukee, Wisconsin when
she was only nine years old and later lived in Madison, Wisconsin. She was a concert singer, hymnist, and composer,
and wrote more than four hundred hymns. For many years
she traveled the Chautauqua Circuit as a member of a quartet which she organized. In 1904 she moved to Seattle, Washington where she joined the Ballard Baptist Church there.
She died in Seattle on November 1, 1961, just two weeks'
short of her 98th birthday. Her hymn appeared in the American Service (1968); Baptist (1975); Broadman (1977); and
Family of God (1976) hymnals, and Hymns for the Living
Church (1974).

LEONARD, MARY HALL (1847-1921)
        "On His altar lay it down,
        Burden hard to carry. "

Sister of Caroline Leonard Goodenough, she was born on a
farm in Bridgewater, Massachusetts and became a school
teacher. She wrote two books on grammar and education,
a local history, three southern stories and four books of poetry, including Rest and Unrest which included three of her
hymns. She died on her mother's family farm at Rochester,
Massachusetts, two days before Thanksgiving Day in 1921.

LEONARDA, ISABELLA (c. 1620- c. 1700)

Composer of church music, she was born at Novara, Italy
and entered the Convent of St. Ursula there and later became abbess of the convent. She composed several masses,
motets, and other pieces of church music. Her last composition was published at Bologna, Italy in 1700.

LESLIE, MARY ELIZA (b. 1831)
"They are gathering homeward from every land. "

Daughter of Andrew Leslie, a Baptist missionary in India,
she was born at Monghyr, India on January 13, 1831. She
was a school superintendent in India for eight years, and
later worked in Calcutta. Her hymn appeared in her Heart
Echoes from the East; or, Sacred Lyrics and Sonnets (London: Nisbet, 1861) and later in W. R. Stevenson's School
Hymnal (1880). She wrote numerous books. We have been
unable to locate the place and date of her death, and the public library in Calcutta has been unable to supply any information.

LEWIS, LUCY S. (1904-1971)
"Chapel Bells. "

She was born in Shanghai, China on March 18, 1904 and educated at the Springside School in Philadelphia, Pennsylvania.
There are two recordings of her hymn listed in Phonolog Reports (1978) of Los Angeles, California. The music was
composed by Esther Fuller. Lucy died on December 30,
1971.

LEYDA, IDA F
"In the early morning. "

Tune--MORNING PRAYER

The wife of H. M. Leyda, she had charge of the Children's
Division of the State Sunday School Council of Religious Education in Chicago, Illinois and published three songbooks,
Carols, Melodies and Junior Hymns and Carols. Later she
resided in Wapello, Iowa and was superintendent of the Primary Department of the Presbyterian Sunday School there.
Her hymn appeared in the Presbyterian Hymnal (1933).

LILLENAS, BERTHA MAE WILSON (1889-1945)
"Jesus took my burden. "

"Jesus is always there. "

Hymnist and composer, she was born in Hanson, Kentucky on March 1, 1889 and was ordained a minister in the Church of the Nazarene in 1912. She married Haldor Lillenas, an evangelist preacher, and they traveled for ten years (1914-24). In 1924 he founded the Lillenas Music Company in Indianapolis, Indiana which was purchased by the Nazarene Publishing Company in 1930. Her hymn, "When the clouds are hanging low, " was included in The Hymnbook (Presbyterian, 1955). Her hymns above appear in Phonolog Reports of Los Angeles, California. She died at Tuscumbia, Missouri on March 13, 1945.

LIVERMORE, MARY ASHTON RICE (1820-1905)
"Jesus, what precept is like Thine,
Forgive, as ye would be forgiven. "

She was born in Boston, Massachusetts on December 19, 1820 and at age fourteen joined the First Baptist Church of Boston, but on May 6, 1845 she married the Reverend Daniel P. Livermore, a Unitarian minister. She spent the Civil War years working for the Sanitary Commission (hospitals). She was one of the founders of the Massachusetts Woman Suffrage Association in 1870. She died on May 23, 1905 and her funeral was held in the First Congregational Church of Melrose, Massachusetts. Her hymn appeared in the Christian Science Hymnal (1937).

LIVERMORE, SARAH WHITE (1789-1874)
"Glory to God and peace on earth. "

She was born at Wilton, New Hampshire on July 20, 1789 and was the aunt of Abiel Abbot Livermore, D. D. , a Unitarian Minister in Keene, New Hampshire from 1836-50. She was a school teacher. Her hymns appeared in the Cheshire Pastoral Association Christian Hymns (1844) and Putnam's Singers and Songs of the Liberal Faith (1875). She died at Wilton on July 3, 1874.

LIVOCK, JANE ELIZABETH (1840-1925)
"My soul awake! Thy rest forsake. "

Born in Norwich, England, she wrote her hymn in 1880 for a prize competition and it was published in the Sunday School Chronicle and later in the Congregational Church Hymnal (1887). She died on February 28, 1925.

LLOYD, EVA BROWN (b. 1912)
"Come, all Christians, be committed to the service of the Lord. "

Born in Jameson, Missouri on March 9, 1912, she was educated at Northwest Missouri State University (B. A.), at Maryville, Missouri and the University of Missouri at Kansas City (M. A.) and at the University of Colorado at Boulder, Colorado. She taught in schools and colleges and married Clarence Lloyd. They resided in Maryville, Missouri and were members of the First Baptist Church there. Her hymn appeared in the Baptist (1975); Broadman (1977); and Family of God (1976) hymnals. As of June 1982 she was involved in Christian education and in the Woman's Missionary Union in Maryville, Missouri. [Letter from Mrs. Lloyd dated 6/1/82.]

LOCKWOOD, CHARLOTTE MATHEWSON (1903-1961)
Tune--ROCK OF AGES

Organist and composer, she was born at Granby, Connecticut, but was raised in Reidsville, North Carolina. She was graduated from the School of Sacred Music at Union Theological Seminary in New York City (Master S. M.) and studied with Widor in Paris and with Ramin at Leipzig, Germany. She was organist at the Crescent Avenue Presbyterian Church in Plainfield, New Jersey when she wrote her tune based on an old Hebrew melody for the hymn "Men and children everywhere" written by the Rev. John J. Moment, minister of her church. The hymn with her tune appeared in The Baptist Hymnal (1973). "Charlotte Lockwood Garden was killed in a very tragic automobile accident on May 19, 1961. " [Information from Kathleen M. Upton, Director of Music, Crescent Avenue Presbyterian Church, Plainfield, New Jersey.]

LUCKHARDT, MILDRED CORELL (b. 1898)
"In tongues of every nation. "

Daughter of Philip George and Mildred McCaffrey Corell, she

was born at New York City on November 20, 1898 and educated at Columbia University and at the Union Theological
Seminary.   On September 20, 1921 she married Gustav
George Luckhardt, a consulting engineer, and they had two
daughters and one son.   She was director of Christian Education at the Presbyterian Church in Rye, New York (1941-
48), worked part time at the Rye Library (1957-65), and
wrote over 20 books--Light on Our Path (1945); Guide to Old
Testament Study (1945); Walk in the Light (1947); The Church
Through the Ages (1951); The Bells Ring Out (1952); Brave
Journey (1974); etc.   She has written study courses and worship material for boards of Christian education of five major
denominations, also several hymns, and lyrics for several
published cantatas and choral numbers.   "I will have a very
small book published [in 1983] by Paulist Press called Brother Francis (from Assisi)." [Letter, 9/6/83.] Her hymn
"How shall we speak, O God?" was published in Christian
Education Hymns (1959); "Great Ruler Over Time and Space"
by the Society (1962) and in the Book of Worship for United
States Forces (1974), and the above hymn in Bible Hymns
(1966), all published by The Hymn Society of America.

LUKE, JEMIMA THOMPSON (1813-1906)
     "I think when I read that sweet story of old. "

The daughter of Thomas Thompson, a leading figure in the
founding of the British and Foreign Sailors' Society, the Sunday School Union and the Bible Society, she was born in Islington, London on August 19, 1813.   Her hymn was written
while traveling in a stagecoach from Taunton to Wellington
to attend a missionary meeting and first appeared in the Sunday School Teachers' Magazine (1841) and in Leed's Hymn
Book (1853).   In 1843 she married Samuel Luke, a Congregational minister who led a church in Bristol, England.   For
a number of years she edited a missionary magazine for
children, and she died at Newport on the Isle of Wight on
February 2, 1906.   Her hymn appeared in the American
(1968); Baptist (1973); Christian (1953); Episcopal (1940);
Family of God (1976); Presbyterian (1955) hymnals and The
Pilgrim Hymnal (1958).

LUNN, CAROLINE SOPHIA GRUNDY (1822-1893)
     "Day and night the blessings fall. "

She was married to the Rev. John Calbraith Lunn, a Unitarian minister at Lancaster, England. She wrote Poems by Linus (1860) and her hymns were published in her husband's Hymns for Religious Services (Leicester, England, 1880).

LYNCH, ROBERTA B. (d. 1959)
"Science, the angel with the flaming sword,
God's gift, the glory of the risen Lord. "

She joined the Church of Christ, Scientist on November 3, 1922 and her hymn first appeared in the Christian Science Sentinel on February 2, 1929 and then in the Christian Science Hymnal (1937). She died on June 12, 1959.

LYON, MARY WHEATON (1844-1892)
"My heart is tired, so tired tonight. "

Born at Fabius, New York she was graduated as valedictorian of her class at Cazenovia College (a Junior woman's college) in Cazenovia, New York in 1865. She wrote articles which were published in the Philadelphia Ledger and other newspapers. In 1868 she married the Rev. A. Judson Lyon, a Baptist minister of Delaware, Ohio. Her poem, "The gates of life swing either way" appeared in Nicholas Smith's Songs from the Heart of Women.

MacALISTER, EDITH FLORENCE BOYLE, LADY (1873-1950)
"Father, hear us as we pray. "

Daughter of Alexander MacAlister, Professor of Anatomy at Cambridge University, England, she was raised a Presbyterian. In 1895 she married her cousin, Sir Donald MacAlister, M. D. (1854-1934) of Cambridge, editor of the Practitioner (1882-95). He was the Cambridge representative on the General Medical Council for 44 years and its president (1904-31), and was principal of the University of Glasgow, Scotland (1907-14 and 1918-29). She wrote Uncle Hal. Deeply interested in the religious training of primary aged school children, she served as a Sunday School superintendent at St. Columbia's Presbyterian Church in Cambridge, England. Her hymn was published in the Presbyterian USA Hymnal (1933).

McALLISTER, LOUISE (1913-1960)
Tune--BOURBON

An old folk-hymn melody, the tune was harmonized by Miss McAllister. Composer and arranger, the daughter of the Professor of English Bible at the Louisville Presbyterian Theological Seminary in Louisville, Kentucky, she was born there. In 1925 the family moved to Richmond, Virginia where her father became a professor at Union Theological Seminary. After graduating from the Collegiate School in Richmond, she attended Mary Baldwin College in Staunton, Virginia, but was unable to continue her studies after she injured her hands. She then studied privately with Mrs. Crosby Adams and John Powell. Her tune with the hymn "'Twas on that dark and doleful night" appeared in The Pilgrim Hymnal (1958). Her tune, AYLESBURY, harmonized from a melody in the Hesperian Harp (1848), together with the hymn, "O love of God most full," appeared in the Presbyterian Hymnbook (1955).

McCAW, MABEL NIEDERMEYER (b. 1899)
    "The church of God is people
    Who live throughout the earth. "

Born at Bloomington, Illinois on March 13, 1899, she was educated at Illinois Wesleyan University (B. S. , 1924) and Yale University (M. A. , 1926). She served as Director of Education at the First Christian Church in Bloomington (1927-35) and was National Director of Children's Work of the United Christian Missionary Society in Indianapolis, Indiana (1935-48). She was a member of the Disciples of Christ, and on February 3, 1948 she married the Reverend Clayton C. McCaw. She has had a number of books published on religion, especially for children: Sometime Every Day, This is God's World, My Friend Next Door, A Friend at Church, and Guiding Children in Christian Stewardship. Her hymn, "Our church proclaims God's love and care" was published in Christian Worship (1953) and the above hymn, with the tune CHURCH IS PEOPLE with music by her daughter-in-law, Maxine Gambs McCaw, appeared in Joyfully Sing (1968). "As of December 1981, Mabel was very much alive and living at Ramsey Memorial Home, Des Moines, Iowa. I received a Christmas card with a letter written on it at that time. " [Letter from Ms. Dorothy Shaffer of Bloomington, Illinois.]

McCAW, MAXINE GAMBS (b. 1919)
    Music--CHURCH IS PEOPLE

Composer and concert pianist, she was born at Des Moines, Iowa on November 14, 1919. "Regarding Maxine Gambs Mc-Caw, she is the wife of Dr. John E. McCaw who is retiring from his professorship at Drake University, Des Moines, next month. I am John's second mother, making Maxine my daughter-in-law. She was born in Des Moines and has lived most of her life here. She is an accomplished concert pianist, and currently teaching music in her home. She, too, feels honored to be included in your forthcoming book. Accept our best wishes for success in this enterprise. " [Letter dated April 20, 1982 from Mrs. Mabel N. McCaw, Des Moines, Iowa.] With words by Mabel McCaw, her tune appeared in the hymnal, Joyfully Sing (1968).

McCOLLIN, FRANCES (1892-1960)
    Anthem--The Lord is Kind

Composer and conductor, she was born at Philadelphia, Pennsylvania on October 24, 1892 and educated at the Institute for the Blind, and at Bryn Mawr College, Bryn Mawr, Pennsylvania, as well as studying music privately. She was chorus conductor at the Burd School in Philadelphia (1922-33), and at Swarthmore College in Swarthmore, Pennsylvania (1923-24). Her anthem above won the Clemson award; O Sing unto the Lord won the Philadelphia Manuscript Society award; Then Shall the Religious Shine won the Mendelssohn Club prize; Come Hither Ye Faithful won the Dayton Westminster Choir prize. She died at Philadelphia, Pennsylvania on February 26, 1960.

MACDONALD, MARY McDOUGALL (1789-1872)
    "Child in the manger, Infant of Mary. "

Born at Ardtun, near Bunessan, Mull, Scotland, she had no formal education but was a devout Baptist and well versed in the Scriptures. Her brother was a Baptist preacher on the island of Mull, who wrote Gaelic poems. She wrote many hymns, married Neill MacDonald, a tenant farmer, and they lived in the village of Cnocan on the island of Mull, where she died. Her hymn appeared in the Baptist (1975); Broadman (1977); and Family of God (1976) hymnals.

MACE, FRANCES P. LAUGHTON (1836-1899)
    "Only waiting till the shadows. "

She was born at Orono, Maine on January 15, 1836 and in 1855 she married Benjamin H. Mace, an attorney in Bangor, Maine. Her hymn was written before her marriage while she was living in Waterville, Maine and first appeared in the Waterville Mail on September 7, 1854, and later in Ira D. Sankey's Sacred Songs and Solos (1878). She moved to California in 1885, became paralyzed in 1891, and died at Los Gatos, California.

MACE, NELLIE B. (d. 1943).
"To Thee, O God, we bring our adoration."

She joined the Church of Christ, Scientist on June 3, 1899 and two of her hymns appeared in the Christian Science Hymnal (1937). She died on March 6, 1943.

MACKAY, MARGARET (1802-1887)
"Asleep in Jesus! Blessed sleep,
From which none ever wakes to weep."

Daughter of Captain Robert Mackay of Hedgefield, Inverness, Scotland, in 1820 she married Major William Mackay, of the 68th Light Infantry. Of her hymns 72 were published in her book, Thoughts Redeemed; or Lays of Leisure Hours (1854). Her hymn (above) first appeared in The Amethyst; or Christian's Annual (1832); later in the Scottish Presbyterian Hymnal (1876); Thring's Collection (1882); and other hymnals. She died at Cheltenham, England on January 5, 1887. Her hymn was published in the Baptist (1973) and Lutheran (1941) hymnals.

McKEEVER, HARRIET BURN (1807-1887)
"Jesus, high in glory."

Born in Philadelphia, Pennsylvania on August 28, 1807 she was a school teacher there for 36 years and was also a Sunday School teacher most of the time. She wrote a number of hymns for St. Andrew's Episcopal Church in Philadelphia which were published in Twilight Musings (1857). She died at Chester, Pennsylvania on February 7, 1887. More recently, her hymn appeared in the English Baptist Hymn Book (1962).

MACKEN, JANE VIRGINIA (1912-1975)
"The cross on the hill. "

Born at St. Louis, Missouri on January 14, 1912, she was
educated at St. Mary-of-the-Woods and Ursuline Academy.
She died on July 1, 1975.

MacKENZIE, ELIZABETH RUMSBY (1853-1943)
"Love divine, from Jesus flowing. "

Born in England, she rose in ranks to Captain in The Salvation Army and commanded the corps at Battersea and Wool-
wich.   She was in charge of the Hendon Corps when she
wrote the above hymn.   Later she married Staff-Captain
George MacKenzie, the aide-de-camp to the Divisional Commander.   Colonel MacKenzie later became Chief Secretary
to Mr. Herbert Booth, the Territorial Commander for Canada,
then for twenty years was a minister at Stratford, Ontario.
Mrs. MacKenzie died at London, Ontario, Canada at the age
of 90.   Her hymn appeared in The War Cry (November 26,
1887) and in The Song Book of The Salvation Army (1899;
1953).

MACONCHY, ELIZABETH (b. 1907)
        Choral work--A Hymn to Christ

Composer and pianist of Irish ancestry, the daughter of Violet M. Poe and Gerald E. C. Maconchy, she was born at
Broxbourne, Herts. , England on 19 March 1907 and studied
at the Royal College of Music in London (1923-27).   In 1930
she married William Richard Le Fanu, a past president of
the Huguenot Society, and they had two daughters.   Her motets,
for unaccompanied double chorus, 1) A Hymn to Christ and
2) A Hymn to God the Father were written in 1931.   She
composed numerous songs, chamber music, two ballets, orchestral works, etc.

MADAN, JUDITH COWPER (1702-1781)
        "In this world of sin and sorrow. "

The daughter of Judge Spencer Cowper, she was an aunt of
William Cowper the poet.   She married Colonel Martin Madan
and they had two sons, the Rev. Martin Madan, born in 1726
and Dr. Spencer Madan, who became Bishop of Peterborough

(England). Her daughter, Frances Maria Madan Cowper
(1727-1797), was also a hymnist. Judith's hymns appeared
in the Appendix to her son's Psalms and Hymns (1763) and
later in Lyra Britannica (1867).

MALIN, ANNIE PINNOCK (1863-1935)
   "God our Father, hear us pray. "

The daughter of William and Sarah Ann Pinnock, she was
born in London, England in May of 1863. When Annie was
only six years old her parents were converted to the Mormon
belief and set sail for America. The sea voyage lasted sev-
en weeks. Their trip from Missouri to Salt Lake City was
by ox-team in covered wagons. In 1884 she married Millard
Fillmore Malin and bore him five children. She wrote stories, hymns, and poems which were published in Latter-day
Saint church magazines. Her hymn appeared in Hymns, The
Church of Jesus Christ of Latter-day Saints (1948). She
died at her home in the Ninth Ward in Salt Lake City, Utah
on March 20, 1935.

MARCY, ELIZABETH EUNICE SMITH (1821-1911)
   "Out of the depths to Thee I cry. "

Daughter of Nathanial Smith, who conducted a school in East-
haven, Connecticut, she was born there on December 22,
1821. Later she attended Wilbraham Academy in Wilbraham,
Massachusetts where she met Oliver Marcy. On July 2,
1847 she married Mr. Marcy, who was a teacher at the
Academy and their four children were born there, but only
one daughter lived to adulthood. In 1862 they moved to
Evanston, Illinois, where Mr. Marcy was a longtime professor of geology at Northwestern University and acting president (1876-81). She was an active member of the Women's
Foreign Missionary Society and the Women's Home Mission-
ary Society, and an assistant superintendent of the Sunday
School of the Methodist Episcopal Church in Evanston. Her
favorite motto was: "Get thy spindle and thy distaff and the
Lord shall send thee flax. " She died at Evanston, Illinois
on January 26, 1911. [Information from Patrick M. Quinn,
University Archivist, Northwestern University Library,
Evanston, Illinois.] Her hymn appeared in the Methodist
Hymnal (1878; 1911).

MARSHALL, JANE MANTON (b. 1924)
    Tune--NORTHAVEN

Composer, she was born at Dallas, Texas on December 5,
1924 and educated at Southern Methodist University (B. M. ,
1945; M. M. , 1968) in Dallas, Texas.   She married Elbert
Marshall, an engineer with Texas Instruments.   An active
member of the Northaven Methodist Church, she served as
choir director and organist there (1957-60).   She taught music
at Southern Methodist University (1969-74), then at Perkins
School of Theology.   She has composed numerous anthems,
three collections of children's choir music, and has contributed
to church music journals.   In 1974 the Southern Baptist Church
Music Conference awarded her a certificate for distinguished
service to church music.   Her tune above appeared in the Baptist Hymnal (1975).

MARSTON, ANNIE WRIGHT (1852-1937)
    "It shall be now, Lord, from my heart I say it. "

Daughter of Dr. C. H. Marston, she was born at Uley,
Gloucestershire, England and later resided at Devizes, Wilt-
shire.   She wrote several hymns for Conventions at Keswick,
England and elsewhere, which appeared in the second edition
of Hymns of Consecreation and Faith (1890).   She died on
September 20, 1937.

MARTH, HELEN JUN (b. 1903)
    Anthem--You taught me how to pray

Composer, hymnist and pianist, she was born at Alton, Illinois on May 24, 1903 and toured the Chautauqua circuit as a
pianist accompanist.   She also worked in Little Theatres for
30 years.   As of March 1982 she was enjoying her retirement.

MARTIN, CIVILLA DURFEE HOLDEN (1866-1948)
    "Be not dismayed whate'er betide
    God will take care of you. "

Born in Jordan, Shelburne, Nova Scotia, Canada on August
21, 1866, she was a village schoolteacher and married evangelist Walter Stillman Martin (1862-1935), an ordained Baptist
minister, who later became a member of the Disciples of
Christ.   She wrote the words for a number of gospel songs,

and her husband composed the music, the tune MARTIN for
the above hymn. For a time her husband taught Bible at the
Atlantic Christian College in Wilson, North Carolina, then in
1919 resided in Atlanta, Georgia. She died in Atlanta on
March 9, 1948. Her hymn appeared in The American Service Hymnal (1968); Broadman (1977); Hymns for the Family
of God (1976); Methodist (1966); Presbyterian (1955); and Baptist (1975) hymnals.

MARTINEAU, HARRIETT (1802-1876)
        "Faith grasps the blessing she desires,
        Hope points the upward gaze. "

She was born in Norwich, England on June 12, 1802. She
was educated mostly at home, contributed to the Unitarian
Monthly Repository (1821), and also wrote a number of books.
She visited America, sailing on August 4, 1834; the trip to
New York City took 42 days. She returned to Liverpool on
August 26, 1836 and wrote a book, Society in America. She
never married and died at Clappersgate, Westmoreland, Eng-
land on June 27, 1876. Five of her hymns appeared in A
Collection of Hymns for Christian Worship printed in 1831;
others in J. R. Beard's Collection (1837); the Rev. W. J.
Fox's Hymns and Anthems (1841); and the Christian Science
Hymnal (1937).

MARTINEZ, MARIANNE (1744-1812)
        Oratorio--Santa Elena at Calvario

Composer of Spanish descent, she was born at Vienna, Austria on 4 May 1744, the daughter of the master of ceremonies
to the Papal nuncio there. Young Haydn, while poor and unknown, occupied a garret in their house and gave her lessons
on the harpsichord. The Italian poet and librettist, Pietro
Metasyasio, also lived in the same house, and was her private tutor. She also composed a Psalm to an Italian translation by Metastasio, for four to eight voices, a Mass, arias,
cantatas, and various sacred music. She died at Vienna on
13 December 1812.

MASON, CAROLINE ATHERTON BRIGGS (1823-1890)
        "O God, I thank Thee for each night. "

Daughter of Dr. Calvin Briggs, she was born in Marblehead,

Massachusetts on July 27, 1823. In 1853 she married
Charles Mason, an attorney, residing in Fitchburg, Massa-
chusetts. Her hymns appeared in her Lost Ring and other
Poems (1891), and the hymn above in Putnam's Singers and
Songs (1875). More recently her hymn was included in The
Student Hymnary (1937) and Hymns of the Spirit (1937, Uni-
versalist/Unitarian). She died at Fitchburg on June 13, 1890.

MASSEY, LUCY FLETCHER (1842-1924)
        "Sweet day of worship, day of rest."

She was the daughter of J. Fletcher of Norwich, England,
and in 1865 she married the Rev. R. Massey, Vicar of
Wareham, Norfolk. Her hymn appeared in her Later Lyrics
of the Christian Church (1870) and The Baptist Church Hymnal (1900). She died on September 16, 1924.

MASSON, ELIZABETH (1806-1865)

Composer and singer, born in Scotland, she was the pupil of
Mrs. Henry Smart and later of Guiditta Pasta in Italy. She
wrote the music for several hymns by Adelaide Ann Procter
(1825-1864). She founded the Royal Society of Female Musicians in London in 1839, and died at London on 9 January
1865.

MASTERS, MARY (1733-1759)
        "'Tis Religion that can give,
        Sweetest pleasures while we live."

She published her Poems in 1753 and Familiar Letters and
Poems on Sacred Occasions, (London: D. H. Cave, 1755).
Her hymn (above) appeared in Rippon's Selection in 1787,
with additional lines. She was a friend of Dr. Samuel Johnson who edited her books of poems for her. More recently
her hymn was published in the Church of Brethren Hymnal
(1923).

MATHESON, ANNIE (1853-1924)
        "Lord, when we have not any light."

Daughter of the Rev. James Matheson, a Congregational min-

ister, she was born at Blackheath, London, England on
March 29, 1853. Her father served in Nottingham, and later
she resided in London. Her hymns appeared in W. R. Stevenson's School Hymnal (1880) and her poems and hymns
were included in Margaret's Year Book (1887). Other hymns
appeared in the Sunday School Hymnary (1905). She died at
London on March 16, 1924. More recently her hymn appeared in the Methodist Hymnal (1935).

MATTERS, MARGARET MURNEY GLENN (d. 1965)
    "O Jesus, our dear Master,
    Thy works now understood. "

Daughter of Major General Edwin F. Glenn, U. S. Army, she
spent her childhood in various army posts in the United States
and in the Far East. She attended public schools in several
places, then was sent to Miss Porter's School in Farmington,
Connecticut. While studying music in Boston, Massachusetts,
she learned of Christian Science and joined the Mother Church
on November 5, 1909. Later she went to Germany for fur-
ther music study, but because of the great demand for Christian Science practitioners there she gave up her musical career to devote her time to the healing work. She served as
a Christian Science practitioner (1924-64) and as a teacher,
lecturer, and a member for the last revision of the Christian
Science Hymnal. Two of her hymns appeared in the 1937
edition. She died on May 7, 1965.

MAUDE, MARY FAWLER HOOPER (1819-1913)
    "Thine forever! God of love,
    Hear us from Thy throne above. "

Daughter of George Henry Hooper of Stanmore, Middlesex,
she was born in London, England on October 25, 1819.
While still in her teens she wrote three textbooks on Scripture Manners and Customs, Scripture Topography and Scripture Natural History which were published by the (Evangelical)
Society for Promoting Christian Knowledge, and the books
were widely used by Sunday School teachers. In 1841 she
married Joseph Maude, a vicar on the Isle of Wight, who
later became Vicar of Chirk, near Ruabon, Wales, and Honorable Canon of St. Asaph. He died in February 1887. Her
hymns were published in her Twelve Letters on Confirmation
(1848); Memorials of Past Years (1852); the Society for Promoting Christian Knowledge Church Hymns (1871); the Hymnal

Companion; Hymns Ancient and Modern (1871); Thring's Collection (1882); and other hymnals. She died at Overton, Wales. More recently her hymn appeared in the Baptist (1973); Lutheran (1941); and Episcopal (1940) hymnals. She taught Sunday classes for young men at Overton, and at age 93, as she lay dying, her former students sang outside her door, "Thine forever, God of love" and a hymn by Priscilla Owens, "Will your anchor hold?" Her dying words were: "Tell them that it does not fail, it holds!"

MAURICE, JANE (1812-1892)
  "Glory to God, for the Day-spring is dawning."

She was born at Tyddyn Tudor, Denbighshire, Wales on October 19, 1812. She was the sister of Peter Maurice, D. D., Curate of Kennington, Berks from 1829-1854. Jane contributed 20 hymns to her brother's The Choral Hymn Book ... 1861. She died October 29, 1892.

MAXWELL, MARY ELIZABETH BRADDON (1837-1915)
  "How I praise Thee, precious Savior."

She was born in England on October 4, 1837 and married John Maxwell in 1874. She was associated with the followers of the Keswick Convention; her hymns appeared in the Keswick Hymn Book. She died at Richmond, Surrey, England on February 4, 1915. More recently her hymn appeared in Hymns for the Living Church (1974).

MAXWELL, MARY FRANCES ROBERTSON (1808-1898)
  "Saints of God! the dawn is brightening."

Daughter of Frances Ferebe and Robert Robertson, a merchant, she was born at Norfolk, Virginia. Her father, a Scotsman, was ruling elder of the first Presbyterian Church established in that part of Virginia. In 1839 she married William Maxwell, President of Hampden-Sydney College. Later he was a member of the State Senate of Virginia and edited the Virginia Historical Register. He died in 1857. At the outbreak of the Civil War, she moved to Danville, Virginia. She won first prize of $100.00 for her hymn in a contest sponsored by the Presbyterian Board of Home Missions which was awarded to her on September 28, 1875. More recently her hymn was included in the Moravian (1920);

Reformed; Lutheran (Missouri Synod); and Concordia (1932,
Lutheran) hymnals. She died in 1898. [Information from
Howson W. Cole, Virginia Historical Society, Richmond,
Virginia.]

MAXWELL, MARY HAMLIN (1814-1853)
     "God hath said, 'For ever blessed.'"

In 1840 she published 107 of her hymns in Original Hymns
(New York), which included the above hymn; it also appeared
in the Methodist Episcopal Hymnal (1878). Her hymn, "I'm
a pilgrim and a stranger" (similar beginning lines by Mary
Shindler) appeared in The Song Book of The Salvation Army
(1953).

MAY, CATHERINE ELIZABETH MARTIN (1808-1873)
     "O Saviour, where shall guilty man...."

The only daughter of Sir Henry William Martin, Bart, she
was born at Lockinge Park, near Wantage, England on February 19, 1808 and in 1837 she married the Rev. George May,
later Vicar of Lyddington, Wilts. Her hymn appeared in Dr.
Maurice's Choral Harmony (1858). More recently her hymn
was published in the Presbyterian Church of Canada (1918)
and Songs of Praise (Anglican, 1931) hymnals. She died at
Totland, on the Isle of Wight, England, on September 12,
1873.

MERCER, MARGARET (1791-1846)
     "Not on a prayerless bed
     Compose thy weary limbs to rest."

Daughter of Sophia Sprigg and Congressman John F. Mercer,
she was born at Annapolis, Maryland on July 1, 1791 and
raised an Episcopalian. Her father served as Governor of
Maryland (1801-03). She devoted her life to the anti-slavery
cause and upon her father's death in 1821, she freed her
share of her father's slaves. She taught in public schools
for twenty-five years and published Popular Lectures on Eth-
ics or Moral Obligations for the Use of Schools (1837) and
Studies for Bible Classes. Her hymn appeared in An American Anthology 1787-1900 (Houghton Mifflin, c. 1900) and in
Evenings with Sacred Poets. In her later life she lived on a
farm at Belmont, near Leesburg, Virginia and died there of
tuberculosis on September 17, 1846.

MERRYLEES, RACHEL BATES (1838-1916)

Daughter of Stewart Bates, D. D., minister of the Reformed Presbyterian Church, she was born at Kelso, England and in 1864 married a Scottish musician. Her hymns appeared in The Dayspring: Hymns Old and New (1875); Wreath of Praise; and J. Paisley & R. Parlane's Gospel Choir (1887). She died on July 28, 1916.

MESECHRE, MARY I. (d. 1935)
"Arise, arise and shine."

She joined the Church of Christ, Scientist on November 7, 1899. Her hymn appeared in the Christian Science Journal for February 1908 and in the Christian Science Hymnal (1937). She died on June 21, 1935.

MEYER, ANNA MAGDALENA PLEHN (1867-1941)
"He's risen, He's risen, Christ Jesus the Lord."

Daughter of George and Ottilie Kassube Plehn, she was born at Alt-Rüdnitz, Germany on November 14, 1867, where her father taught school from 1859 to 1869, when he emigrated to America and settled in St. Louis, Missouri. He entered the Lutheran Practical Seminary there and was admitted to the ministry in 1871. For several years he served at churches in Lake Ridge and Tecumseh, Michigan, then at Chippewa Falls, Wisconsin for 22 years. On July 25, 1893 she was married to the Rev. Christian Meyer of Howard, South Dakota. Her husband served in churches in Nebraska, Illinois, and Wisconsin, and died in 1939 at Sheboygan, Wisconsin. She translated hymns from the German, and also wrote some original poems and hymns which were published in church magazines. She died at Milwaukee, Wisconsin on August 18, 1941. Her hymn appeared in The Lutheran Hymnal (1941).

MEYER, LUCY RIDER (1849-1922)
Tune--Northfield Benediction

A composer born at New Haven, near Middlebury, Vermont on September 9, 1849, she was educated in public schools and while still in her teens she taught in the high school at

Brandon, Vermont and in a school for freedmen at Greensboro, North Carolina. She entered the Junior class at Oberlin College in Ohio (1869). After becoming engaged to a young man studying to become a medical missionary, she decided to follow his career and enrolled in the Women's Medical School in Philadelphia. But her fiancé died, and she abandoned that career. She served as Principal of the Troy (Methodist) Conference Academy in Poultney, Vermont and as Professor of Chemistry at McKendree College in Illinois, and taught at Northfield Seminary. In 1885 she married Josiah S. Meyer, a Methodist Episcopal minister of the Rock River Conference, and they opened the Chicago Training School for City, Home and Foreign Missions where she served as Principal (1885-1917). She died at Chicago, Illinois on March 16, 1922. Her musical setting for "The Lord bless thee and keep thee" appeared in the Methodist Hymnal (1935).

MEYNELL, ALICE CHRISTIANA GERTRUDE THOMPSON (1847-1922)
"To the Mother of Christ, the Son of Man. "

Daughter of Christiana Weller and Thomas J. Thompson, she was born at Barnes, England on September 22, 1847. She became a Roman Catholic about 1872 and published her first book of poems, Preludes, in 1875. She married Wilfred Meynell and bore him eight children. She wrote The Rhythm of Life (1893); Poems (1893); The Colour of Life (1896); Later Poems (1902); and other books. She was a friend of Katharine Hinkson and other literary personages of the time, and died at London, England on November 22, 1922. Her hymn appeared in I Sing of a Maiden, the Mary Book of Verse, edited by Sister M. Thérèse (Macmillan, 1947).

MIEIR, AUDREY MAE WAGNER (b. 1916)
"His name is Wonderful. "

The daughter of Marie Elizabeth Dorsey and Dow C. Wagner, she was born at Leechburg, Pennsylvania on May 12, 1916 and educated at L. I. F. E. Bible College. In 1936 she was married to Charles B. Mieir and in 1937 she was ordained a minister in the International Church of Foursquare Gospel. She has played gospel songs on the piano on radio and made personal appearances (1937-45), director and organizer of various choirs (1946-58), director of the Mieir Choir Clinic

and vice-president of Mieir Music Foundation, Inc., Hollywood, California since 1960. She wrote "The desert shall
bloom like a rose" and other beautiful songs while suffering
with cancer. A member of the Bethel Chapel, Assembly of
God Church in San Jose, California, she was active as of
April 1982. Her hymn appeared in the Baptist (1975); Family of God (1976); and Broadman (1977) hymnals.

MILES, ELIZABETH APPLETON (1807-1877)
   "The earth, all light and loveliness."

She was born at Boston, Massachusetts on March 28, 1807
and in 1833 she married Solomon P. Miles, Headmaster of
the Boston High School. After her husband died in 1842 she
resided with her son in Brattleboro, Vermont. Her hymn appeared in The Christian Examiner (1828) and other hymns appeared in the Unitarian Book of Hymns (Boston, 1846); Hymns
of the Spirit (Boston, 1864); and Putnam's Singers and Songs
of the Liberal Faith (1875). She died on January 23, 1877.

MILLER, ANNE LANGDON (b. 1908)
   Tune--VERMONT

Composer and violinist, she was born at New York City on
January 6, 1908 and educated there at the Institute of Musical
Art and the David Mannes School of Music. After several
years as first violinist in the Vermont State Symphony Orches-
tra, in 1948 she entered the Community of Poor Clares.
Her tune appeared in The Hymnal of the Protestant Episcopal
Church (1940).

MILLER, EMILY HUNTINGTON (1833-1913)
   "I love to hear the story
   which angel voices tell."

Daughter of the Rev. Thomas Huntington, D.D., a Methodist
minister, she was born at Brooklyn, Connecticut on October
22, 1833 and obtained her A.B. at Oberlin College, Oberlin,
Ohio in 1857. On September 5, 1860 she married Professor
John E. Miller of Greentown, Ohio. She published numerous
books, Captain Firth, Little Neighbors, etc., and From Ava-
lon and Other Poems. Her hymn, "Enter thy temple, glorious King" was written for the dedication of the Methodist
Episcopal Church in Akron, Ohio in 1861 and appeared in the

Methodist Hymnal (1878). She was joint editor of The Little
Corporal, a children's magazine which became St. Nicholas,
and her hymn above called "Angel's Story" appeared in the
1867 edition and later in Hymns Ancient and Modern (1875).
Other hymns appeared in E. Hodder's New Sunday School
Hymn Book (2nd edition, 1868); Common Praise (1879); Barrett's Book of Praise for Children (1881); and other hymnals.
In 1891 she became Dean of Women at Northwestern University, Evanston, Illinois. She died at Northfield, Minnesota
on November 2, 1913. More recently her hymn appeared in
the Presbyterian Hymnal (1933); and the English Baptist Hymn
Book (London, 1962).

MILLER, LILLIAN ANNE (b. 1916)
    "I will call upon God. "

Composer, hymnist, pianist, and teacher, she was born at
North Haddonfield, New Jersey on May 31, 1916 and was educated at the Sternberg School of Music, Rutgers University in
New Brunswick, New Jersey and studied privately. She
taught at the North Haddonfield branch of the Sternberg School
and was a pianist-accompanist for the Philadelphia Light Opera Company. She had her own trio with the Cosmopolitan
Opera Company and was a teacher in Newark, New Jersey.
She also wrote "Blessed land of mine, " "O Lord behold the
earth, " "Exult in Glory, " etc.

MILLS, ELIZABETH KING (1805-1829)
    "O land of rest, for thee I sigh!
    When will the moment come. "

Daughter of Philip King, she was born at Stoke Newington,
England and was later married to Thomas Mills, a member
of Parliament. The hymn appeared as "Sweet land of rest"
by G. M. -1829 in Hatfield's Church Hymn Book (1872) and in
other hymnals as by Elizabeth Mills. It was in Sankey's
Sacred Songs and Solos (1881). Her hymn "We speak of the
realms of the blest" appeared in Miller's Singers and Songs
... (1869) and as "We sing of the land of the blest" in other
hymnals. It appeared in almost every children's hymn book
published in England or in America. She died in London,
England on April 21, 1829. More recently her hymn above
appeared in the American Service Hymnal (1968).

MILNER-BARRY, ALDA MARGUERITE (1875-1941)
"Good Joseph had a garden. "

The youngest daughter of the Rev. Edward Milner Barry,
she was born at Scothorne Vicarage, near Lincoln, England,
and studied at St. Christopher's College, Blackheath, where
she later taught. She was the author of Prayers and Praises
in the Infant Sunday School and The Joyful Life. She was a
member of the Church of England and six of her hymns, including the one above, were published in the Church School
Hymnal (1926) and in Hymns Ancient and Modern. She died
at Weston-super-Mare, England on April 15, 1940. More
recently her hymn appeared in the English Baptist Hymn Book
(1962).

MITCHELL, ELIZABETH HARCOURT ROLLS (1833-1910)
"Come to the manger in Bethlehem. "

Daughter of John E. W. Rolls of the Hendrie, Monmouth,
Wales, she was born on December 15, 1833. In 1860 she
married F. J. Mitchell of Llanfrechfa Grange, Caerleon,
Monmouthshire, Wales. Five of her hymns appeared in Mrs.
Brock's Children's Hymn Book (1881); other original hymns
of hers appeared in the Altar Hymnal (1884) and she also
translated hymns from the Latin. She died on September 16,
1910.

MINGA, ANN BARCUS (1903-1976)
"Christ, by whom twelve humble men. "

Daughter of J. Sam Barcus, President of Southwestern Uni-
versity, Georgetown, Texas, she was born at Clarendon,
Texas on July 10, 1903 and received degrees from South-
western University and Columbia University in New York
City, and did graduate work at Duke University in Durham,
North Carolina. She taught English and speech at Wesley
College, Centenary College, Southwestern University, North
Texas State College at Denton and East Texas State Univer-
sity at Commerce, Texas. She married the Rev. T. Herbert
Minga, at Georgetown, Texas on May 30, 1932. He was a
Chaplain in the Air Force during World War II, and later
pastor of the White Rock United Methodist Church in Dallas,
Texas. She published several books of poetry; her third
book was called Roses are Velvet. She died at Dallas, Texas
on July 27, 1976. [Information from Mrs. J. Huston, Secre-

tary, Methodist Church, Denton, Texas.] Her hymn appeared in Christian Education Hymns published by The Hymn Society of America (1959).

MISTRAL, GABRIELA (1899-1957)
"Thou knowest, Lord, with what flaming boldness. "

Born Lucila Godey-Alcayaga at Vicuna, Chile, on April 7, 1899, she was director of schools in Santiago, Chile and advisor to the Ministry of Education (1922-24) at Mexico City. She was made a consul for life by the Chilean Congress (1935) and served in Madrid, Lisbon, Nice, Petropolis (Brazil), Los Angeles, and Santa Barbara, California (1947-54). She was Roman Catholic and wrote numerous books. She won the Nobel Prize in Literature in 1945. Her hymn appeared in an Anthology of Contemporary Latin American Poetry (New Directions, 1947). She resided at Roslyn Harbor, New York.

MOODY, MAY WHITTLE (1870-1963)
Tune--WHITTLE

Composer and daughter of evangelist Daniel W. Whittle (1840-1891), she was named "Mary" but chose "May" and at age 15 attended the Girl's School in Northfield, Massachusetts which was founded by evangelist Dwight L. Moody. Later she attended Oberlin College (1888-89) in Oberlin, Ohio and the Royal Academy of Music in London, England (1890-91). She sang gospel songs in the evangelistic campaigns of Moody and Whittle. On August 29, 1894 she married William R. Moody, son of the famous evangelist, and they had six children, two of whom died in infancy. They lived at Northfield where Will Moody headed the Northfield Schools and also the Mount Hermon Conference center which had been founded by his father. With Charles M. Alexander, she was co-editor of Northfield Hymnal No. 3. Her tune appeared in Sacred Songs No. 1 edited by Ira D. Sankey, James McGranahan, and George C. Stebbins (1896) and with the hymn, "Dying with Jesus" in Hymns for the Living Church (1974). She died at Northfield on August 20, 1963.

MOORE, JESSIE ELEANOR (1886-1969)
"Our thoughts go 'round the world. "

Daughter of Edwin M. and Jessie Chander Moore, she was
born at Newark, New Jersey on December 1, 1886 and educated at the Newark Normal School, Columbia University
(B. S. , 1919; M. A. , 1922) and the Union Theological Seminary
in New York City (B. D. , 1943). After teaching kindergarten
in Newark schools (1907-18) and elsewhere, she was editor
of The Pilgrim Press, Boston (1930-47) and assistant editor
of the Methodist Publishing House in Nashville, Tennessee
(1947-57). For years she was a member of the First Methodist Church of Asbury Park, New Jersey. She wrote numerous books, Prayers for Little Children (1937), etc. Her
hymn was included in A Hymnal for Friends (1955, Quakers).
She resided at Ocean Grove, New Jersey.

MORE, HANNAH (1745-1833)
    "The angry word suppressed; the taunting thought?"

Daughter of the schoolmaster Jacob More, she was born at
Stapleton, Gloucestershire, England on February 2, 1745,
the fourth of five daughters. She was educated at Bristol,
where her elder sisters ran a boarding school. None of the
five daughters married. She made numerous trips to London
and was a friend of David Garrick, Dr. Samuel Johnson, Edmund Burke, and Sir Joshua Reynolds. She was a member
of the famous "Bluestocking" crowd of Elizabeth Montagu,
and she called herself Mrs. More, since in 18th century England it was considered a disgrace to be a spinster. She
wrote several plays produced in England by David Garrick
and her book Sacred Dramas (1782) went into 19 editions.
She became an anti-slavery advocate and friend of William
Wilberforce, and retired to live at Cowslip Green, Wrington,
Somerset. She outlived her sisters and died at Clifton, Bristol, England on September 7, 1833.

MORGAN, ANGELA (1873-1957)
    "God does do such wonderful things. "

Daughter of Carol Baldwin and Alwyn Morgan, an attorney,
she was born at Washington, D. C. and educated at Chautauqua, New York. She wrote for newspapers in Chicago, New
York City, and Boston and became the first woman to occupy
the pulpit of Chapel Royal, Savoy, London in author's reading.
She was a member of the Poetry Society of America and the
Poetry Society of London and wrote The Hour Has Struck
(1914); Utterance and Other Poems (1916); Selected Poems

(1927); Drum Beats Out of Heaven (1941); and numerous other books. She was awarded an honorary Litt. D. by Golden State University, Los Angeles, California (1942). Later she resided at Mount Marion, Vesta County, New York and died on January 24, 1957 and was buried at Saugerties, New York. Her hymn appeared in A Treasury of Religious Verse (Fleming H. Revell, 1962).

MORGAN, CAROL McAFEE (b. 1899)
"Humbly now we come before thee."

Born at Rockville, Missouri on July 2, 1899, she married Barney Morgan who served four years as Dean of the Polytechnic Institute, San German, Puerto Rico and twenty years as Superintendent of the Board for Christian Work in Santo Domingo, Dominican Republic. She wrote the mission study book, Rim of the Carribbean, and later was Director of Christian Education in the First Presbyterian Church in Mt. Vernon, New York, subsequently working as a Mobile Parish Worker for the Presbytery of Westchester, New York. After her husband died, she married Dr. John Appleby on October 1, 1960. Her hymn appeared in Christian Education Hymns published by The Hymn Society of America (1959). As of May 1982 she was living in Alhambra, California. [Information from the First Presbyterian Church, Mount Vernon, New York.]

MORRIS, ELIZA FANNY GOFFE (1821-1874)
"God of pity, God of grace."

Born in London, England, she married Josiah Morris in 1849. Her poetical ability was realized when a poem she wrote on "Kindness to Animals" received the Band of Hope award. She edited a Bible Class Hymn Book, contributed words to School Harmonies, published by her husband, and wrote The Voice and the Reply (Worcester, 1858) which included the above hymn, and also Life Lyrics. Her husband was sub-editor of the Malvern News. Her hymns appeared in Miller's Singers and Songs of the Church (1869); the Anglican Hymn Book (2nd edition, 1871); and more recently in the Evangelical and Reformed Church Hymnal (1941). She died at Malvern, England.

MORRIS, LELIA NAYLOR (1862-1929)
   "Jesus is coming to earth again. "
   Tunes--SECOND COMING, McCONNESVILLE, and
      MORRIS

A composer and hymnist, born at Pennsville, Morgan County,
Ohio on April 15, 1862, she moved with her family to Malta,
Ohio, just across the Muskingum River from McConnelsville
in 1866 when her father returned from the Civil War.   After
her father died, with her mother and sister, the three wom-
en opened a millinery shop in McConnelsville.   She was a
member of the Methodist Protestant Church, but after her
marriage in 1881 to Charles H. Morris, she joined the Methodist Episcopal Church with her husband.   She attended various Methodist camp meetings--Old Camp Sychar in Mt. Vernon, Ohio, Sebring Camp at Sebring, Ohio and at Mountain
Lake Park, Maryland.   She also wrote the music for her
hymns, and when her eyesight failed in 1913, her son erected
a large blackboard, 28 feet long, with music staff lines on
it, so she could continue her hymn writing.   She died at Auburn, Ohio on July 23, 1929.   Her hymns appeared in Baptist
(1975); Broadman (1977); and Family of God (1976) hymnals.

MORRIS, MARION LONGFELLOW (1849-1924)
   "He knows the bitter, weary way. "

A niece of Henry Wadsworth Longfellow, she was born at
Portland, Maine on April 1, 1849 and spent most of her life
in Brookline, Massachusetts.   On May 9, 1876 she married
W. F. Morris of Boston.   Her hymn was written on Septem-
ber 15, 1874.   She was a newspaper reporter, and an ac-
credited press representative at The White House during the
administrations of presidents William McKinley and Theodore
Roosevelt.   Her hymn was included in the Broadman Hymnal
(Baptist, 1940).   She was a charter member of the Daughters
of the American Revolution, and died at the home of her son,
H. W. Morris, in Shawmut, California on June 23, 1924.
[Obituary in The New York Times and information from Edith
H. McCauley, Special Collections, Public Library, Portland,
Maine.]

MORRISON, MARGARET (d. 1954)
   "We lift our hearts in praise. "

She was born and educated in Canada and later the family

moved to the United States. She was taught by private tutors. She became a Shakespearean actress and headed a company of Shakespearean actors until she became interested in Christian Science. In 1913 she entered the full-time public practice of Christian Science healing. Her tour of duty as a Christian Science lecturer began in 1935 and in 1944 she became an associate editor of the Christian Science periodicals. Two of her hymns appeared in the Christian Science Hymnal (1937). She died on May 1, 1954 in Pigeon Cove, Massachusetts.

MORSE, ANNA JUSTINA (1893-1979)
         Tunes--CONSECRATION and KEMPER

Composer and organist, she was born at Haverhill, Massachusetts on July 29, 1893 and was educated at Wellesley College (B. A., 1919), Wellesley, Massachusetts with graduate study at Yale University, New Haven, Connecticut and at Northwestern University, Evanston, Illinois. She taught in high schools in Washington, D. C. and in New Haven, Connecticut, where she was assistant organist at Christ Church until 1925. Later she was in charge of the junior school at Kemper Hall in Kenosha, Wisconsin (1925-38) and from 1938 director of studies and choir director. Her two hymn tunes mentioned above appeared in The Hymnal (1940) of the Protestant Episcopal Church. She died on December 15, 1979.

MOULE, HARRIOT MARY ELLIOTT (1844-1915)
         "Cast thou thy care upon the Lord."

The youngest daughter of the Rev. C. Boileau Elliott, M. A., F. R. S., rector of Tatingstone, Suffolk, England, she was born in Paris, France on September 29, 1844. In 1881 she married Handley Carr Glyn Moule (1841-1920), principal of Ridley Hall at Cambridge University (1880-99), who became Bishop of Durham in 1901. Her hymn was first published in her husband's Songs in the House of the Pilgrimage (1896) and then in Hymns of Consecreation and Faith (1902). She died on July 14, 1915.

MOULTRIE, MARY DUNLAP (1837-1866)
         "Dormi, Fili! dormi, Mater."
         "Sleep, my Babe! O sleep, the Mother."

She was the daughter of John Moultrie, who was presented by the Earl of Craven to the Rectory of Rugby, England in 1825 and where he remained until his death in 1874. She was born at the Rectory in July 1837. She was the sister of Gerald Moultrie, who was Chaplain to the Dowager Marchioness of Londonderry, North Ireland (1855-59) and later Vicar of Southleigh (1869). Her translations of hymns from the Latin were published in her brother's Hymns and Lyrics (1867). More recently her hymn was published in the Oxford Book of Carols (Anglican, 1964). She died at Rugby on June 15, 1866.

MOZLEY, HARRIET ELIZABETH NEWMAN (c. 1806-1852)
    "When safely on dry land once more. "

Daughter of John Newman, partner in the banking firm of Ramsbottom, Newman and Company of London, England, she was also the sister of Cardinal Newman. On September 27, 1836 at St. Werburgh's, Derby, England, she was married to Thomas Mozley (1806-1893), perpetual curate of Moreton-Pinkey, Northamptonshire and junior treasurer of Oriel. They had one daughter. He contributed articles to the London Times for a number of years. Her hymns, 28 in all including the above, were published in her Hymns for Children on the Lord's Prayer, Our Duty towards God, and Scripture History (1835). It reached a sixth edition in 1856. Some of her hymns were included in the Child's Christian Year (1841) and in subsequent hymnals. She died in Guilford Street, Russell Square, London on July 17, 1852.

MUNGER, HARRIETT KING OSGOOD (1857-1925)
    "O my father, I would know Thee. "

Born in Salem, Massachusetts on March 14, 1857, she entered Wellesley College in its first year of founding, but she was unable to continue her courses due to poor health, and so turned to study art. She studied abroad and at the Boston Museum of Fine Arts School, then became a teacher at the Burnham School for Girls at Northampton, Massachusetts. On March 5, 1889 she married the Rev. Theodore Thornton Munger, a Congregational minister of the United Church of New Haven, Connecticut, serving from 1885 to 1900. She was his second wife. She organized the Pleasant Sunday Afternoon Class when the mothers were free and helped organize the New Haven Nurses' Association. After her husband died in 1910 she returned to her old home in Salem,

Massachusetts where she died.   Her hymn appeared in the
Presbyterian Hymnal (1933).

MURPHY, ANNE S. (1877-1942)
    Tune--CONSTANTLY ABIDING
    "There's a peace in my heart. "

Composer and hymnist, she was born at Sebring, Ohio and
was the wife of Will L. Murphy, who at one time had a successful pottery business, but then the depression years came,
her husband died, and she lost all her money.   Penniless,
she went to live with a sister in Burbank, California.   She
was a singer, musician, composer, evangelist, and had written many hymns, both the words and music.   Despite her
problems and heartaches, she came through her bad times
with an inner peace reflected in her hymns.   She died at
Burbank on March 30, 1942.   Her hymn appeared in Hymns
for the Living Church (1974).   [Information received from
the Public Library, Burbank, California.]

MUSGRAVE, THEA (b. 1928)
    Opera--A Christmas Carol

Composer, conductor, she was born at Edinburgh, Scotland
and educated at Edinburgh University and the Paris Conservatory (Mus. B.).   In 1971 she married Peter Mares.   She
wrote several operas, including the above which was first
produced by the Virginia Opera Association in 1979.   She resided in Norfolk, Virginia.

NAIRNE, CAROLINA OLIPHANT, BARONESS (1766-1845)
    "The Land o' the Leal. "

Composer, hymnist and songwriter, daughter of Laurence
Oliphant, she was born at Gask, Perthshire, Scotland on August 16, 1766 and was a Jacobite (devoted to the Royal House
of Stuart).   She married a Jacobite, Major William Nairne
in 1806, who became the 5th Baron Nairne in 1824.   Using
the pen-name "Mrs. Bogan of Bogan, " her poems were published in The Scottish Minstrel (1821-24).   She is known for
her songs "Charlie is My Darling, " "The Hundred Pipers, "
"The Laird O' Cockpen, " etc.   She died on October 26, 1845
and her collected poems were published in Lays from Strath-
earn (1846) and more recently in Masterpieces of Religious

Verse (Harper, 1948) and The World's Greatest Religious
Poetry (Macmillan, 1934). In Scotland a laverock is a lark,
and she wrote:

> Sweet's the laverock's note and lang,
> Lilting wildly up the glen!
> But aye to me he sings ae sang,
> Will ye no' come back again?

NAVARRE, MARGUERITE, QUEEN OF (1492-1549)
"A Godly Meditation of the Christian soul, etc. "

Translator and versifier, daughter of Charles d'Orleans,
Count of Angoulême, she was born at Angoulême, Navarre
on April 11, 1492. In 1509 she married Charles, Duke
d'Alençon, who died in 1525. Then in 1527 she married
Henri d'Albret, King of Navarre, an ancient kingdom which
by then consisted of just a small area north of the Pyrénées.
She published her poems, Les Marguerites de la marguerite
des princess (1547), and fourteen psalms which were translated from the French by the Princess Elizabeth (afterwards
Queen Elizabeth I) which appeared in The Psalmists of Great
Britain (1843) and in Select Poetry Chiefly Devotional of the
Reign of Queen Elizabeth (Cambridge, 1845). Queen Marguerite died at Odot-en-Bigorre on September 21, 1549. Marguerite was a strong Protestant, and endeavored to keep her
country that way. Her grandson, Henri, the last King of
Navarre, became King Henry IV of France in 1589. In order to maintain peace, he gave up Protestantism and was accepted into the Roman Catholic Church. In 1598 he issued
the Edict of Nantes which gave rights and privileges to the
Protestant French Huguenots.

NEVILL, EDITH MILDRED (1889-1976)
"God is good. "

She was born in England on August 20, 1889 and educated at
Westhill, Birmingham, and London University. She was an
educational psychologist and one of the pioneers of modern
Sunday School methods. Her hymn was written for the junior
departments at Kingsley Hall, Bow, England. [At the Riverside Presbyterian Church in Cocoa Beach, Florida recently
and during the winter months the gospel sing-along, led by
the Cocoa Beach High School choir director, Deacon Milton
Borens, starts off with everybody singing "God is good. "]

Her hymn was published in the English Baptist Hymn Book (1962). She died on August 29, 1976, just nine days after her 87th birthday.

NEVIN, ALICE (1837-1925)
Tunes--RESURRECTION, CECIL, and ELSIE

Composer and organist, the daughter of Martha Jenkins and Dr. John Williamson Nevin, she was born at Allegheny (now Pittsburgh), Pennsylvania on August 1, 1837, where her father occupied the chair of biblical literature at Western Theological Seminary (1828-40). She was raised in Mercersburg, Pennsylvania where her father was a professor at the Reformed Church Theological Seminary (1840-51), when he became a professor at Franklin and Marshall College, Lancaster, Pennsylvania until his death in 1892 at age 86. Unfortunately, while an infant, she was dropped by a nurse and the rest of her life she walked with a limp. For many years she was organist and choir director at Franklin and Marshall College and also at the First Reformed Church in Lancaster, Pennsylvania. In 1879 she published Hymns and Carols for Church and Sunday School which included her tunes RESURRECTION, CECIL, ELSIE and two unnamed tunes and three arrangements, WILLIAMSON, COBLENTZ and CORNISH MELODY. She also published her Poems (1922). She was active in founding St. Luke's Reformed Church. She died at Lancaster on November 19, 1925. Her tunes RESURRECTION and WILLIAMSON appeared in the Evangelical and Reformed Church Hymnal (1941).

NEWELL, LAURA E. PIXLEY (1854-1916)
"Across the years."

Composer, hymnist, poet, and songwriter, the daughter of Ann Laura Osborne and Edward A. Pixley, she was born at New Marlborough, near Great Barrington, Massachusetts on February 5, 1854. When she was only four years old, her mother died, and she was adopted by an aunt, Mrs. Hiram Mabie, who took her to a farm near Wamego, Kansas. On August 30, 1871 she married Lauren Newell at Zeandale, Kansas. He entered the Civil War as a Sergeant in May 1862, served with the 2nd Regiment, Company F, Kansas State Volunteer Cavalry, and discharged as a 1st Lieutenant on April 30, 1865. He was a carpenter and builder, and they resided near Manhattan, Kansas. She was active in the

Sunday School of the Congregational Church. Her first poem was published when she was only 14, and she wrote many songs. She wrote the hymn above for which she also composed the music. Laura and her husband had four sons and two daughters. "A city awaits us" was included in the Evangelical Lutheran and Presbyterian (1955) hymnals. She died at Manhattan, Kansas on October 13, 1916. [Information from Cheryl Collins and Jean C. Dallas of the Riley County Historical Society & Museum, Manhattan, Kansas.]

NEWTON, MAUD DE VERSE (d. 1970)
    "He sent His Word, His holy Word. "

She joined the Church of Christ, Scientist on May 30, 1913 and her hymn appeared in the Christian Science Sentinel for March 22, 1930 and in the Christian Science Hymnal (1937). She died on May 15, 1970.

NIEDERMEYER, MABEL   see   MABEL N. McCAW

NITSCHMANN, ANNA   see   ANNA N. VON ZINZENDORF

NOEL, CAROLINE MARIA (1817-1877)
    "At the name of Jesus, Every knee shall bow. "

Daughter of the Honorable Gerald T. Noel, she was born in London, England on April 10, 1817. She was the niece of the Honorable Baptist W. Noel. Her hymns were published in her book The Name of Jesus and Other Verses for the Sick and Lonely (1861). Various editions were published; there were 78 hymns and poems in the 1878 edition, The Name of Jesus and Other Poems, published after her death. She died at London on December 7, 1877. More recently her hymn appeared in the Broadman (1977); Episcopal (1940); Family of God (1976); Methodist (1966); Presbyterian (1955) hymnals and The Pilgrim Hymnal (1958).

NORFLEET, MARY WINSTON CROCKETT (b. 1919)
    "Long ago God's chosen men,
    Working for His glory. "

She was born in Glen Burnie, Maryland on November 21,

1919 and married Marmaduke W. Norfleet, Jr. in 1944.
They had four sons and two daughters. She was graduated
from the University of Virginia in 1940 and at the Presbyterian School of Christian Religion received a Master's of
Religious Education in 1943. She has served as a part-time
writer for the Presbyterian Board of Christian Education
since 1945. Her hymn was published in Joyfully Sing--A
Hymnal for Juniors (1968).

NOURSE, LAURA C. (d. 1929)
     "Now sweeping down the years untold. "

She studied with Mary Baker Eddy in 1888 and joined the
Church of Christ, Scientist on July 1, 1893. She was a
resident of Pompey, New York, then moved to Escanaba,
Michigan (1893) and then to Eau Clair, Wisconsin (1897),
where she was a Christian Science practitioner until 1925.
She died at Eau Clair on October 17, 1929. Her hymn appeared in the Christian Science Journal (January, 1890) and
in the Christian Science Hymnal (1937).

NUNN, MARIANNE (1778-1847)
     "One there is above all others, O how He loves. "

Daughter of John Nunn of Colchester, England, she was born
there on May 17, 1778. She was the sister of the Rev. John
Nunn, Domestic Chaplain to the Earl of Galloway from 1849
and Rector of Thorndon, Suffolk from 1854. Her hymn appeared in her brother's Psalms and Hymns from the most ap-
proved Authors... (1817) and later in Lyra Britannica (1867).
She wrote The Benevolent Merchant and other books. She
never married. Variations on her hymn appeared: "There's
a friend above all others" in John Curwen's The New Child's
Own Hymn Book (1874), and "One is kind above all others"
in other juvenile songbooks. More recently her hymn appeared in The Song Book of The Salvation Army (1953).

OAKEY, EMILY SULLIVAN (1829-1883)
     "Sowing the seed by the daylight fair,
     Sowing the seed by the noonday glare. "

Born in Albany, New York, she wrote hymns for Philip Bliss,
which appeared in his Gospel Songs (1874) and in Ira D.
Sankey's Sacred Songs and Solos. She died in her home town,

Albany, New York. More recently her hymn appeared in
the Southern Baptist Hymnal (1973).

O'BRIEN, MARY L. (b. 1896)
"Creator of the world we know, and worlds beyond
our ken. "

She was born at Cincinnati, Ohio on November 22, 1896 and
was graduated from Miami University in Oxford, Ohio. On
March 24, 1926 she married Dr. Henry R. O'Brien. They
served in Thailand for four years under the auspices of the
Presbyterian Board of Missions. Dr. O'Brien was ordained
an elder in the Presbyterian Church of Olean, New York and
Mrs. O'Brien was ordained an elder in the Camp Hill, Pennsylvania, Presbyterian Church. Her husband became senior
surgeon of the U.S. Public Health Service and director of
the Division of Professional Education for the Pennsylvania
Health Department until his retirement in 1964. She wrote
poetry, short plays, and pageants. Her hymn appeared in
Lord's Day Hymns published by The Hymn Society of America (1968). As of May 1982 she was enjoying her retirement. [Letter from her son, James P. O'Brien of Somer-
ville, Massachusetts.]

OGDON, INA DULEY (1872-1964)
"Do not wait until some deed of greatness you may
do. . . .
Brighten the corner where you are. "

Her name has often been misspelled as Ina Dudley Ogden.
Born in Rossville, Illinois on April 3, 1872, she became a
member of the Disciples of Christ Church. On September 2,
1896 she was married to James Weston Ogdon, and was a
resident of West Toledo, Ohio for many years. "Brighten
the corner where you are" was written in 1913 and popu-
larized by Homer Rodeheaver (1880-1955), the famous gospel
singer. She died in May 1964. Her hymn appeared in Joyfully Sing--A Hymnal for Juniors (1968) and there were nine
recordings of the gospel song listed in Phonolog Reports
(1978). She also wrote "I've cast my heavy burdens down
on Canaan's happy shore" which appeared in the American
Service Hymnal (1968); "He hears when my soul to Him
cries" and three other hymns which appeared in Rodeheaver's
Gospel Solos and Duets No. 3.

OPIE, AMELIA ALDERSON (1769-1853)
"There seems a voice in every gale. "

Daughter of Dr. Alderson, a physician, she was born at Norwich, England on November 12, 1769. In May 1798 she married John Opie, the painter. She wrote numerous novels and
books of poetry, including Father and Daughter (1801), and
Tales of Real Life (1813). Then her husband died in 1807.
She had been a Unitarian, but joined the Society of Friends
in 1814. She wrote Lays for the Dead in 1833. She lived
at Castle Meadow, Norwich, where she died on December 2,
1853.

ORTLUND, ELIZABETH ANNE SWEET (b. 1923)
"The vision of a dying world is vast before our eyes. "

Composer, hymnist, and organist, the daughter of Brigadier
General Joseph B. Sweet, she was born at Wichita, Kansas
on December 3, 1923, and was educated at the University of
Redlands, California. She was married to Raymond C. Ortlund, pastor of the Lake Avenue Congregational Church in
Pasadena, California. She held the A. A. G. O. certificate
from the American Guild of Organists and served as organist for the "Old Fashioned Revival Hour" radio broadcasts,
and also with the successor broadcasts, "The Joyful
Sound. " She has written 25 hymn text and tunes, about 100
anthems, sacred and secular solos, and various instrumental
works. Her hymn appeared in Hymns for the Living Church
(1974).

OSGOOD, FRANCES SARGENT LOCKE (1811-1850)
"To labor is to pray,
Let thy great deed be thy prayer to thy God. "

Daughter of Mary Ingersoll and Joseph Locke, she was born
at Boston, Massachusetts on June 18, 1811 and raised in
Hingham, Massachusetts. She contributed poems to Mrs.
Child's Juvenile Miscellany. On October 7, 1835 she married Samuel S. Osgood, a portrait painter, and they sailed
for England where they made their home in London. She
was introduced into London literary circles by the Honorable
Mrs. Norton. They later returned to America, and she met
Edgar Allan Poe in March 1845. Mrs. Osgood and Poe
wrote verses to each other. She had numerous books published and died in New York City on May 12, 1850.

OWEN, FRANCES MARY SYNGE (1842-1883)
"Lighten the darkness of our life's long night."

She was born in England on April 16, 1842 and married the
Rev. J. Albert Owen, Assistant Master at Cheltenham College. She wrote several books, including John Keats: A
Study; Soldier and Patriot: A life of George Washington; Essays and Poems (1887). The hymn above appeared in Tre-
foil, Verses by Three (1868) and with other hymns in Hymns
for the Use of the Chapel at Cheltenham College (1890). She
died on June 19, 1883. More recently her hymn above appeared in The Pilgrim Hymnal (1958).

OWENS, PRISCILLA JANE (1829-1907)
"We have heard the joyful sound."

The daughter of Isaac and Jane Stewart Owens, she was born
in Baltimore, Maryland on July 21, 1829 and spent her entire life there. A public school teacher for forty-nine years,
she was also a Sunday School teacher at the Union Square
Methodist Episcopal Church. Her hymns appeared in the
Scotch Church Hymnary (1898) and another hymn, "Will your
anchor hold in the storms of life?" appeared in the American
Service Hymnal (1968). She died at Baltimore on December
5, 1907. The hymn above appeared in the American Service
(1968); Baptist (1975); Broadman (1977); Christian Worship
(1953); Family of God (1976); Joyfully Sing (1968); and Presbyterian (1955) hymnals.

PAGE, KATE STEARNS (1873-1963)
"We, thy people, praise thee,
God of every nation."

She was born in Brookline, Massachusetts on August 21, 1873
and taught at the Dennison House Settlement School in Boston
and at the Parke School in Brookline, Massachusetts. Later
she taught the pre-school music classes at the Diller-Quaile
School of Music in New York City (1933-41). With Agnes
Diller, one of the founders of the music school, she wrote
a number of books. Her hymn appeared in The Methodist
Hymnal (1966). She died at New York City on January 19,
1963.

PAGE, MARY JUDD (b. 1818)
"Ye who are called to labor."

The daughter of Arza and Lucinda Adams Judd, she was born at Leeds, Ontario, Canada on November 26, 1818 and was married to John E. Page, an early apostle of The Church of Jesus Christ of Latter-day Saints. Her hymn appeared in their Hymns (1948). John E. Page (1799-1867) was born in Oneida County, New York, and on 26 December 1833 he married Lorain Stevens. He was sent on a mission to Canada in May 1836 by the Prophet Joseph Smith, and except for three weeks early in 1837, he remained there until May 1838, when he traveled with a party of saints southward in thirty wagons arriving at DeWitt, Carroll County, Missouri in October 1838. Ruthless mobs attacked the Mormons and the saints were driven away to Far West, Caldwell County, where Page's wife and two children died of cold and hunger. We assume it was Lorain who died there. (Letter of 12/2/83 from Carol H. Cannon, Genealogy World, Salt Lake City, Utah.) The date of his marriage to Mary Judd is unknown, and we have been unable to determine her date and place of death, although her husband died in Sycamore, Illinois in the fall of 1867.

PALMER, ALICE FREEMAN (1855-1902)
   "How sweet and silent is the place. "

She was born at Colesville, New York on February 21, 1855 and was graduated from the University of Michigan (1876), with her Ph. D. at Michigan (1881), L. H. D. Columbia (1887), and LL. D. , Union College (1895). In 1887 she married George H. Palmer, LL. D. She was Professor of History at Wellesley College (1879-81), President there (1881-87), and Dean of Women at the University of Chicago (1892-95). She died at Paris, France on December 6, 1902. In 1920 she was elected to the Hall of Fame for Great Americans. Her hymn was included in the Reformed Church in America; Unitarian (1914); The Student Hymnary (1937); and Army and Navy (1942) hymnals.

PALMER, PHEBE WORALL (1807-1874)
   "O when shall I sweep through the gates. "

Born in New York City on December 18, 1807, the fourth of ten children, she was raised a Methodist. On September 28, 1827 she married Walter C. Palmer. In New York City in 1835 she started, with her sister, a Thursday Afternoon Prayer Meeting for women which she conducted for 37 years.

Her daughter, Phebe Palmer, the composer, married Joseph
F. Knapp, who founded the Metropolitan Life Insurance Company. Her hymn above appeared in Ira D. Sankey's Sacred
Songs and Solos (1878). She also wrote "Blessed Bible, how
I love thee," called "The Cleansing Stream," with music by
her daughter, Mrs. Knapp, and also "Welcome to Glory,"
with music by Mrs. Knapp, which appeared in the Revivalist
(1868). Her hymn "Blessed Bible, how I love thee" was included in the Eastern Mennonite, Church of the Brethren
(1925) and Mennonite (1959) hymnals. She died in New York
City on November 2, 1874.

PARENTE, SISTER ELIZABETH (b. 1918)
     Works--Mass in Honor of Our Lady of Victory

Composer, choir conductor, and pianist, she was born at
Cambridge, New York on March 20, 1918 and educated at
Georgian Court College, Lakewood, New Jersey (M. B., 1938),
New York University, and Catholic University of America in
Washington, D. C. (M. M., 1962). She was music department
head of Villa Victoria Academy in Trenton, New Jersey
(1938-66), and Principal (1967-73); Music Department head
at Bethlehem University in Bethlehem, Israel (1973-79).
Her Mass (above) was published by G. Schirmer (New York,
1959). She also wrote an Ave Maria (vocal) for the centenary
of Our Lady of Lourdes (1958) and more than ten piano
pieces. She performed at Town Hall (1943) and Carnegie
Hall (1959-63) in New York City, at the NEMC Convention
in Atlantic City, New Jersey (1959); N. J. Performing Arts
Festival in Princeton (1963-64); N. J. State Symphony at South
Orange (1972) and numerous other concert performances.
[Letter from Sister Elizabeth from Our Lady of Mercy Convent, where she was residing in March 1982, Park Ridge,
New Jersey.]

PARKER, ALICE STUART (b. 1925)
     Tune--HAWLEY

Composer, conductor, and teacher, she was born at Boston,
Massachusetts on December 16, 1925 and was educated at
Smith College (B. A., 1947), Northampton, Massachusetts and
at the Juilliard School (M. S., 1949), in New York City. On
August 20, 1954 she married Thomas Pyle and they had two
sons and three daughters. She was an arranger for the
Robert Shaw Chorale (1948-67), taught privately in New York

from 1951, was conductor at the Mennonite Church Center in Laurelville, Pennsylvania (1961-70), lecturer at Meadowbrook, Michigan (1967), Blossom Festival School (1964-71). She composed various choral works and carols. The tune above is a choral setting for "A Hymn for Confirmation" (text by Fred Kaan) in the "Hymn Concerto Series" published by The Hymn Society of America (1982).

PARKER, ANN NESBITT (1828-1863)

She was born at Horsley-on-Tyne, England, and in 1851 married the Rev. Dr. Parker, who later served as Minister to the City Temple in London. She contributed 18 hymns to the Cavendish Hymnal (1864) which was edited by her husband and by the Rev. R. A. Bertram. She died on September 20, 1863.

PARR, HARRIET (1828-1900)
        "Hear my prayer, O heavenly Father. "

She was born in York, England and became a well-known novelist. Her hymn appeared as a prayer of a young man in her story The Wreck of the Golden Mary, off the coast of California in the days of the gold rush, which appeared in the Christmas edition of Charles Dickens' Household Words in 1856. Later it appeared in the New Congregational Hymn Book of 1859 and in Thring's Collection of 1882 as "Hear our prayer. " Her hymn was also included in The Evangelical Lutheran Book of Worship (1899); and in Songs of Praise (1931, Anglican). She died at Whittle Meade, Shanklin, Isle of Wight on February 18, 1900.

PARSON, ELIZABETH ROOKER (1812-1873)
        "Angels round the throne are praising. "

Daughter of the Rev. W. Rooker, Congregational Minister at Tavistock, England for nearly 50 years, she was born there on June 5, 1812. From 1840 to 1844, in the vestry of her father's chapel, Miss Rooker conducted a class for young people. During this period she wrote several hymns, which later appeared in the Baptist Psalms and Hymns (1858). Since the students came willingly, she called her students the "Willing Class, " and later 18 of her hymns were published as Willing Class Hymns, by one of her former students.

In 1844 she married T. Edgecombe Parson. She died at Plymouth, England.

PARTRIDGE, SYBIL FARISH (SISTER MARY XAVIER) (1856-1917)
> "Lord, for tomorrow and its needs I do not pray;
> Keep me, my God, from stain of sin of Jesus, just
> for today. "

She spent her adult life as a nun in the convent of Notre Dame, on Mount Pleasant in Liverpool, England. She was one of the few Roman Catholics to write Protestant hymns. Her hymn appeared in the Christian Worship (1953) and Baptist (1956) hymnals. She was the sister of cartoonist Sir Bernard Partridge (1861-1945) whose drawings appeared in the humorous London magazine, Punch.

PATTERSON, CORDELIA M. (b. 1907)
> "The first Christmas. "

A hymnist and songwriter, she was born at St. Mary's, Kansas on November 17, 1907 and had a high school education. She also wrote the words for "St. Philomena, the Beloved. "

PATTERSON, JOY F. (b. 1931)
> "Isaiah the prophet has written of old. "

Composer and hymnist, she was born at Lansing, Michigan on October 11, 1931 and was educated at the University of Wisconsin (B. A. ; M. A.) and was a Fulbright scholar at the University of Strasbourg, France. She was married to C. Duane Patterson, an attorney, and they had one son and two daughters. Despite the lack of formal musical training, she began composing music in 1970 with the assistance of Sterling L. Anderson, Minister of Music at the First Presbyterian Church of Wausau, where she is an active member, and now has six sacred choral works in print. The above hymn was published in the booklet, New Hymns for Children, as one of seven winning hymns, by the Choristers Guild and The Hymn Society of America (1982).

PATTERSON, WILEY (b. 1910)
> "The baby Jesus stirred in sleep. "

Composer, hymnist, and choral director, she was born at
Chatham, Virginia on July 20, 1910 and was educated at
Chatham Hall, Hollins College in Hollins, Virginia and at the
Cincinnati Conservatory in Ohio. She taught music and drama
at the Low-Heywood School in Stamford, Connecticut and was
director of the junior choir at the First Congregational Church
in Darien, Connecticut. She married Maurice J. Reis.

PATTINSON, JANET STEEL (1848-1930)
    "Come to me, O my Saviour. "

She was born at Paisley, Scotland, but as a child was raised
in Bradford, Yorks, England. Her hymn was first published
in The Teacher at Work (1886), then in the Sunday School
Hymnary (1905). Other hymns appeared in C. Bonner's Garland of Sunday School Music (1886 edition); Horder's Hymns
Supplement (1894); and Worship Song (1905). In 1899 she
published Far-Ben, or Poems in Many Moods. She died on
March 29, 1930.

PATTON, ABIGAIL JEMIMA "ABBY" HUTCHINSON (1829-
1892)
    "Kind words can never die. "

Composer, contralto, and hymnist, daughter of Mary Leavitt
and Jesse Hutchinson, one of sixteen children, she was born
at Milford, New Hampshire on August 29, 1829 and was educated at Hancock Academy and later at Edes Seminary in
Plymouth, Massachusetts. At age ten she made her first
public appearance as a singer at a concert given in the Baptist church in Milford. Thirteen of the sixteen children survived to adulthood, and all were singers, but the quartet of
Abby, Asa, John, and Judson became famous in the 1840s.
They toured New England (1841-43), and made their first visit to New York City in May 1843. Their concerts were given
in the old Broadway Tabernacle, and they took the city by
storm. The "Hutchinson Family Singers" toured England and
Scotland (1846) and were the guests of Charles Dickens, Harriet Martineau, John Bright, the Honorable Mrs. Norton, and
others. On February 28, 1849 she married Ludlow Patton,
a stock broker in New York City. The Hutchinsons were
abolitionists, temperance leaders, and advocates of woman
suffrage. They sang in the Republican campaigns of 1856
and 1860. They sang in The White House for President John
Tyler and later in the Green Room of The White House for

President Lincoln (1862). She composed the music for Alfred Tennyson's "Ring Out Wild Bells" and other songs. She founded the first kindergarten in America in Orange, New Jersey. Her hymn appeared in Schaff's Christ in Song (1869). Abby died in New York City on November 24, 1892.

PAUL, DORIS A. (b. 1903)
    Works--Remember Now Thy Creator

Composer, conductor, hymnist, and teacher, she was born at Upland, Indiana on August 16, 1903 and educated at Taylor University (B. A. ; B. Mus. Ed.) in Upland; at Northwestern University; University of Michigan (M. M.) and with Fred Waring at the Fred Waring Workshop. She taught in public schools, at Taylor University and at Iowa State Teachers College in Ames, Iowa; also conducted the Lansing Matinee Musicale Chorus in Lansing, Michigan. Her works include Thou Art My Lamp; We Give Thee Thanks; and with Esther Fuller, A Book of Responses (38 introits and responses). As of March 1982 she was enjoying her retirement.

PEABODY, JOSEPHINE PRESTON (1874-1922)
    "Dear Lord, whose serving maiden. "

Daughter of Josephine Merrill and Charles K. Peabody, she was born at Brooklyn, New York on May 30, 1874 and educated at Girls' Latin School, Boston, and Radcliffe College (1896), Cambridge, Massachusetts. On June 21, 1906 she married Lionel S. Marks. She was an instructor at Wellesley College (1901-03). She wrote Wayfarers--A Book of Verse (1908); Pan--A Choric Idyll (for music-1904); The Piper (drama-produced in England 1910 and in America 1911); Harvest Moon (war poems 1916); etc. She resided at Cambridge, Massachusetts and died on December 4, 1922. Her hymn appeared in A Treasury of Poems for Worship and Devotion (Harper, 1959).

PEARCE, LYDIA FREEMAN MOSER (1841-1925)
    "O Son of Man! Great Sower. "

Daughter of Roger Moser, she was born at Kendal, England and in 1870 married the Reverend R. J. Pearce, D. C. L. , who later became Vicar of Bedlington, Northunberland. Her hymns and poems were published in the Church Missionary

Society Gleaner. Her hymn above was written for the Durham Sower's Band in 1893 and later appeared in the Church
Missionary Hymn Book (1899). She died on June 16, 1925.

PEARCE, SELINA P. (b. 1845)
　　"Be our joyful song today. "

The daughter of a Baptist minister, she was born at Lowell,
Ohio on December 29, 1845 and later resided in Marietta,
Ohio. "In 1891 Miss Selina Pearce was elected corresponding secretary of The Young Peoples' Union of the Marietta
Baptist Association. " [Information from Louise Zimmer of
the Washington County Public Library, Marietta, Ohio.] We
have been unable to locate the place and date of her death.

PECK, KATHRYN BLACKBURN (1904-1975)
　　"God, give us Christian homes,
　　Homes where the will of the Master is sought. "

Born in Jacksonville, Illinois on July 9, 1904, she was the
author of numerous books on religion. On August 23, 1919
she was married to Harlan C. Peck. From 1946 she worked
for the Department of Church Schools, Church of the Nazarene in Kansas City, Missouri. The above hymn, plus three
more, appeared in Joyfully Sing--A Hymnal for Juniors
(1968).

PEMBROKE, MARY SIDNEY HERBERT, COUNTESS OF
(1561-1621)
　　"O Lord, in me there lieth naught. "

The sister of Sir Philip Sidney, she was born at Ticknell,
Worcestershire, England and in 1577 married Henry Herbert,
the 2nd Earl Pembroke. She wrote A Discourse on Life and
Death and a translation of R. Garnier's tragedy, Antonie.
The Countess and her brother translated and versified the
Psalms of David, of which only the first 43 were by Philip,
the Countess having finished the manuscript after his death.
The manuscript was not published until 1823, and was entitled The Psalms of David, Translated into Divers and Sun-
dry Kinds of Verse ... Begun by the Noble and Learned
Gent, Sir Philip Sidney, Knt. , and Finished by the Right Honorable the Countess of Pembroke, His Sister. Her hymn
above was published in Songs of Praise (London, 1931).

PENNEFATHER, CATHERINE KING (1826-1893)
"I'm journeying through a desert world. "

Daughter of Admiral King of Angley, England, on September
16, 1847 she was married to the Rev. William Pennefather,
son of an Irish Baron and a great philanthropist, the pro-
moter of the Midmay Conferences. Mr. Pennefather was one
of two men who, in 1873, invited the evangelist, Dwight L.
Moody to England, and when Moody and singer Ira D. Sankey
landed at Liverpool, both sponsors were dead. Her hymn
appeared in The Enlarged London Hymn Book (1863). She
died on January 12, 1893.

PENSTONE, MARIA MATILDA (1859-1910)
"God has given us a book. "

Born in London, England, she served on the staff of the
Home and Colonial Training College for Teachers, then be-
came Headmistress of Highbury School for Girls in England.
A pioneer of modern school training, she served on the
Board of the National Froebel Union and was a member of
the Teachers' Guild. Her hymn was first published in The
Sunday Kindergarten and later in the English Baptist Hymn
Book (1962). She died at Highgate.

PERCY, FRANCES COAN (b. 1843)
"As swiftly, silently draws near the night. "

Daughter of Richard D. Coan of Guilford, Connecticut, she
was an Episcopalian and taught at a school for freedmen in
Norfolk, Virginia. The principal of the school was Henry
Clay Percy, whom she married in 1866. After her husband's
death in 1898, she lived in Hartford, Connecticut and then in
New York City. In her later life she was an invalid. Two
of her hymns appeared in The Pilgrim Hymnal (prior 1931).

PERKINS, EMILY SWAN (1866-1941)
Tune--LAUFER

Composer and hymnist, she was born at Chicago, Illinois on
October 19, 1866 and later resided at Riverdale-on-Hudson,
New York. She initiated the idea of a society devoted to
hymns, and was one of the five organizers of The Hymn Society of America (1922) and became its recording secretary.

She was a member of the Presbyterian Church in the U. S. A.
Four of her hymns, with 54 of her hymn tunes, were published in Stonehurst Hymn Tunes (1921). Her hymn, "Thou
art, O God, the God of might" appeared in the Presbyterian
Hymnal (1933) and her tune above in the Methodist Hymnal
(1935).

PESCARA, VITTORIA COLONNA, MARCHESA (1490-1547)
"When the breath of God that moved above the tide. "

The daughter of Fabrizio Colonna, Grand Constable of Naples,
she was born at Castillo di Marino, near Rome. In 1509
she married Captain Fernando Francisco d'Avalos, Marchese
de Pescara, later a famous Italian General who died at Pavia
in 1525. She knew all the literary and artistic personages
of her time, and was a friend of Michelangelo Buonarroti
(1475-1564), who sent her sketches and addressed sonnets to
her. She published her poems and hymns in Rime Spirituali
(about 1540). Although a Roman Catholic, she was a devotee
of the evangelist preacher Bernardino Ochino (1487-1564) who
preached the liberty of the Spirit. The Roman Inquisition in
1542 was a crisis in her life and she went on fasts and was
reduced to skin and bones. Ochion fled across the Alps and
sent her a letter, but she could not turn against her religion.
She turned over the unopened letter to Cardinal Pole who for-
warded it to the Inquisition in Rome. Upon her death in
1547, Michelangelo wrote a sonnet about her:

> The sculptor's hammer according to his will
> Gives to the rugged stone a human form....
> Beauty alone creates, invests with form,
> Able to recreate and also kill....

PETERS, MARY BOWLY (1813-1856)
"Through the love of God our Saviour,
All will be well;
Free and changeless in His favor. "

She was born in Cirencester in Gloucestershire, England on
April 17, 1813. She married John M. Peters, rector of
Quenington in Gloucestershire and later vicar of Langford in
Oxfordshire. She was only 21 years old when he died in
1834. Two of her most popular hymns in England are "A-
round Thy table, Holy Lord" and "Through the love of God
our Saviour. " Fifty-eight of her hymns appeared in Hymns

intended to help the Communion of Saints (London, 1847).
She wrote The World's History from the Creation to the Ac-
cession of Queen Victoria published in seven volumes. Her
hymns were published in the Plymouth Brethren's Psalms,
Hymns and Spiritual Songs (London, 1842); Dr. Walker's
Cheltenham Psalms and Hymns (1855); Snepp's Songs of Grace
& Glory (1872); and numerous other hymnals. She died at
Clifton, England on July 29, 1856. More recently her hymn
above appeared in the Christian Science Hymnal (1937) and
Hymns for the Family of God (1976).

PETRE, KATHARINE HOWARD, LADY (1831-1882)
    "Behold the Handmaid of the Lord. "

Daughter of the fourth Earl of Wicklow, she married the
Hon. Arthur C. A. Petre of Coptfold, Essex, England in
1855. She was Roman Catholic. Her hymns appeared in
her Sacred Verses (1864), her Hymns and Verses (1884),
and in Arundal Hymns (1902). She died at Ryde, England on
December 28, 1882.

PHILLIPS, EDNA MARTHA (b. 1904)
    "Teach me to serve Thee, Lord. "

Born at Sandycroft, Flintshire, Wales in 1904, she was educated at Queensberry Council School and Hawarden County
School, Flintshire. She taught at Queensberry Council School
from 1924 to 1946. Her husband was minister of the Alpha
Presbyterian Church in Builth Wells, Brecon, Wales.

PHILLIPS, HARRIET CECILIA (1806-1884)
    "We bring no glittering treasures. "

Born in Sharon, Connecticut, she was a Sunday School teacher in New York City for many years. Her hymn above appeared in the Methodist Episcopal Hymns (1849) and her other hymns in the Rev. W. C. Hoyt's Family and Social Melodies (1853). More recently her hymn appeared in The Song
Book of The Salvation Army (1953).

PIGOTT, JEAN SOPHIA (1845-1882)
    "Jesus, I am resting, resting
     In the joy of what Thou art. "

Composer and hymnist, born in Ireland in 1845, she attended
an evangelistic Keswick Convention at Brighton, England in
July 1875, after which she was afflicted with invalidism.
Despite her illness, she wrote the above hymn of hope and
confidence. She discarded all her medicines, relying on God
for help in her prayers. Two of her brothers went to China
as missionaries, one of them to a martyr's grave. She was
not only a hymnist, but also a composer of music and an
artist. Her hymns appeared in the Keswick Hymn Book;
Hymns for the Family of God (1976); the Presbyterian Hymnal (1933); and Hymns for the Living Church (1974).

POHJOLA-SALMIO, JENNY (b. 1899)
        "Jesus, hear my humble pleading. "

A farmer's daughter, she was born at Orivesi, Finland.
She said she was inspired by God to write this hymn (1919)
and later many more hymns. Her hymn first appeared in a
collection of choir anthems called Zion Tunes and more recently in the Lutheran Hymnal (1958).

POLLARD, ADELAIDE ADDISON (1862-1934)
        "Have thine own way, Lord! Have thine own way!
        Thou art the potter, I am the clay. "

Born Sarah A. Pollard at Bloomfield, Iowa on November 27,
1862, she changed her given name to Adelaide. She attended
schools in Denmark, Iowa, Valpariso, Indiana, and at the
Boston School of Oratory in Massachusetts. During the
1880's she taught in girls' schools in Chicago, then at the
Missionary Training School in Nyack, New York. She served
as a missionary in Africa and in Scotland before and during
World War I. Her hymn appeared in The American Service
Hymnal (1968); Broadman (1977); Christian Worship (1953);
Hymns for the Family of God (1976); Methodist (1966); Pres-
byterian (1955) hymnals and Phonolog Reports of Los Angeles,
California listed 15 recordings. She died at New York City
on December 20, 1934.

POLLARD, JOSEPHINE (1840-1892)
        "Joy-bells ringing, Children singing. "

She was born in New York City. She wrote The Gypsy series
in six volumes (1873-74); A Piece of Silver (1876); Vagrant

Verses (1886); and other books.   Her hymn appeared in Ira
D. Sankey's Sacred Songs and Solos in 1878.

POPPLE, MARIA (1796-1847)
   "Restore, O Father, to our times restore. "

She was the daughter of the Rev. Miles Popple, Vicar of
Welton, near Hull, England.   Her hymn appeared in Beard's
Unitarian Collection of Hymns (1837).

PORTER, ETHEL K. FLENTYE (b. 1901)
   Descant for EASTER HYMN

A composer, she was born in Wilmetee, Illinois and after
her graduation from Northwestern University, Evanston, Illinois (A. B. , 1923), where she met her husband, Hugh Porter,
she graduated with honors from the American Conservatory
of Music (B. M. , 1927) in Chicago, Illinois.   From 1927 to
1931 she studied piano with Olga Samaroff-Stokowski on a
fellowship at the Graduate School of the Juilliard Music
Foundation in New York City.   After teaching at the Dalton
School in New York City from 1931 to 1945, she gave up
teaching at Dalton when her husband became director of the
School of Sacred Music at Union Theological Seminary.   Her
husband died in 1960.   The above descant for "Christ the
Lord is risen today" was written with her husband and appeared in The Pilgrim Hymnal (1958).   As of April 1982 she
was enjoying her retirement.

POSEGATE, MAXCINE WOODBRIDGE (b. 1924)
   Tune--WOODBRIDGE

A composer and organist, born at Modesto, California on
June 5, 1924, she was educated at Modesto Junior College,
Wheaton College (B. S.) and California State University at
Long Beach (M. A.).   She is married to Robert Posegate,
Director of Admissions and Records at Northwestern College,
Roseville, Minnesota.   He also teaches hymnology, and she
teaches music theory and class piano at the college.   She
has been a church organist, and has composed over fifty an-
thems that have been published.   Her tune above, set to the
hymn, "Gentle Mary laid her child" (words by Joseph S.
Cook, 1919), was published by The Hymn Society of America
in The Hymn for July 1981.

POSSE, KATARINA ELIZABETH EHRENBORG, BARONESS
(1818-1890)
"When Christmas morn is dawning. "

She was born of an aristocratic family in Sweden, and established a Sunday School in the Kungsholm district (1853).
In 1856 she married Baron J. A. Posse. Her hymn appeared
in Hemlandssånger (1891), a Swedish evangelistic hymn book.
She also translated hymns. Her hymn more recently appeared in the Lutheran Hymnal (1958).

POTTER, (ETHEL OLIVE) DOREEN (1925-1980)
Tune for--"Jesus, where can we find you?"

A composer, she was a citizen of Jamaica, born in Panama,
and taught music and English at St. Katharine's College,
Liverpool, England. Licentiate of Music degree at Trinity
College, London. She wrote the music for Fred Kan's
hymns: "Break not the circle, " "God has set us free, "
"God of Bible and Tradition, " "Help us accept each other, "
"Let us talents and tongues employ. " Her tunes were pub-
lished in Pilgrim Praise, Cantate Domingo, Sing a New Song,
New Songs of Asian Cities, Praise for Today, Break not the
Circle and Creation Sings (1979). She died at Geneva, Swit-
zerland. [Information from Ann Lodge of Riley, Kansas,
editor of Creation Sings (Philadelphia: Geneva Press, 1979).]

POUNDS, JESSIE BROWN (1861-1921)
"I know that my Redeemer liveth. "

Born at Hiram, Ohio on August 31, 1861, she began writing
for religious periodicals at age fifteen. In 1897 she was
married to the Rev. John E. Pounds, pastor of the Central
Christian Church, Indianapolis, Indiana. For more than
thirty years she wrote hymns for James H. Fillmore, a
founder of the Fillmore Brothers Music House in Cincinnati,
Ohio. Mrs. Pounds' hymns appeared in his Songs of Glory
(1874) and in subsequent publications. She published nine
books, fifty cantata librettos, and more than four hundred
gospel hymns, including "Anywhere with Jesus I can safely
go" written with Mrs. C. M. Alexander (Helen C. Alexander
Dixon) and "I must needs go home by way of the cross. "
Her hymn, "Somewhere the sun is shining ... Beautiful Isle
of Somewhere, " was a favorite of President William McKinley.
Her hymn above appeared in the American Service (1968);

Baptist (1975); Broadman (1977); and Christian Worship (1953) hymnals.

PRENTISS, ELIZABETH PAYSON (1818-1878)
"More love to thee, O Christ!"

She was born in Portland, Maine on October 26, 1818 the fifth of eight children. When she was only 16 she began contributing poetry and prose to the Youth's Companion. She taught school in Portland, Maine; Ipswich, Massachusetts; and in Richmond, Virginia before marrying George L. Prentiss, a Congregational minister, who became a Presbyterian minister in New York City in 1851. He served as professor of homiletics and polity at Union Theological Seminary in New York. She wrote numerous books, the most popular being Stepping Heavenward (1869). She died at her summer home in Dorset, Vermont on August 13, 1878. Her hymns appeared in Schaff's Christ in Song (1869); Hatfield's Church Hymn Book (1872); Golden Hours: Hymns and Songs of the Christian Life (1874); and the hymn above more recently in The American Service Hymnal (1968); Baptist (1973); Broadman (1977); Christian Worship (1953); Episcopal (1940); Family of God (1976); Methodist (1966); Presbyterian (1953); and The Pilgrim Hymnal (1958) of the United Church of Christ; also there are two phonograph recordings listed by Phonolog Reports of Los Angeles (1978).

PRESTON, NOVELLA DILLARD (b. 1901)
"My singing is a prayer, O Lord."

Born in Putnam County, Tennessee on May 25, 1901, she attended public schools in Lebanon, Tennessee. She taught public school in Thomas, Oklahoma for one year, then attended a business college in Nashville, Tennessee. Starting in 1922 she worked for the Baptist Sunday School Board for forty-five years and was also the assistant editor of The Church Musician (1951-66). She married Floyd E. Preston, and several years after his death she married K. Brooks Jordan, and they were both active members of the First Baptist Church in Nashville, Tennessee. Her hymn appeared in the Baptist (1975) and Broadman (1977) hymnals. Mrs. Jordan is still very active and is in regular attendance at church. [March 10, 1982 letter received from Mrs. Rita Hedquist, Secretary of the First Baptist Church, Nashville, Tennessee.]

PRICE, MARION JAMES (b. 1913)
    "The Church of Christ has work to do."

Born at Aurora, Illinois on February 3, 1913 she was educated at Vassar College in Poughkeepsie, New York (A. B.)
and married Roy William Price.   They had three children
and resided in Aurora where she was a communicant of the
Trinity Episcopal Church.   She wrote a number of hymns with
tunes by John Leo Lewis which won the Drexel Award (1955);
second place in the Moravian Contest (1956); and Harvey Gaul
Award (1957).   "O Jesus, who once heard the plea, " published by The Hymn Society of America (1961), appeared in
the Advent Christian Hymnal (1968).   Her children's hymns
were published by the Oxford Press, London, the United
Church of Canada, Seabury Press, and the Lutheran Church
of America, with recordings by the latter (1966-69).   The
hymn above appeared in Hymns for the 70s (The Hymn Society of America, 1970).

PROCTER, ADELAIDE ANN (1825-1864)
    "My God, I thank Thee, who hast made
    The earth so bright."

Daughter of Anne Skepper and Bryan Waller Procter, who
wrote under the pseudonym "Barry Cornwall, " she was born
at London, England on October 30, 1825.   Her father was a
friend of Charles Dickens and Charles Lamb.   Adelaide sent
her early poems, signed "Mary Berwick, " to Charles Dickens
when he was editor of Household Words (1853-59) and they
were so good that Dickens published the poems; it was two
years before he discovered that they were written by the
daughter of a friend of his.   She joined the Roman Catholic
faith when she was 26 years old and published her Legends
and Lyrics, a Book of Verse (1858; 1862).   Also a writer of
popular songs, she is best known for "The Lost Chord" (with
music by Sir Arthur Sullivan).   In 1847 Fanny Kemble, the
actress, wrote: "Her character and intellectual gifts, and
the delicate state of her health, all make her an object of interest to me. "   Ms. Procter died of tuberculosis at Malvern,
London, England on February 2, 1864.   Her hymn above appeared in Christian Worship (1953); Methodist (1966); Presbyterian (1955); hymnals and in The Pilgrim Hymnal (1958).

PROCTOR, EDNA DEAN (1829-1923)
    "Through storm and sun the age draws on."

Born at Herkimer, New York on September 18, 1829, she
never married. Her hymn was written for the Women's
Congress of Missions at the Columbian Exposition in Chicago,
Illinois in 1893. President Benjamin Harrison asked her to
write a poem on protecting the forests of the White Mountains
and she wrote a striking poem, "The Doom of the White
Hills." She resided in Brooklyn, New York for a number
of years, then in Framingham, Massachusetts. She wrote
Poems (1866; 1890); Songs of America (1906); The Glory of
Toil (1916); and other books. She died on December 18,
1923.

PRUSSIA, ANNA AMALIA, PRINCESS OF (1723-1787)
    Passion oratorio--Tod Jesu

Composer, and sister of Frederick the Great, she was born
at Berlin, Germany on November 9, 1723. She studied music with her brother and with the cathedral organist, Gott-
leib Hayne, and with Johann P. Kirnberger. She composed
many chorals and some instrumental works, but is best
known for her music for Tod Jesu, which was later also set
to music by Karl H. Graun. She died at Berlin on March
30, 1787.

PULLEN, ALICE MURIEL (b. 1889)
    "At work, beside His father's bench."

Daughter of a Baptist missionary in Italy, she became a
teacher and settlement worker. She was on the staff of the
children's house at Bow, England, and was one of the pioneers of the Graded Sunday School. After writing stories
for children, hymns, and biographies, she turned to become
a farmer, and was believed to be still living in 1982. Her
hymn was included in the Evangelical Reformed Hymnal
(1941).

PYPER, MARY (1795-1870)
    "We shall see Him, in our nature."

Born at Greenock, England on May 25, 1795, she did needle-
work for a living and resided in Edinburgh, Scotland. Her
hymns were published in Select Pieces (1847). She died on
May 25, 1870.

RAILE, VILATE SCHOFIELD (1890-1954)
"Upon the cross of calvary."

Born in Salt Lake City, she was educated at Brigham Young
University, the University of Utah, the Utah State University
at Logan, and at Mills College in Oakland, California. She
was instrumental in the founding of the Primary Children's
Hospital. Her poem "Pioneers" was placed on "This is the
Place Monument" at the mouth of Emigration Canyon near
Salt Lake City, and she also published a book of poems.
Her hymn appeared in Hymns (1948) of The Church of Jesus
Christ of Latter-day Saints.

RANDALL, LAURA LEE (d. 1966)
"This is the day the Lord hath made."

She joined the Church of Christ, Scientist on June 4, 1909
and her hymn appeared in the Christian Science Hymnal
(1937). She died on October 28, 1966.

RANYARD, ELLEN HENRIETTA WHITE (1810-1879)
"Mark that long dark line of shadows."

Daughter of John B. White, a cement maker, she was born
in the district of Nine Elms in London, England on January
9, 1810. The family moved to Swanscombe, Kent, and on
January 10, 1839 she was married there to Benjamin Ranyard. She wrote The Book and Its Story ... of the Jubilee
of the British and Foreign Bible Society (1852) which was
extraordinarily popular. She founded the Female Bible Mission; by 1879 some 170 women worked for it. She wrote ten
other religious books. Her hymns appeared in Shepp's Songs
of Grace and Glory (1872). She died in London on February
11, 1879 and her husband died on March 20, 1879 at age 86.

REED, EDITH MARGARET CELLIBRAND (1885-1933)
"Infant holy, infant lowly,
For His bed a cattle stall."

A versifier, her hymn is from a Polish Christmas Carol.
She was born at London, England on March 31, 1885 and
studied at the Guildhall School of Music in London. She was
an associate of the Royal College of Organists and published
the Story Lives of the Great Composers. She died at London

on June 4, 1933. Her hymn appeared in the Baptist (1975);
Broadman (1977); Family of God (1976); and Presbyterian
(1955) hymnals.

REED, ELIZABETH (ELIZA) HOLMES (1794-1867)
"O do not let the Word depart,
And close thine eyes against the light. "

She was born in London, England on March 4, 1794 and in
1816 she married the Rev. Andrew Reed, who was educated
for the Congregational Ministry. He served as pastor of the
New Road Chapel, St. Georges-in-the-East and then at Wycliffe Chapel. She wrote Original Tales for Children and
The Mother's Manual for Training her Children (1865). Her
hymns appeared in her husband's Wycliffe Chapel Supplement
(1872). She died at London on July 4, 1867. More recently
her hymn appeared in The American Service Hymnal (1968)
and The New Broadman Hymnal (1977).

REED, IDA L. see IDA REED SMITH

REESE, LIZETTE WOODWORTH (1856-1935)
"Glad that I live am I,
That the sky is blue,
Glad for the country lanes,
And the fall of the dew. "

She was born in Huntington (now Waverly), Maryland on January 9, 1856. She attended St. John's (Episcopal) Parish
School, where she later taught. She taught in Baltimore
schools for 48 years (1873-1921). Her poem "Tears" is
considered one of the most famous sonnets written by an
American, and a classic in American literature:

When I consider life and its few years,
A wisp of fog betwixt us and the sun;
A call to battle, and the battle done. . .
I wonder at the idleness of tears.

She died in Baltimore, Maryland on December 17, 1935.
Her hymn above was published in Songs of Praise (1931).

REICHARDT, C. LUISE (1779-1826)
Tune-- ARMAGEDDON

A composer and daughter of the composer-teacher Johann
Friedrich Reichardt, she was born at Berlin, Germany on
April 11, 1779 and studied with her father. She made her
debut as a singer in 1794 and settled in Hamburg, Germany
in 1814 where she taught at a vocal academy. Shortly before her wedding, her fiancé died, and later her voice failed,
so she put her full attention into composing music. She
wrote numerous popular songs in addition to hymn music.
Her tune appeared in Part III of Layriz's Kern des deutschen
Kirchengesangs (1853) and appeared in The Church Psalter
and Hymn-Book (1872). She died at Hamburg on November
17, 1826. More recently her tune was set to the hymn "Who
is on the Lord's side?" and appeared in Hymns for the Living Church (1974). She also wrote the music SCHLAF, KIND-
LEIN, SCHLAF for "Sleep, baby, sleep! Thy mother watch
doth keep. " Her songs were popular in Germany and published as recently as 1922 by G. Reinhardt of Munich.

REINHARDT, JOSEPHINE D. (b. 1921)
     "Father Eternal, we pray for thy blessing. "

Born at Vineland, New Jersey on September 2, 1921, she
was married to Frank R. Reinhardt and they resided in Upper Montclair, New Jersey. She was employed as a dynam-
icist by the Curtiss-Wright Corporation and was an active
member of the Central Presbyterian Church. Her hymn appeared in Marriage and Family Life Hymns (The Hymn Society of America, 1961).

RENDLE, LILY (1875-1964)
     Tune--VESPER HYMN

A composer, born in London, England on May 14, 1875 she
was educated in London and Paris and won a gold medal and
an associateship at the Guildhall School of Music studying
piano, composition, and voice. She taught at the Bechstein
Hall in London for 20 years. She moved to Eastbourne in
East Sussex, England in 1922 to care for her invalid mother
who died in 1944. After her mother's death she taught a few
pupils at Eastbourne and died there on July 27, 1964. Her
hymn tune appeared in the Methodist Hymnal (1964).

RENO, DELMA BEATRICE WHATLEY (b. 1916)
     "Praise the Lord, the King of Glory. "

Born at Long Leaf, Louisiana on September 27, 1916, she
attended public schools in Glenmora, Louisiana. After re-
ceiving the R. N. degree from the Grady Memorial Hospital
School of Nursing in Atlanta, Georgia, she served in the
Army Nurse Corps during World War II. As a member of
the First Baptist Church in Dallas, Texas, she served as
superintendent of the Special Education Department, working
with mentally and emotionally handicapped children. Her
poems and hymns were published in The Meditations of My
Heart (1975) and the hymn above appeared in the Baptist
(1975) and Broadman (1977) hymnals.

RESSLER, MARIAN KISTLER (1892-1970)
     "Hark, the angel voices singing."

Born at Shenandoah, Pennsylvania on May 27, 1892, she was
educated at Wilson College, Chambersburg, Pennsylvania
(B. A., 1914) and raised a Methodist. She married William
H. Ressler and they resided in Shamokin, Pennsylvania where
she directed the Intermediate Choir and served as soloist at
St. John's Evangelical and Reformed Church in Shamokin
where she held membership. She and her husband had five
children, and she was a leader in the Young Women's Christian Association. She wrote the third stanza for the above
Croatian Christmas carol at the request of her pastor, Dr.
Edward O. Butkofsky, which appeared in the Evangelical and
Reformed Hymnal (1941). She died on May 18, 1970 while
vacationing with her husband in Sarasota, Florida. [Informa-
tion from Phyllis Pittman, Alumnae Office, Wilson College,
Chambersburg, Pennsylvania.]

REYNOLDS, MARY LOU ROBERTSON (b. 1924)
     "Praise Him, O praise Him."

The daughter of Ralph and Bessie Rose Mallory Robertson,
she was born at Springfield, Missouri on December 15, 1924
and was graduated from William Jewell College (A. B., 1945)
in Liberty, Missouri. In 1947 she was married to the Rev.
William Jensen Reynolds, minister of the First Baptist
Church of Oklahoma City, Oklahoma. They had two sons.
In 1955 they moved to Nashville, Tennessee, where Mr.
Reynolds became affiliated with the music department of the
Baptist Sunday School Board and she was employed in the
editorial department of the Abingdon Press for five years.
Her hymn appeared in the Baptist (1975) and Broadman (1977)
hymnals.

REUSS-EBERSDORF, BENIGNA MARIA, COUNTESS OF
(1695-1751)
"Komm Segen aus der Höh. "
"Attend O Lord, my daily toil. "

Daughter of Count Heinrich XXVIII of Reuss-Ebersdorf, Germany, she was born at Ebersdorf on December 15, 1695.
She was tutored in the castle, and learned Latin, Greek, and Hebrew.   She was a cousin of Count von Zinzendorf.   Her hymn appeared in the Moravian Hymn Book (1801; 1849); the Württemberg Gesang Buch (1842); and Dr. R. P. Dunn's Sacred Lyrics from the German (Philadelphia, 1859).   After her parents died she lived in a manor house near Pottiga, in the district of Lobenstein, where she died on July 31, 1751.

RHODES, SARAH BETTS BRADSHAW (1829-1904)
"God who made the earth,
The air, the sky, sea. "

Composer, hymnist, and sculptress, she was the wife of
J. Alsop Rhodes, a master silversmith in Sheffield, England.
A Congregationalist, she wrote her hymn for the Sheffield Sunday School Union Whitsuntide Festival in 1870, and also wrote the tune for her hymn which appeared in the Methodist Sunday School Hymn Book (1879).   After her husband's death she became head of a girl's school at Worksop, Notts, England, where she died.   More recently her hymn appeared in Episcopal (1940); Presbyterian (1955) hymnals and in the English Baptist Hymn Book (1962).

RICE, CAROLINE LAURA NORTH (1819-1899)
"Wilt thou hear the voice of praise?"

Daughter of William North of Lowell, Massachusetts, she was married on September 13, 1843 to the Rev. William Rice, Jr. , a Methodist Episcopal Minister of Springfield, Massachusetts and they had three sons and one daughter.
In 1856, when there was a conflict waging in the Methodist councils which led to the separation into the Northern and Southern conferences, the Rev. Rice was a pronounced anti-slavery leader.   He received the honorary D. D. from Wesleyan University (1876) from which college he had received his A. M. (1853).   During the Civil War, she was President of the Soldiers' Aid Society of Springfield.   At the close of

the war she was one of the founders of the Home for the
Friendless. In 1893 Dr. and Mrs. Rice celebrated their
golden wedding anniversary. He died in 1897. "She was living in Springfield in 1898, when she gave the Wesleyan University library a book collection of 564 volumes. I have
seen the bookplate from this gift in volumes of hymns but
had not realized she was a hymnist herself. " [Letter of
8/31/83 from Elizabeth A. Swain, University Archivist, Olin
Library, Wesleyan University, Middletown, Connecticut.]
She wrote her hymn for a Sunday School celebration and it
appeared in the Methodist Episcopal Hymnal (1877; 1911).
She died on August 29, 1899.

RICHARDS, LAURA ELIZABETH HOWE (1850-1943)
      "The little flowers. "

Daughter of Samuel Gridley and Julia Ward Howe, who wrote
"The Battle Hymn of the Republic, " Laura was born at Boston, Massachusetts on February 27, 1850. On June 17, 1871
she was married to Henry Richards and they had five daughters and two sons. She wrote over 90 books, including
Sketches and Scraps (1881); Captain January (1890); Golden
Windows, a Book of Fables for Old and Young (1904); Life of
Florence Nightingale (1909); Life of Julia Ward Howe (with
Maud Howe Elliott, 1916); Life of Elizabeth Fry (1916); Life
of Abigail Adams (1917); Life of Joan of Arc (1919); The Hot-
tentot and Other Ditties (1939). She died at Gardiner, Maine
on January 14, 1943.

RICHARDSON, CHARLOTTE CAROLINE SMITH (1775-1825)
      "O God, to Thee we raise our eyes. "

She was born at York, England on March 5, 1775, and married a shoemaker named Richardson on October 31, 1802,
but he died of tuberculosis in 1804. Her hymn is from her
Poems, published in York in 1896, and entitled "After the
death of my dear husband, 1804. " She died at York on September 26, 1825.

RICHTER, ANNE RIGBY (1792-1857)
      "We saw Thee not when Thou didst come. "

Daughter of the Rev. Robert Rigby, Vicar of St. Mary's,
Beverley, Yorkshire, England from 1791 to 1823, she was

born there and baptized on September 5, 1792. On February
13, 1822 she married the Rev. Henry William Richter, Chaplain of the County Gaol at Kirton, Lindsey, Lincolnshire and
later Rector of St. Paul's, Lincoln. Her hymn appeared as
a long poem in Songs from the Valley. A Collection of Sacred Poetry (Kirkby, Lonsdale, 1834) and in the Friendly Visitor, April 1836 by "Anne R. Kirton." She published The
Nun and Other Poems (Hull, 1841) and was an intimate friend
of Felicia Hemans, the famous poet and hymnist. Her hymn
appeared in J. H. Gurney's Lutterworth Collection of Hymns
for Public Worship (1838); in Hymns Ancient and Modern;
and in other collections. She died at Lincoln, England. Her
hymn, as revised by the Rev. John H. Gurney, appeared
more recently in the English Baptist Hymn Book (London,
1962).

RITTENHOUSE, ELIZABETH MAE (b. 1915)
    "Oh hallelujah Jesus lives within."

Composer, hymnist, and evangelist, she was born at Wood-
lawn, Alabama on July 23, 1915 and was educated at a Bible
Institute. She served as secretary of the Akron Ministerial
Association Chartered Christian Assembly in Akron, Ohio
and conducted a radio ministry covering Akron and also
Clarksburg, West Virginia. She also wrote "A Soldier for
Christ," "Search My Heart," etc.

RITTER, FANNY MALONE RAYMOND (1840-1890)
    "From this dust, my soul, thou shalt rise."

She translated hymns from the German. She was a writer
on musical subjects and a well-known singer in New York
City. She wrote Woman as Musician (1877); Some Famous
Songs (1878); Songs and Ballads (1887). Her translation appeared in Sursum Corda (1898).

ROBERTS, KATHERINE EMILY CLAYTON (1877-1962)
    "O Lord, thy people gathered here
    Uplift their joyful hearts as one."

Daughter of the Rev. L. Clayton, she was born at Leicester,
England and studied singing in London and Paris. In 1913
she married Robert E. Roberts, and he composed the music
for her hymns. They wrote a History of Peterborough; Carol

Stories; and other books. She also wrote plays and pagents which were produced locally, and served as secretary of the Rutland Rural Community Council. Later he was vicar at St. Marks, and several parishes, including Peterborough Cathedral, Knighton, and Leicester. She died at Ashford, Middlesex in 1962. Her hymn appeared in Songs of Praise (London, 1931) and the Lutheran Hymnal (1958). Another hymn, "All poor men and humble," paraphrased and versified from a Welsh Carol appeared in the Oxford Book of Carols (1928) and in The Worship Book (United Presbyterian, 1972).

ROBERTS, MARTHA SUSAN BLAKENEY (1862-1941)
"Be present, Holy Father, to bless our work today."

Daughter of the Rev. J. E. Blakeney, D. D. , Archdeacon of Sheffield, England, she was born there on December 25, 1862. She was married to Samuel Roberts, Justice of the Peace at Sheffield on December 21, 1880. Her hymn was written for the laying of the cornerstone of the North Transept of the Parish Church in Sheffield on July 12, 1880, and she also wrote other hymns. She died on February 25, 1941.

ROBERTSON, NEMI (d. 1926)
"Grace for today, O Love divine."

She studied with Mary Baker Eddy in Boston, Massachusetts in 1889 and again in 1898. She joined the Church of Christ, Scientist on March 31, 1894. After residing in Chicago, Illinois for ten years (1888-98), she lived in East Orange, New Jersey (1899-1910). Her hymn appeared in the Christian Science Journal on June 29, 1912 and in the Christian Science Hymnal (1937). She was a Christian Science practitioner and teacher (1896-1926) and died on February 25, 1926.

ROBINSON, AGNES MARY FRANCES (1857-1944)
"O source and sea of love, O Spirit."

She was born in Leamington, England and married James Darmesteter (1849-1894), Oriental scholar and brother of Arsene Darmesteter, French philologist (1846-1888). In 1901 she married Pierre Emile Duclaux. She wrote A Handful of Honeysuckles (verses-1878); The Crowned Hippolytus (1881); Arden (1883); The End of the Middle Ages (1888); Madame de Sévigné (1914); A Portrait of Pascal (1926); and other books. Her hymn appeared in Songs of Praise (1931).

ROSCOE, MARY ANN see MARY R. JEVONS

ROSCOE, JANE see JANE R. HORNBLOWER

ROSS, MIRIAM DEWEY (b. 1927)
"Give me the eyes to see this child. "

She married James F. Ross, and became a resident of Hanover, New Hampshire. Her hymn appeared in Christian Education Hymns published by The Hymn Society of America
(1959) and in Christian Worship--A Hymnal (1970).

ROSSETTI, CHRISTINA GEORGINA (1830-1894)
"In the bleak mid-winter,
Frosty winds made moan. "

The daughter of Gabriele Rossetti, an Italian refugee who
later became professor of Italian at King's College in London,
England, she was born in London on December 5, 1830. She
was the sister of Dante Gabriel Rossetti, painter and poet.
Numerous of her books of poetry were published between
1842 and 1874, when she devoted herself mainly to hymns
and religious works. She broke her engagement to James
Collinson, a noted London artist, because he was a Roman
Catholic and met with a similar situation when her hand in
marriage was asked by Charles B. Cayly. Considered a
beautiful woman, she posed for several portraits of the ma-
donna for Millais and for her brother, Dante Gabriel. She
died at London on December 29, 1894. Her hymns appeared
in the Episcopal (1940); Methodist (1966); Songs of Praise
(1931); and The Pilgrim Hymnal (1958).

ROUNSEFELL, CARRIE ESTHER PARKER (1861-1930)
Tune--MANCHESTER

Composer and singer, the daughter of Clara and James A.
Parker, she was born at Merrimack, New Hampshire on
March 1, 1861. She was raised in Manchester, New Hampshire where she met and married William E. Rounsefell, a
bookkeeper for a paint and wallpaper firm there. As a singing evangelist, she toured New England and eastern New York
State with a small autoharp. Later she became a member of
the Church of God. Her hymn tune was used for "It may not

be on the mountain's height" by Mary Brown. She wrote her tune while attending a revival meeting of the Baptist Church in Lynn, Massachusetts. She died at Durham, Maine on September 18, 1930. Her hymn tune appeared in the Baptist Hymnal (1956).

ROWE, ELIZABETH SINGER (1674-1737)
"Begin the high celestial strain. "

The daughter of the Rev. William Singer, an independent minister near Frome, Somersetshire, England, she was married to the poet Thomas Rowe in 1710. Her hymns were published after her death in her Miscellaneous Works in Prose and Verse (1739) and in her Hymns and Versions of Psalms (1739). She died in February 1737. Five of her hymns, including the one above, appeared in C. Evans' Collection (fifth edition, 1786).

ROWLAND, MAY (1870-1959)
"The day is slowly wending
Toward its silent ending. "

Named Mary Alice Rowland, she was born at Woodstock, Oxfordshire, England on September 21, 1870 and was educated at Somerset. After moving to Eastbourne in 1902, she was a parish worker at All Souls' Church there. In a hymn contest sponsored by The Hymn Society of America in 1928 she won a prize for her "Hymn for Airmen, " and in 1932 she wrote a "Jubilee Hymn" for All Souls' Church. Lily Rendle (1875-1964), a pianist, singer, and composer, wrote the music for three hymns by May Rowland which appeared in the 1935 Methodist Hymnal. She died at Eastbourne on February 17, 1959. Her hymn above appeared in The Methodist Hymnal (1964).

RUMBAUGH, VIDA FAYE (b. 1927)
"The righteous ones shall be forever blest. "

Translator and versifier, she was born at Lisbon, Iowa on January 23, 1927 and educated at Coe College in Cedar Rapids, Iowa and at the School of Sacred Music at Union Theological Seminary in New York City (M. S. M. , 1949). She served as a Presbyterian missionary to Thailand (1949-58), was director of personnel for the United Fire and Casualty

Company in Cedar Rapids (1958-65), then served as a staff
assistant at St. Michael's Episcopal Church in Cedar Rapids.
Her hymn appeared in The Methodist Hymnal (1964).

RUSSELL, ANNA BELLE (1862-1954)
    "There is never a day so dreary....
    Wonderful, wonderful Jesus. "

The daughter of Chancey and Jane Denson Russell, she was
born at Pine Valley, Chemung County, New York on April
21, 1862. She made her home with her sister, Cora C.
Russell, in Corning, New York, where they were active members of the First Methodist Church. Both Anna and her sister Cora wrote hymns. Anna died at Corning, New York on
October 29, 1954. Her hymn appeared in the Baptist (1975);
American Service (1968); and Broadman (1977) hymnals.

SAFFERY, MARIA GRACE HORSEY (1773-1858)
    "'Tis the Great Father we adore. "

She was the daughter of the Rev. J. Horsey of Portsea,
England and became the wife of the Rev. Mr. Saffery, pastor
of the Baptist Church at Salisbury. She published her Poems
on Sacred Subjects in 1834. Her hymn (above) appeared in
the Baptist New Selection of 1828; other hymns appeared in
Comprehensive Rippon (1844). Her son, the Rev. P. J. Saffery, was a prominent Baptist minister.

SANGSTER, MARGARET ELIZABETH MUNSON (1838-1912)
    "O Christ, forget not them who stand
    Thy vanguard in the distant land. "

Born in New Rochelle, New York on February 22, 1838, she
was a magazine editor for 40 years and wrote 40 books. In
October 1858 she married George Sangster. She had been a
member of the Dutch Reformed Church, but later became a
Congregationalist. She served as editor of Health and Home
(1871-73); held an editorial position with The Christian at
Work (1873-79); was assistant editor of the Christian Intelligencer (1879-88); also editor of Harper's Young People (1882-
89); editor of Harper's Bazaar (1889-99); and a staff contributor to The Ladies' Home Journal (1899-1905), the Woman's
Home Companion (1905-12), and The Christian Herald (1894-
1912). She wrote Manual of Missions of the Reformed Church

in America (1878); The Easter Message (1898); The Daily
Pathway (1904); Good Manners for All Occasions (1904); The
Story Bible (1905); an autobiography, From My Youth Up
(1909); The Women of the Bible (1911); etc. She resided at
Glen Ridge, New Jersey and died at South Orange, New Jer-
sey on June 3, 1912. Her hymn appeared in the Presbyterian
Hymnal (1933); Evangelical and Reformed Church Hymnal
(1941); and in Christian Worship (1953).

SAUNDERS, CARRIE LOU (1893-1976)
    "Stay close to God. "

A composer, she was born at Mexia, Texas on August 13,
1893 and was educated at Texas Technological College in Lub-
bock, Texas. She sang in choirs and also wrote the music
for "My Savior Came" and other hymns. She died on February 3, 1976.

SAXBY, JANE EUPHEMIA BROWNE (1811-1898)
    "O Jesus Christ, the Holy One. "

Daughter of William Browne of Tallantire Hall, Cumberland,
England, she was born on January 27, 1811. She was the
sister of Lady Teignmouth, and in 1862 she married the Rev.
S. H. Saxby, Vicar of East Clevedon, Somersetshire, England.
She wrote numerous poems and hymns published in her The
Dove on the Cross (1849); The Voice of the Bird (1875); and
Aunt Effie's Gift to the Nursery (1876). Her hymn above ap-
peared in the English Presbyterian Psalms and Hymns for
Divine Worship (1867); Dr. W. F. Stevenson's Hymns for the
Church and Home (1873); and other hymnals. Her hymn also
was included in The Book of Praise (Presbyterian Church of
Canada, 1918). She died on March 25, 1898.

SAXONY, PRINCESS MARIA ANTONIA WALPURGIS, ELEC-
TRESS OF (1724-1780)
    Libretto for La Conversione di Sant'Agostino

Daughter of Emperor Charles VII, Elector of Bavaria, she
was born at Munich, Germany on July 18, 1724 and was a
pupil of Hasse and Porpora. She was a librettist and hymnist. She published two Italian operas to her own librettos
and also wrote texts for oratorios and cantatas by Ristori
and Hasse. The music for the above oratorio was composed

by Johann A. Hasse and produced at Dresden on March 30, 1750. She died at Dresden, on April 23, 1780.

SAYLE, AMY (1886-1970)
"Paul the preacher, Paul the poet. "

Born in Kensington, London, England, on April 5, 1886, she was educated at Bremen, Germany; Paris; King's College, London; and Newnham, Cambridge; where she was graduated. She was an active member of St. Mary Abbot's, Kensington, London and churchwarden at St. George's, Bloomsbury (1929-37) and Alderman on the London City Council (1946-49). Her hymn appeared in Hymns Ancient and Modern (1939). She died on June 30, 1970.

SCHLEGEL, KATHARINA AMALIA DORTHEA VON (1697-1752)
"Stille, mein Willie, dein Jesu hilft siegen. "
"Be still, my soul, the Lord is on thy side,
Bear patiently the cross of grief or pain. "

Born on October 22, 1697, she was a lady attached to the small ducal court at Cöthen, Germany, since between 1750 and 1752 she carried on a correspondence with Heinrich Ernest, Count Stolberg Wernigerode. Her hymn appeared in Albert Knapp's Evangelischer Lieder-Schutz (1837); a translation by Jane Borthwick (above) in her Hymns from the Land of Luther; and others. More recently her hymn was published in the Lutheran (1941); Methodist (1966); Presbyterian (1955) hymnals and in The Pilgrim Hymnal (1958).

SCHWARZBACH, ANNA ELISABETH VON SCHÖNBERG, BARONESS VON (c. 1684-1716)
Tune--PSALMS OF DAVID

In 1704 she married G. F. Behaim, Baron von Schwarzbach. She published Die nach den gewöhnlichsten Kirchen-Gesängen eingerichtete Psalmen Davids, Nürnberg, Germany in 1723. She died at Hirschfelde, near Zittan.

SCHWARZBURG-RUDOLSTADT, EMILIE JULIANE, COUNTESS OF (1637-1706)
"Bis hieher hat mich Gott gebracht. "

"The Lord hath helped me hitherto,
By His surpassing favor. "

"Wer weiss, wie nahe mir mein Ende. "
"Who knows when death may overtake me. "

Her father was Count Albert Friedrich of Barby and Mühlingen
on the Elbe, but during the Thirty Years' War, the family
sought refuge in Heideckburg Castle in Schwarzburg-Rudolstadt.
Her mother's sister was the wife of Count Ludwig Günther,
lord of the castle, and Emilie (or Amilie) Juliane was born
there on August 16, 1637. She was only five years old when
both of her parents had died, and she was adopted by her
aunt, the Countess. She was educated at Rudolstadt, along
with her cousins, Ludamilia Elisabeth and Ludamilia's brother and two sisters. On July 7, 1665, she married her cousin, Albert Anton, later the Count. Her hymns first appeared
in the Appendix of 1688 to the Rudolstadt Gesang Buch (1682;
1704); the American Lutheran General Synod's Hymn Book
(1850-52); the Ohio Lutheran Hymnal (1880); the Pennsylvania
Lutheran Church Book (1868); and numerous others. She
died at Rudolstadt on December 3, 1706. More recently her
hymns appeared in The Lutheran Hymnal (1941).

SCHWARZBURG-RUDOLSTADT, LUDAMILIA ELISABETH OF
(1640-1672)
"Jesu, Jesu, nichts als Jesu. "
"Jesus, Jesus, only Jesus,
Can my heartfelt longing still. "

Daughter of Count Ludwig Günther I of Schwarzburg-Rudolstadt,
she was born in the nearby castle of Heidecksburg, Germany
on April 7, 1640. She was the cousin of Emile Juliane, later
the Countess of Schwarzburg-Rudolstadt. In 1665 she went to
the castle of Friedensburg near Leutenberg with her mother;
but her mother died in 1670, and she returned to Rudolstadt.
She became betrothed to Count Christian Wilhelm of Schwarz-
burg-Sondershausen on December 20, 1671, but then tragedy
struck. There was an epidemic of measles in the area, and
her eldest sister, Sophie Juliane, was seized and died on
February 14, 1672. Sophie had been attended to and nursed
by her sisters, Ludamilia and Christiane Magdalene, who
both caught the measles and both died at Rudolstadt on March
12, 1672. Her hymn (above) was published in the Vermehrtes
Gesang-Büchlein (Halberstadt, 1673); A. Fritsch's Jesus Lieder (3rd edition, Jena, 1675); and in the Ohio Lutheran Hym-

nal (1880). Ludamilia's hymns were published by her cousin Emilie, at Rudolstadt in 1687. Her hymn appeared in The Lutheran Hymnal (1941).

SCHWERDTFEGER, LILLIAN (b. 1920)
"Lord, Who art the great Creator. "

She was born at Buckskin, Indiana on February 5, 1920 and spent her entire lifetime there. A member of St. John's United Church of Christ, she also joined the American Association of Retired Persons. Her hymn appeared in 10 New Hymns on Aging and the Later Years (The Hymn Society of America, 1976).

SCOTS, MARY STUART, QUEEN OF (1542-1587)
"O merciful Father, My hope is in Thee. "

Daughter of Mary of Lorraine and King James V of Scotland, she was born at Linlithgow castle on the night of December 7, 1542 and was one week old when she inherited the crown. On April 24, 1558 she was married to the dauphin of France, and in July 1559 he became King Francis II. But she was Queen of France less than 18 months; her husband died in December, 1560. On July 29, 1565 she married her cousin, Lord Darnley. He was murdered on February 10, 1567, and on May 15, 1567 she married Lord Bothwell. The Scots accused Queen Mary of the murder of Darnley, and after her forces were defeated near Glasgow on May 13, 1568, she fled to England, where she was detained, then imprisoned by Queen Elizabeth I and executed in the great hall at Fotheringhay castle on February 8, 1587. She wrote her hymn in Latin the night before her execution, and it was translated by John Fawcett and appeared in Old Favorite Songs and Hymns (Garden City Publishing Co., 1946); The World's Great Religious Poetry (Macmillan, 1934); A Treasury of Religious Verse (Fleming H. Revell, 1962); and other books. There is an interesting anecdote about her. She said, as recorded in Calendar Venetian State Papers A. D. 1562, entry 648: "My only regret is that I am not a man, to know what life it is to lie all night in the fields, to walk on the causeway with a jack and knapschulle, a Glasgow buckler, and a broadsword. "

SCOTT, CLARA H. JONES (1841-1897)
   "Open my eyes, that I may see
   Glimpses of truth thou hast for me. "

   Tune--SCOTT

Composer and hymnist, she was born in Elk Grove, Illinois
on December 3, 1841 and attended C. M. Cady's Musical
Institute in Chicago, Illinois. At age 18 she began teaching
music in the Ladies' Seminary at Lyons, Iowa and in 1861
she married Henry Clay Scott. She published the Royal Anthem Book (1882), which was the first collection of anthems
published by a woman, and she contributed hymns to H. R.
Palmer's Collection. She was thrown from a buggy by a
runaway horse and accidentally killed, while on a visit to
Dubuque, Iowa on June 21, 1897. Her hymn appeared in the
Baptist (1975); The New Broadman Hymnal (1977); Hymns for
the Family of God (1976); The Methodist Hymnal (1966); and
Hymns for the Living Church (1974).

SCOTT, ELIZABETH see ELIZABETH S. W. SMITH

SCOTT, LESBIA LOCKET (b. 1898)
   "I sing a song of the Saints of God. "

Composer and hymnist, born at London, England, on August
11, 1898, she was educated at Raven's Croft School, Sussex
and in 1917 she married John Mortimer Scott, an officer in
the Royal Navy. She wrote poems for her children, which
were published in 1929 under the title Everyday Hymns for
Little Children by the Society of SS Peter and Paul Ltd.,
London. The words, music, and illustrations were all done
by Mrs. Scott. She was also a playwright and produced her
own plays wherever her husband was stationed. Among her
produced plays were Malta Cathedral Nativity Play (1931);
That Fell Arrest (1937); and Then Will She Return (1946).
"I am her daughter and I'm happy to say that my mother is
still alive and well. ... A few years after his retirement
my father took Holy Orders and was appointed Rector of
Gideigh, a tiny village on the Eastern slopes of Dartmoor,
some of the most beautiful scenery in Britain. They were
also there for thirteen years until my father's retirement
from ill-health in 1967 when they went to live near Stratford-
on-Avon, near my sister, their eldest daughter. My father
died three years later and my mother has recently moved to

the ancient market town of Pershore, Worcestershire, where,
I am glad to say, she enjoys excellent health and is still
writing and still painting at the age of eighty-three. " [Letter
of March 1982 from her daughter, Mary Morton, of Chag-
ford, Devon, England.] Her hymn appeared in the (American) Episcopal Hymnal (1940).

SCUDDER, ELIZA (1821-1896)
    "Thou long disowned, reviled, oppressed,
    Strange friend of human kind. "

A niece of Dr. Edmund H. Sears, the prominent Unitarian
minister, she was born in Boston, Massachusetts on November 14, 1821 but joined the Protestant Episcopal Church herself. Some of her hymns appeared in Hymns of the Spirit
(1864), edited by Samuel Longfellow and Samuel Johnson.
She died in Salem, Massachusetts. More recently her hymn
above appeared in Songs of Praise (Oxford University Press,
1931).

SEAL, EMILY F. (d. 1920)
    "What is thy birthright, man. "

She joined the Church of Christ, Scientist on June 3, 1899
and her poem, which she called "The Seal of Love, " appeared
in The Christian Science Journal for June 1890 and in the
Christian Science Hymnal (1937) with another hymn of hers.
She was a Christian Science practitioner and teacher, and
died on April 1, 1920.

SEAVER, BLANCHE EBERT (b. 1891)
    "Just for today. "

Composer, hymnist, and songwriter, daughter of Theodore
Ebert, she was born at Chicago, Illinois on September 15,
1891 and was graduated from the Chicago Musical College
(1911). On September 16, 1916 she married Frank R.
Seaver. Active with the Los Angeles Symphony Association,
Hollywood Bowl Patroness Committee, various hospitals and
orphanages in Los Angeles, California, she was named the
Los Angeles Times "Woman of the Year" in 1964. She received honorary degrees from the University of Southern
California (L. H. D. , 1966) Pomona College (L. L. D. , 1970)
at Claremont, California and Oklahoma Christian College

(D. Humanities, 1972) at Oklahoma City, Oklahoma. Hymnist and composer, one recording of her hymn was reported by Phonolog Reports of Los Angeles (1978). She also wrote "Close at Thy feet, my Lord" and other hymns, and a Pontifical Mass. As of March 1982 she was still active and enjoying life. Her hymn was sung at the Eucharistic Congress in Dublin, Ireland. [Information from the Public Library, Los Angeles, California.]

SEEBACH, MARGARET REBECCA HINES (1875-1948)
    "Thy kingdom come! O Father hear our prayer. "

Born at Gettysburg, Pennsylvania on July 5, 1875, she was educated at Gettysburg College (B. A.; M. A., 1897). In the same year she married the Rev. Julius F. Seebach, a Lutheran pastor, and they had two sons. She published Missionary Milestones, Martin of Mansfield, Land of All Nations, etc. She was editor of Lutheran Woman's Work (1917-37). She was awarded the Doctor of Literature degree by Carthage College (1943), Carthage, Illinois and by Gettysburg College (1944). Her hymn appeared in the Missionary Society's publication Here We Have Stars and in the Lutheran Hymnal (1958). She also wrote the refrain: "All hail, our glorious Saviour" for Lillian Cassaday's hymn "O Christians leagued together" which also appeared in the Lutheran Hymnal (1958).

SENITZ, ELIZABETHE VON (1629-1679)
    "O du Liebe meiner Liebe. "
    "The holiest love, whom most I love. "

She was born at Rankau, Brieg, Silesia, Poland. Her hymn apparently was adapted from one by Girolamo Savonarola (1454-1498). It appeared in Wagner's Gesang-Buch (Leipzig, 1697); the Geistreiches Gesang-Buch (Halle, 1697); Freylinghausen's Gesang-Buch (1704); Miss Winkworth's Lyra Germanica (1855); Schraff's Christ in Song (1869); Whiting's Hymns for the Church Catholic (1882); the American Dutch Reform Hymn Book (1869); and the Baptist Praise Book (1871). She died at Oels, Silesia (now Slask), Poland.

SERVOSS, MARY ELIZABETH (b. 1849)
    "When the storms of life are raging,
    Tempests wild on sea and land. "

She was born in Schenectady, New York. Lines from her hymn "He Will Hide Me" (above) appeared in Ira D. Sankey's Sacred Songs and Solos (1881). Other hymns she wrote appeared in the Sunday School Union Voice of Praise (1887) and in other hymnals. More recently her hymn was included in The Broadman Hymnal (Baptist, 1940).

SEWELL, ELIZABETH MISSING (1815-1906)
"O Saviour, when Thy loving hand. "

Daughter of Thomas Sewell, a solicitor at Newport on the Isle of Wight, England, she was born there on February 19, 1815, one of twelve children (seven sons and five daughters). Influenced by Henry Wilberforce and others of the Oxford (religious) Movement, she published The Cottage Monthly (1840) and Stories Illustrative of the Lord's Prayer (1843). In 1844 she moved to Bonchurch. Elizabeth and her sister Ellen (1813-1905) ran a school there (1852-1891). In 1866 she founded St. Boniface School at Ventnor, England. She died at Ashcliff, Bonchurch, England on August 17, 1906. Her hymn appeared in the Supplemental Hymns to Hymns Ancient and Modern (1889).

SEWALL, HARRIET WINSLOW (1819-1889)
"Why this longing, this forever sighing. "

Daughter of Comfort Hussey and Nathan Winslow, she was born at Portland, Maine on June 30, 1819 and educated at Friends' boarding school in Providence, Rhode Island. In 1848 she married Charles List and in 1856 she married Samuel Sewall. She was a founder of the New England Women's Club, edited the letters of her friend, Lydia Maria Child (1833) and was a leader in the woman's suffrage movement. Her poems were collected and published by Ednah D. Cheyney (1889) and her hymn appeared in W. J. Fox's Hymns and Anthems and in Whittier's collection Songs of Three Centuries. She died at Wellesley, Massachusetts on April 19, 1889.

SHAPCOTE, EMILY MARY STEWARD (1828-1909)
"Queen of the Holy Rosary. "

She was born in Liverpool, England and in 1856 she married the Rev. E. G. Shapcote, Minister of the Church of England and Curate of Odiham, Hants, later a missionary in South

Africa. In 1866 she joined the Roman Catholic Church, and her husband joined in 1868. She was one of three sisters who published their hymns in Hymns for Infant Children by A., C. and E (1852). She was "E," her aunt, Mary Steward was "A," and her sister, Eleanor Steward was "C." Other hymns appeared in her Eucharistic Hours (1886). Her hymn above appeared in A. E. Tozer's Catholic Hymns (1898).

SHARPE, EVELYN (1884-1969)
    Tunes--BULSTRODE and PLATT'S LANE

Composer, the daughter of an architect, she was educated privately, and was born at Battersea, England on September 2, 1884. In 1919 she married Lewis John Saville. Her publications include many songs, and part-song stage performances, and as test-pieces at several musical festivals in England and in the Dominions. Her tunes appeared in Songs of Praise (London, 1931). She died on August 25, 1969.

SHEARER, WINIFRED JACOBS (1883-1966)
    Tune-- FILIA

Composer, daughter of the Rev. Henry E. Jacobs, a Lutheran pastor, she was born at Gettysburg, Pennsylvania on September 3, 1883 and was educated at the Philadelphia Conservatory of Music and at the Leefson-Hills Holdander Conservatory in Philadelphia. In 1907 she married Mr. Shearer, a violinist. She was first organist at the Church of the Ascension, Mt. Airy, on the campus of the Lutheran Theological Seminary in Philadelphia. Later she was organist at St. Peter's Church in North Wales, Pennsylvania. She died at Gwynedd Valley, Pennsylvania, a Welsh settlement, on June 24, 1966. Her tune appeared in the Lutheran Common Service Book (1917; 1958).

SHEAROUSE, FLORINE W. (1898-1974)
    "Jesus Has a Birthday."

Hymnist, she was born at Atlanta, Georgia on December 19, 1898 and educated at Kate Baldwin Kindergarten Training School and at a Vocational Training School. She was a charter member of the Poetry Society of Georgia, and later resided in Miami, Florida. Olive Dungam composed the music for her hymns and songs. She died on February 14, 1974.

SHEKELTON, MARY (1827-1883)
     "It passeth knowledge,
     that dear love of mine. "

She lived in Dublin, Ireland and was Secretary of the Inva-
lid's Prayer Union.   Her hymn was first published in 1863.
More recently her hymn was included in the English Baptist
Hymn Book (1962).   After her death, her poems were col-
lected by her sister and published in Chosen, Chastened,
Crowned; Memorials of Mary Shekelton, late Secretary of the
Invalid's Prayer Union, by her Sister (1884).   She died in
Dublin, Ireland.

SHELLY, MARTHA EVANS JACKSON (1812-1901)
     "Lord, a little band and lowly. "

Daughter of John Jackson, she was born at Stockport, Cheshire, England and in 1846 was married to J. W. Shelly of
Yarmouth.   Her hymn was published in the Rev. John Curwen's Child's Own Hymn Book (1844) and in subsequent publications, with other hymns.   More recently her hymn was published in the Mennonite; Church of Scotland (1927); and Presbyterian Church of Canada (1918) hymnals.

SHEPHERD, ANNE HOULDITCH (1809-1857)
     "Around the throne of God in heaven. "

Daughter of the Rev. E. H. Houlditch, late Rector of Speen,
Berkshire, England, she was born at Cowes on the Isle of
Wight on September 11, 1809 and in 1843 was married to S.
Saville Shepherd.   She wrote religious novels, Ellen Seymour
(1848) and others, and her 64 hymns were published in her
Hymns Adapted to the Comprehension of Young Minds (1847)
and by 1855 there was a fifth edition.   Her hymn above appeared in Dr. J. M. Neale's Hymns for Children (1842);
Thring's Collection (1882); and others.   She died at Blackheath, Kent, England on January 7, 1857.   More recently
her hymn appeared in The Song Book of The Salvation Army
(1953).

SHINDLER, MARY STANLEY BUNCE PALMER DANA (1810-
1883)
     "I'm a pilgrim, and I'm a stranger,
     I can tarry, I can tarry but a night. "

Born in Beaufort, South Carolina on February 15, 1810, she
was married to Charles E. Dana of New York City in 1835
and lived in Muscatine, Iowa. After her husband died in
1839, she married Robert D. Shindler, professor at Shelby
College in Kentucky in 1851. She published Southern Harp
(1840) and Northern Harp (1841). Eight of her hymns were
published in T. O. Summer's Songs of Zion 1852). Originally a Presbyterian, then a Unitarian, she later joined the
Protestant Episcopal Church. The hymn above was published
in the Baptist Hymnal (1973) and there were four recordings
of the hymn listed in Phonolog Reports (1978) of Los Angeles,
California. Her hymn also appeared in the Augustana Lutheran (1925); Concordia (Lutheran, 1932); Christian Science
(1937); and Seventh-Day Adventist (1940) hymnals. She died
in Texas.

SHIPTON, ANNA (1815-1901)
    "Jesus, Master, hear my cry. "

The above hymn was included in her Whispers in the Palms,
Hymns and Meditations (London: W. Yapp, 1855; second edition, 1857). She also wrote Precious Gems for the Saviour's
Diadem (1862) and other books. She died at St. Leonard's-
on-Sea, England on November 5, 1901.

SHIRREFF, EMILY ANNE ELIZA (1814-1897)
    "Gracious Savior, who didst honor. "

Born in England on November 3, 1814, she was largely self-
educated. Working with her sister, they helped establish
Girton College (for women) and the National Union for Im-
proving Education of Women of all Classes in 1871. She
also taught kindergarten classes, and wrote the Principles of
the Kindergarten System (1876; 1880) and The Kindergarten
at Home (1884; 1890). Her hymn appeared in Hymns for the
Living Church (1974). She died at London, England on
March 20, 1897.

SIDEBOTHAM, MARY ANN (1833-1913)
    Tune--EUROPA

Composer, organist and hymnist, she was born at London,
England and spent most of her life with her brother, the vicar
of St. Thomas-on-the-Bourne in Surrey, England, serving as

his housekeeper and organist in his church. She was also a
pianist and lifelong friend of Henry Smart. She contributed
twelve tunes for Mrs. Carey Brock's Children's Hymn Book
(1881), published under the auspices of the Society for Promoting Christian Knowledge, of which Miss Sidebotham was
editor. She wrote The Bird's Nest, a collection of fifty songs
for children, and with Mrs. Carey Brock compiled A Collection of Twelve Christmas Carols (1894). She died on the
Isle of Wight on February 20, 1913. Her hymn tune appeared in the Supplement to Hymns Ancient and Modern. Her
hymn, "Lord, Thy mercy now entreating, " appeared in the
Children's Hymn Book (1881); the Scottish Hymnal (1884); and
more recently in The Pilgrim Hymnal (1958).

SIEDHOFF, EDNA ELIZABETH (b. 1885)
    Tune--BOSTON

Composer, pianist and organist, she was the daughter of
Fredericka Levi and William H. Siedhoff, an upholsterer,
and was born at Lockport, New York and studied piano at
the Longy School in Boston, Massachusetts and was a pupil
in composition with Frank Converse. [Information from letter dated June 10, 1982 from L. Richard Reed, County Historian, Niagara County, Lockport, New York.] She left
Lockport in 1911 and studied piano in Berlin, Germany with
Breithaupt and Schnabel, composition with Leichtentritt, and
organ with Walter Fischer during her three-year stay there.
She was the first woman organist to play at the American
Church in Berlin. She left Germany at the outbreak of World
War I. Her tune to the hymn, "Thou art the way, " appeared
in the Christian Science Hymnal (1932). We have been unable
to locate her place and date of death.

SIGOURNEY, LYDIA HOWARD HUNTLEY (1791-1865)
    "Fill the fount with roses. "

She was born in Norwich, Connecticut on September 1, 1791
and married Charles Sigourney on June 16, 1819. Although
she was reared a Congregationalist, she became an Episcopalian upon her marriage. She wrote numerous books of poetry, biographies, and stories. She wrote for Godey's Lady's
Book and for Graham's Magazine when Edgar Allan Poe was
the editor. Her hymns appeared in Nettleton's Village Hymns
(1824); Ripley's Selection (1829); Cheever's Common Place
Book (1831); Winchell's Baptist Additional Hymns (1832);

Christian Lyle Supplement (1833); Linsley and Davis' Selected Hymns (1836); Connecticut Psalms and Hymns (1845); Universalist Hymns for Christian Devotion by Adams and Chapin (Boston, 1846); and Lyra Sacra Americana (London, 1868). At the height of her popularity she was known as the "Sweet Singer of Hartford." Her hymn, "Go to thy rest fair child" was included in the Moravian and Mennonite (1940) hymnals. She died in Hartford, Connecticut on June 10, 1865.

SIMPSON, JANE CROSS BELL (1811-1886)
"Pray when the morn is breaking,
Pray when the noon is bright.
Pray with the eve's declining,
Pray in the hush of night. "

She was born in Glasgow, Scotland on November 12, 1811. Her hymns were published in the Scottish Christian Herald. In 1837 she married her half-cousin, J. Bell Simpson, librarian of the Sterling Library in Glasgow (1851-60). They had eight children, but she survived all but two daughters. Her hymns appeared in Rogers' Lyra Britannica (1867); Matineau's Hymns (1873); Prout's Psalmist (1878); and the Scottish Evangelical Hymnal (1878). She died at Aberdeen, Scotland on June 17, 1886. More recently her hymn appeared in Songs of Praise (Oxford, 1931).

SKEMP, ADA (1857-1927)
"I love to think that Jesus saw
The same bright sun that shines today. "

Co-principal of Hale High School in Cheshire, England, she married the Rev. J. G. Skemp, a Baptist minister. Later she was co-principal of Ansdell College, Lytham St. Anne's in Lancashire. Her hymn first appeared in Carey Bonner's Child Songs (1908); in A Student's Hymnal by the University of Wales (1923); in School Worship (1926); and finally in The Pilgrim Hymnal (1958).

SLADE, MARY BRIDGES CANEDY (1826-1882)
"Sweetly, Lord, have we heard thee calling. "

Born in Fall River, Massachusetts in 1826, she became a schoolteacher and served as assistant editor of The New England Journal of Education. She married a clergyman, and

spent her entire lifetime in her home town. Her hymn,
"From all the dark places of earth's needy races" appeared
in The American Service Hymnal (1968). Another hymn,
"Who at my door is standing, patiently drawing near" and the
hymn above appeared in the Baptist (1975); and Broadman
(1977) hymnals. She died at Fall River in 1882.

SMITH, CAROLINA LOUISA SPRAGUE (1827-1886)
"Tarry with me, O my Saviour. "

She was born at Salem, Massachusetts and later married the
Rev. Charles Smith, pastor of the South Congregational
Church in Andover, Massachusetts. She wrote her hymn in
the summer of 1852 and sent it to Mr. Hatfield, editor of
The Messenger, but he rejected it. It was included in Rev.
Henry Ward Beecher's Plymouth Collection of 1855. More
recently her hymn was published in the Eastern Mennonite
(1902); Reformed (1902); and Presbyterian U.S. (1927) hymnals.

SMITH, ELEANOR (1858-1942)
"In another land and time,
Long ago and far away. "

Composer, hymnist, singer, and songwriter, daughter of
Matilda Jasperson and Willard N. Smith, she was born at
Atlanta, Illinois on June 15, 1858 and was educated in Chi-
cago where she took lessons in voice with Fannie Root and
studied composition with Frederick G. Gleason. Then she
studied voice under Julius Hey and composition with Moritz
Moszkowski, in Berlin for three years. She taught at the
Chicago Kindergarten College and Chicago Normal School for
Teachers, then at the University of Chicago (1902-04). After
meeting Jane Addams, she founded the Hull House School of
Music and headed the school (1893-1935). She was an Episcopalian. She wrote Songs for Little Children (1887); Songs
of Life and Nature (1899); Modern Music Series (1905); and
the Eleanor Smith Series (1909-11). She never married, and
died at Midland, Michigan on June 30, 1942. Her hymn appeared in Songs of Praise (London, 1931).

SMITH, ELIZA ROXEY SNOW (1804-1887)
"O my Father, thou that dwellest in the high and
glorious place. "

The daughter of Oliver and Rosetta L. Pettibone Snow, she
was born in Becket, Berkshire County, Massachusetts on
June 21, 1804, the second of seven children, all raised Baptists. The family moved to Mantua, Portage County, Ohio
in 1806. She was baptized in the Church of Jesus Christ of
Latter-day Saints (Mormons) on April 5, 1835 by the prophet
himself, Joseph Smith, in Kirkland, Ohio. In 1836 the family moved to Quincy, Illinois, then to La Harpe, and settled
in Commerce, Illinois (later named Nauvoo). On June 29,
1842 she became one of the plural wives of Joseph Smith.
He was assassinated on June 27, 1844, and she was in the
exodus of February 28, 1846. Both her parents died at Wal-
nut Grove, Illinois. She traveled by covered wagon westward,
arriving in Salt Lake City in October 1847, and became the
plural wife of Brigham Young in 1849. Her first book of
poems was published in 1856. She died at Salt Lake City,
Utah on December 5, 1887. Several of her hymns appeared
in Hymns (1948) of the Church of Jesus Christ of Latter-day
Saints.

SMITH, ELIZABETH LEE ALLEN (1817-1898)
      "I greet thee, who my sure Redeemer art. "

Translator and versifier, the daughter of Dr. William Allen,
President of Dartmouth University (1817-20) and of Bowdin
College (1820-39), she was born at Hanover, New Hampshire.
In 1843 she was married to Dr. H. B. Smith, who later be-
came a professor at the Union Theological Seminary in New
York City (1850). He died in 1877. Her hymns appeared
in Schraff's Christ in Song (1869) and more recently in the
Evangelical and Reformed Church Hymnal (1941); The Pil-
grim Hymnal (1958); and Hymns for the Living Church (1974).

SMITH, ELIZABETH SCOTT WILLIAMS (1708-1776)
      "Thy bounties, gracious Lord,
      With gratitude we won. "

The sister of hymn-writer Thomas Scott (1705-1775), she
was born at Hitchin, England about 1708. In January 1751-
52 she married, at Norwich, Elisha Williams, formerly rector of Yale College, and they moved to Connecticut in March
1752. After his death, she married the Honorable William
Smith of New York City in 1761. She died at Wethersfield,
Connecticut on June 13, 1776 at age 68. Her hymns appeared
in The Christian Magazine (1763) and 19 of her hymns ap-

peared in Ash and Evans' Collection (Bristol, Connecticut, 1769) and 20 in Dobell's New Selection (1806). More recently her hymn above appeared in Christian Worship--A Hymnal (1953).

SMITH, FLORENCE MARGARET (1886-1958)
"Lord and Master, who hast called us. "

Daughter of Charles Ward Smith, she was born at Hull, England and educated at Palmers Green High School and at St. Christopher's College, Blackheath (1914). She wrote novels, Novel on Yellow Paper (1936); The Holiday (1949); books of verse, and contributed to various magazines, Time and Tide, Punch, the Spectator, to the Times Literary Supplement and to Country Life, she died on February 24, 1958. Her hymn appeared in Hymns Ancient and Modern (1939).

SMITH, IDA L. REED (1865-1951)
"I belong to the king. "

Born on a farm near Philippi, Barbour County, West Virginia on November 30, 1865, her poems and hymns were published in various religious magazines. After her father died she had to work the farm and take care of her invalid mother. She married a Mr. Smith. Eventually she became bedridden herself, and after her husband died she was without any income to provide for her needs, and no one to help her. When the American Society of Composers, Authors and Publishers (ASCAP) were informed of her situation, they provided a monthly income for her until her death in Philippi, West Virginia on July 8, 1951. Her hymn was published in Great Hymns of the Faith (1972) and Hymns for the Living Church (1974). Another hymn, "Come to the Father, O wanderer come" appeared in Rodeheaver's Gospel Solos and Duets No. 3.

SMITH, MARY LOUISE RILEY (1842-1927)
"Scatter seeds of kindness. "

"Let us gather up the sunbeams. "

Born at Brighton, New York on May 27, 1842, she was married to Albert Smith. She wrote A Gift of Gentians and Other Verses (1882), The Inn at Rest (1888) and several booklets.

SMITH, RUBY MAE (b. 1902)
"When Jesus shall come. "

Composer, hymnist, publisher, teacher, songwriter, she was
born at Joplin, Missouri on March 20, 1902 and educated in
public schools and private musical study. She organized and
led the vocal quartet, "Ruby Smith and the Rubytones" and
taught guitar, organ, piano, voice and was owner and president of the Rubytone Record and Publishing Company of Portland, Oregon. She also wrote "The Lord Wilt Come" and
other hymns and published Come Heed the Call and Beyond
the Gateway.

SMITH, SALLY M. pen name of FANNY CROSBY

SMITH, WILLIE MAE FORD (b. c. 1908)
"A sword in his right hand. . . .
Lord you said you'd fight my battles,
if I just keep still. "

Black singer and hymnist. "She was born at Rolling Fork,
Mississippi, and was brought to St. Louis when she was 12,
which was some time before 1922. She married a Smith in
the hauling business but no Christian name is given. She
formed the 'Ford Sisters Quartet' which sang at the National
Baptist Convention in 1922. She was living in 1975 working
as a paraprofessional in a mental hospital in St. Louis. "
[Information from the St. Louis Public Library, St. Louis,
Missouri.] There was one recording of her hymn listed in
Phonolog Reports (1978).

SMYTH, DAME ETHEL MARY (1858-1944)
Mass in D Major

A composer and daughter of General J. H. Smyth of the
Royal Artillery, she was born at London, England on April
23, 1858 and studied under Heinrich von Herzogenberg at the
Leipzig Conservatory. Her Quintet for Strings (1884) and a
Sonata for Violin and Pianoforte (1887) were performed at
Leipzig, Germany. Her Mass in D Major was performed at
Albert Hall in London under Barnby's direction on January 18,
1893. Her three-act opera, The Wreckers, was performed
at Leipzig on November 11, 1906. She was active in the
cause of Woman's Suffrage and her March of the Women be-

came popular at processions of the Women's Social and Political Union. She composed many other works and was considered the greatest woman composer of her time. She died
at Woking, England on May 9, 1944.

SOUTHEY, CAROLINE ANN BOWLES (1786-1854)
"I weep, but not rebellious tears. "

Daughter of Charles Bowles of Buckland, near Lymington,
England, she was married in 1839 to Robert Southey, the
poet. She was Southey's second wife. They lived at Greta
Hall, Keswick, Cumberland, England. He died March 21,
1843. She published Solitary Hours (1826); The Birth-day,
a Poem (1836); Poetical Works (1867); etc. Her hymn appeared in the Baptist Psalms and Hymns (1858). She is
best known for having written the "Mariner's Hymn":

> Launch thy bark, mariner!
> Christian, God speed thee!
> Let loose the rudder-bands,
> Good angels lead thee!
> Set thy sails warily,
> Tempests will come;
> Steer thy course steadily,
> Christian steer home!

SPAETH, HARRIETT REYNOLDS KRAUTH (1845-1925)
"Ye lands, to the Lord make a jubilant noise. "

The daughter of the Rev. Dr. Charles P. Krauth, Vice-
Provost of the University of Pennsylvania (Philadelphia), she
was born at Baltimore, Maryland on September 21, 1845.
She played the piano and organ and sang (contralto). On
October 12, 1880 she married the Rev. Adolph Spaeth, a
Lutheran minister, and they had four sons and one daughter,
but two sons died as infants. Her most notable son was Dr.
Sigmund Spaeth. Her books included The Church Book with
Music, published by the General Council Publication Board
(1893); Pictures from the Life of Hans Sachs; and the Life
of Adolph Spaeth (General Council Publication House, 1916).
Her translations from the German appeared in the Pennsyl-
vania Lutheran Little Children's Book (Philadelphia, 1885)
and the Southern Lutheran Service & Hymns for Sunday
Schools (Philadelphia, 1883). She died at Philadelphia,
Pennsylvania on May 10, 1925. More recently, three of her

hymns, translations from the German, appeared in The Lutheran Hymnal (1941) and one hymn appeared in the Evangelical and Reformed Church Hymnal (1941).

SPRATT, ANN BAIRD (b. 1829)
   Tune--KEDRON

A composer, she was born in England and her tune is used for Horatius Bonar's hymn "No, not despairingly, I come to Thee." It is one of two of her hymn tunes first published in the Book of Common Praise (1866). It also appeared in J. Ireland Tucker's The Parish Hymnal (New York, 1870); in Tucker's Tunes Old and New (1872); the American Presbyterian Hymnal (1874) where it is called BETHEL; The Methodist Hymnals (1905; 1911; 1935); and in the Baptist Hymnal (1956). We have been unable to locate her date of death.

STAINER, ROSALIND F. BRIDGE (1884-1966)
   Tune--BETHSAIDA

Composer, and daughter of Sir Frederick Bridge, she was born at the Cloisters, Westminster Abbey, London, England, on February 10, 1884 and studied music at home, studying the piano and viola with visiting masters, and harmony with her father. In 1907 she married Dr. Edward Stainer, F. R. C. P. , second son of Sir John Stainer, who was organist at St. Paul's Cathedral in London. Her hymn appeared in the English Methodist Hymn-Book (1904; 1935). She died on July 1, 1966.

STEAD, LOUISA M. R.   see   LOUISA WODEHOUSE

STEELE, ANNE (1716-1778)
   "Father of mercies, in thy Word,
   That endless glory shines. "

   "Father, whate'er of earthly bliss,
   Thy sov'reign will denies. "

Daughter of William Steele, an unsalaried Baptist preacher and timber merchant, she was born at Broughton, Hampshire, England in May 1716. Her fiancé was drowned just a few hours before they were to be married, and she never fully

recovered from this tragic event. Her first book of devotional poems was published in 1760 under the pseudonym
"Theodosia," again at Bristol in 1780 and in America in 1808.
Some of her poems were printed in the Spectator but only
under the name "Steele." Later 144 of her hymns were published in Hymns, Psalms and Poems by Anne Steele (London,
1863). She died at Hampshire on November 11, 1778. Her
hymns appeared in the Baptist (1973); Episcopal (1940); Lutheran (1941); Methodist (1966); and Presbyterian (1955) hymnals.

STEELE, HARRIETT BINNEY (1826-1902)
        "Children, loud hosannas singing."

Daughter of the Reverend Amos Binney, D.D., she was born
at Kingston, New Hampshire on September 23, 1826 and later
lived in Wilbraham, Massachusetts. On August 8, 1850 she
married the Reverend Daniel Steele, D.D., pastor of the
Methodist Episcopal Church in Fitchburg, Massachusetts.
They had two sons and two daughters. He was professor at
Genesee College in Lima, New York (1862-71) and acting
president. The college moved to Syracuse, New York and
he taught there (1871-72) and was acting Chancellor. Later
they lived in Milton, Massachusetts where she died on February 24, 1902. [Data from Eileen C. Piazza, Reference Librarian, Public Library, Milton, Massachusetts.] Her hymn
appeared in the Methodist Episcopal Hymnal (1878).

STEELE, HELEN (b. 1904)
        "High towering mountains,
        fields gold with grain."

A composer, choral director, pianist, teacher, and hymnist,
she was born at Enfield, Connecticut on June 21, 1904 and
was educated at Mt. Holyoke College, South Hadley, Massachusetts. Her hymn was published in Hymns for the Family
of God (1976). "In reply to your request for the information
with regard to Helen Steele (Mrs. Wager S. Harris), Class
of 1915, I am happy to report that Mrs. Harris is still living." [April 1982 letter from Mrs. Nancy C. Lech, Alumnae Administrator--Records of Mount Holyoke College.]

STEPHENSON, ISABELLA STEPHANA (1843-1890)
        "Holy Father, in thy mercy,
        Hear our anxious prayer."

Daughter of an army officer, she spent most of her life as an invalid, residing in Cheltenham, England, where she was born and died. She was a member of the Church of England and her hymn appeared in the Supplemental Hymns to Hymns Ancient and Modern (1889). It was extremely popular with British troops in France during World War I. More recently her hymn appeared in the Episcopal (1940) and Lutheran (1941; 1958) hymnals.

STEVENSON, LILIAN (1870-1960)
"Fairest Lord Jesus."

Translator and versifier, daughter of an Irish Presbyterian minister, she was educated at the Slade School of Art. She was active in the Fellowship of Reconciliation and was editor of the journal of the Student Christian Movement for several periods between 1896 and 1903. Her hymn appeared in the English Baptist Hymn Book (1962).

STEVENSON, MATILDA BOYLE DAVIS (b. 1838)
"Sweet flowers are blooming in God's sight."

Daughter of the Rev. G. H. Davis, Secretary of the Religious Tract Society, she was born at Weymouth, England in September 1838. In 1863 she was married to the Rev. John Frederick Stevenson, D. D., Congregational Minister at Brixton. Her hymn first appeared in W. R. Stevenson's School Hymns (1880). Her husband died in Montreal, Quebec, Canada in 1891. We have been unable to locate her date of death.

STILLMAN, MILDRED WHITNEY (1890-1950)
"Now once again for help that never faileth."

She was born at San Francisco, California on August 19, 1890 and educated at Barnard College in New York City. On June 7, 1911 she was married to Ernest G. Stillman. Although the mother of six children, she found time to write numerous books, collections of poems, Woodnotes (1922); Unknowing (1925); Queens and Crickets (1927); Apology to My Neighbors (1934); and Tuesday at Prime (1940); a novel of Christ; A Boy at Galilee (1929); essays, The Parson's Garden (1931); Re-discovering the Creed (1938); and several children's books. She died of a heart attack at her home in

Cornwall-on-Hudson, New York on August 21, 1950. Her hymn appeared in The Hymnal of the Protestant Episcopal Church in the USA (1940) and in the Evangelical and Reformed Church Hymnal (1941).

STIRLING, ELIZABETH (1819-1895)
   Psalm 130

Composer and organist, she was born at Greenwich, England on February 26, 1819 and studied piano and organ with Edward Holmes and harmony with G. A. Macfarren and J. A. Hamilton. At the age of twenty she was appointed organist at All Saints', Poplar, and held this position for almost 20 years, then at St. Andrew's, Undershaft. During the early 1850s she attended Oxford University and in 1856 passed the examination for the degree of Mus. Bac. , and composed the work, Psalm 130 for five voices with orchestra, which Oxford accepted as satisfactory. But the University refused to give her the degree she had earned, stating they could not give a degree to a woman. In 1863 she married F. A. Bridge, and continued as organist at St. Andrew's until 1880. Besides organ transcriptions from classical works, she also composed organ pieces and part-songs, "All among the barley" being very popular. She died at London, England on March 25, 1895.

STOCK, SARAH GERALDINE (1838-1898)
   "Let the song go round the earth. "

   Also Tune--MOEL LLYS

Composer and hymnist, the elder sister of Dr. Eugene Stock, editorial secretary of the Church Missionary Society, she was born at Islington, London, England on December 27, 1838 and became active in missionary work for the Church of England. Her hymns appeared in the Church Missionary Hymn Book (1899) of which she was co-editor and in the enlarged 1902 edition of Hymns of Consecration and Faith. Julian's Dictionary of Hymnology lists 29 of her hymns in common use by 1915. She died at Penmaenmawr, Wales, on August 27, 1898. More recently her hymn appeared in the Baptist (1975); Broadman (1977); and Christian Worship (1953) hymnals. Her hymn and tune appeared in the English Baptist Hymn Book (London, 1962).

STOCKTON, MARTHA MATILDA BRUSTAR (1821-1885)
"God loved the world of sinners lost. "

Born on June 11, 1821, she married the Rev. W. C. Stockton of Ocean City, New Jersey. Her hymn appeared in Laudes Domini (1884). She died on October 18, 1885. More recently her hymn appeared in The Song Book of The Salvation Army (1953).

STODDART, BARBARA WILSON (1865-1915)
"Blessed Lamb of Calvary. "

Born at Fair Isle, one of the Shetland Islands, Scotland on September 16, 1865, she was raised at Kirkwall in the Orkney Islands, Scotland. Soon after The Salvation Army corps was opened there, Barbara was converted and became a soldier in the army. She became an officer in 1886 and married a Mr. Stoddart. They were both active in the British corps. Mrs. Stoddart became Brigadier at Middlebrough, England and was the Divisional Chancellor there. She died there on January 28, 1915. Her hymn appeared in The War Cry (August 12, 1893) and with the lines "Spotless Lamb, O wilt Thou make me" appeared in the 1899 and 1953 editions of The Song Book of The Salvation Army.

STONE, ELLA A. (d. 1915)
"O sweet and tender as the dawn. "

She joined the Church of Christ, Scientist on November 3, 1903 and her hymn appeared in the Christian Science Hymnal (1937). She died on March 21, 1915.

STONE, MARY KENT ADAMS (b. 1835)
"Lord, with a very tired mind. "

She was the daughter of J. S. Stone, D. D. , Dean of the Theological School of the Protestant Episcopal Church in Cambridge, Massachusetts. Her hymn appeared in Horder's Congregational Hymns (1884). We have been unable to locate her place and date of death.

STOWE, HARRIET BEECHER (1811-1896)
"Still, still with Thee, when purple morning breaketh, When the bird waketh, and the shadows flee. "

"Knocking, knocking, who is there?
Waiting, waiting, oh how fair. "

Daughter of the Reverend Lyman Beecher, she was born at
Litchfield, Connecticut on June 14, 1811. In 1832 her father
became president of Lane Seminary in Cincinnati, Ohio and
in 1836 she married Calvin E. Stowe, professor of language
and biblical literature at the seminary. Later he was a professor at Bowdoin College in Brunswick, Maine and at Andover Theological Seminary. Her brother, the Reverend
Henry Ward Beecher, pastor of the Plymouth Church in
Brooklyn, New York City, included three of her hymns in
his Plymouth Collection (1855); her hymns were published in
her Religious Poems (1867); the Boston Hymns of the Spirit
(1864); Sankey's Sacred Songs and Solos (1881). She obtained
world fame with her novel, Uncle Tom's Cabin (1852). She
died at Hartford, Connecticut on July 1, 1896. More recently her hymns appeared in The American Service Hymnal
(1968); Baptist (1973); Christian Worship (1953); Methodist
(1966); and The Pilgrim Hymnal (1958) and one recording
listed by Phonolog Reports of Los Angeles (1978).

STRATFORD, ELIZABETH (1828-1868)
"We praise Thee, we bless Thee, O Father in heaven. "

She was born in London, England on October 30, 1828 and
her hymns appeared in her Hymns for the Collects Throughout the Year for the Use of Children (1857) and in W. F.
Stevenson's Hymns for Children and Home (1873). She died
at Belper, England on April 4, 1868.

STRATTON, LOVIE RICKER (1841-1910)
"O Lord, our God, almighty King. "

Born at Somersworth, New Hampshire on October 31, 1841,
she was graduated from high school there and taught in public schools in Dover, New Hampshire for eleven years. On
June 19, 1872 she married Dr. Frank K. Stratton, pastor of
the Dorchester Street Methodist Episcopal Church in South
Boston, Massachusetts. Her poems and hymns were published in Zion's Herald, the Christian Witness, and other
publications. She died at Melrose, Massachusetts on September 6, 1910. Her hymn appeared in the Methodist Hymnal
(1911).

STREATFIELD, CHARLOTTE SAINT (1829-1901)
"How beautiful the hills of God. "

Tune--LANGTON

Daughter of the Rev. J. J. Saint, Rector at Speldhurst, England, she was born there on December 31, 1829. In 1862 she married Lieutenant Charles N. Streatfield, Royal Navy, eldest son of Major General Streatfield of the Royal Engineers. She published Hymns and Verses on the Collects (1865); Hymns on the Love of Jesus ... (1877); A Little Garland of the Saints and Other Verses (1877); The Story of the Good Shepherd (1885); and prose works, Meditations on the Seven Last Words (1874) and Words of Comfort (1875). Her hymns appeared in Mrs. Brock's Children's Hymn Book (1881). Her tune LANGTON was included in The Magnificat (New Church, 1893) and the Book of Worship (Evangelical Lutheran, 1899). She died on September 27, 1901.

STRONG, ANNA LOUISE (1885-1970)
"The City of God. "

Daughter of Ruth Maria Tracy, formerly of Mansfield, Ohio and Dr. Sydney Strong, a Congregational minister, she was born at Friend, Nebraska on November 24, 1885 and was educated in Germany (1902), Bryn Mawr College in Pennsylvania (1903), and at Oberlin in Ohio (A. B. , 1905), University of Chicago (Ph. D. , 1908). She was director of child welfare exhibits in Kansas City, St. Louis, Rochester, Louisville, Providence, Montreal, Northampton, Massachusetts and Dublin, Ireland, etc. She resided in Seattle, Washington (1916-21), was a correspondent for Hearst newspapers in Eastern Europe (1922-26), went to Russia and founded a newspaper there, The Moscow News, then went to China and wrote a newsletter, Letter from China (1958-70). She wrote Songs of the City (1906); Psychology of Prayer (1909); Children of Revolution (1925); China's Millions (1928); This Soviet World (1936); My Native Land (1940) and numerous other books. She resided in Peking, China. Her hymn appeared in Masterpieces of Religious Verse (Harper, 1948).

STRUTHER, JAN (1901-1953)
"We thank you, Lord of Heaven. "

Born Joyce Anstruther in London, England, she adopted "Jan

Struther" as her pen-name. In 1923 she married Anthony M. Graham. She wrote five books of poetry which included Betsinda Dances and Other Poems (1931); Sycamore Square and Other Poems (1932); and Glass Blower (1941); but is best known for her novel Mrs. Miniver (1939). Twelve of her hymns appeared in Songs of Praise (London, 1931) and three of her hymns appeared in The Hymnal of the Protestant Episcopal Church in the USA (1940). During World War II she lived in New York City and was in much demand for her lectures. She once said: "My children are delighted when they hear taxi drivers say 'foist' and 'thoid,' just as in the films." In 1948 she was married to A. K. Placzek, and she spent several years on the editorial board of The Times of London. She died of cancer in New York City on July 20, 1953. Her hymn "When Stephen, full of power and grace" was published in the Baptist Hymnal (1975).

STUTSMAN, GRACE MAY (1886-1970)
  "In Bethlehem 'neath starlit skies."

    Tune--WAITS' CAROL

Composer and hymnist, she was born at Melrose, Massachusetts on March 4, 1886 and was educated at Boston University and the New England Conservatory of Music in Boston. A concert pianist, she received a scholarship for graduate study at the conservatory and also won the Endicott prize in song composition. Although not a Christian Scientist, she contributed articles for the Christian Science Monitor for 25 years. A symphony, choruses, songs, hymns, and string quartets are among her compositions. Her hymn and tune above appeared in the Methodist Hymnal (1964). "Our records show that she was enrolled in the Conservatory program from 1920 to 1922. She had teachers with the following surnames: Bridge, Johns and Mason. And she gave a piano recital in 1922 that included three of her own works. Our records indicate that she died on April 30, 1970." [April 1982 letter from Katherine Gonzales, Director of Alumni Relations at the New England Conservatory of Music.]

SUMMERS, HELEN (1857-1943)
  "Master of the vineyard, hear."

She was born in England. Her hymn first appeared in the Sunday School Chronicle, then with other hymns in the Christian Endeavor Hymnal of 1896. She died on November 22, 1943.

TARR, FLORENCE (1908-1951)
"God is ever beside me. "

Born at New York City on March 14, 1908, she was educated at Columbia University, City College of New York, and studied piano with Gustave Becker. Fay Foster composed the music for hymns by Florence Tarr including "We are all His Children. " She also wrote the words for the cantatas The World of Tomorrow and O Wondrous Star. She died at New York City on May 23, 1951.

TAYLOR, ANN MARTIN (1758-1830)
"There is a sacred, hallowed spot. "

She was the wife of Isaac Taylor of Ongar, Essex, England and the mother of hymnists Jane Taylor and Ann Taylor Gilbert. Her hymn first appeared in the Youth's Magazine (1812) and later in the Scottish Presbyterian Hymnal (1876).

TAYLOR, CLARE (c. 1710-1778)
"Who can condemn, since Christ hath died?"

Reported that she was a member of the Church of England, residing in Westminster, and she translated Moravian hymns from the German which appeared in the Moravian Hymn Book (1742-1789). D. Sedgewick published 39 of her hymns in Hymns composed chiefly on the Atonement of Christ and Redemption through His Blood (1865).

TAYLOR, EMILY (1795-1872)
"O Father through the anxious fear. "

She was the great granddaughter of Dr. John Taylor, the Hebraist; and daughter of Samuel Taylor of New Buckenham, Norfolk, England and a niece of John Taylor of Norwich, the hymnist. She wrote numerous books of prose, and her hymns appeared in the Unitarian Collection of Psalms and Hymns (Liverpool, 1818); the Norwich Unitarian Hymn Book (1826); the Rev. J. R. Beard's Collection of Hymns for Public and Private Worship (1837); Horder's Congregational Hymns (1884); etc. Although raised a Unitarian, she joined the Church of England in later life.

TAYLOR, FLORENCE MARIAN TOMPKINS (b. 1892)
"Gladly we lift our hearts and voices
Unto Thee, O God, in pray'r. "

Born in Brooklyn, New York City on March 4, 1892, she was
graduated from Montclair State College and taught in New Jersey public schools (1909-17). On December 18, 1916 she
married George R. Taylor and they had two daughters and
one son. Later she lived in Columbus, Ohio. The following
article appeared in the Columbus Dispatch for October 30,
1976:

> "Retired" Author Finishes 15th Book.
>
> An 84-year old author is still going strong and is
> about to have her 15th religious book published in
> the spring. Mrs. Taylor explained she turned to
> writing books while working in Christian education
> at the Protestant Council of churches headquarters
> in New York City.... After two or three years
> she was asked to write a vacation church school
> textbook. That was the beginning of her 38-year
> career as an author. Most of the books Mrs. Tay-
> lor has had published are daily devotionals.... It
> is her belief that a Christian family not only wor-
> ships together on Sunday but during the week as
> well. Although Mrs. Taylor has a membership in
> a Congregational church in Montclair, New Jersey,
> she has attended services at First Congregational
> and the Redeemer's Church since moving to Colum-
> bus in 1958.

Her hymn appeared in Children's Religion (June, 1944), the
Pilgrim Press and in Joyfully Sing--A Hymnal for Juniors
(1968). She was still living and active in February 1982.
[Letter dated February 22, 1982 from Mrs. Florence Taylor
from Columbus, Ohio.]

TAYLOR, HELEN (1818-1885)
"Father, the little offering take. "

She was the daughter of Martin Taylor and was born in England. She wrote The Child's Book of Homilies; A Series of
Simple Lays for Christian Children; Missionary Hymns for
the Use of Children (1846).

TAYLOR, HELEN (1875-1943)
"Bless this house, O Lord, we pray. "

Born in England, she married Sydney H. Rothschild. Her
hymn, written in 1927, became popular in America as a
Thanksgiving hymn. Singer John McCormack made it famous;
when he appeared at the London Ballads Concerts in 1935 for
their 25th anniversary, he was asked to sing "Bless the
House, " but immediately suggested the title be changed to
"Bless this House, " which was done, and the song became
popular. It was sung many times in British homes during
the bombings in World War II.

TAYLOR, JANE (1783-1824)
"Lord, I would own thy tender care. "

The daughter of Isaac and Ann Martin Taylor, the hymnist,
she was born in London, England on September 23, 1783 and
was the younger sister of hymnist Ann Taylor Gilbert. She
wrote Display; a tale (1815); Essays in Rhymes (1816); etc.
With her sister she wrote Original Poems (1805); Hymns for
the Sanctuary (1806); etc. More recently her hymn was included in Hymns Ancient and Modern (Anglican); Church of
Scotland Hymn Book (1927); and the Anglican Hymn Book
(1965). She died at Ongar, Essex, England, the family
home, on April 13, 1824.

TAYLOR, MARY VIRGINIA (b. 1912)
"Sleep my little Lord Jesus. "

Hymnist, she was born at Muskogee, Oklahoma on August 7,
1912 and educated at Northeastern State College (B. A.) in
Tahlequah, Oklahoma. She was dean of the Muskogee Junior
High School in Muskogee and married Lionel Taylor, the
composer and pianist, who composed the music for her
hymns and the anthem above. They lived in the Los Angeles,
California area. As of March 1982 she was enjoying her
retirement.

TAYLOR, REBEKAH HOPE MORLEY (1800-1877)
"Thou art the way, O Lord. "

The eldest daughter of E. Morley, Member of Parliament,
she was born in England and married Herbert W. Taylor, a

member of the Plymouth Brethren. Her hymn appeared in
the Enlarged London Hymn Book (1873) and the Plymouth
Brethren Collection.

TAYLOR, SARAH ELLEN (1883-1954)
   "O God of light, thy Word, a lamp unfailing. "

The daughter of a Methodist preacher, William B. Taylor,
she was born at Stockport, England on December 30, 1883
and was brought to America when she was eight years old.
After she was graduated from Brown University, Providence,
Rhode Island (B. A. , 1904; M. A. , 1910), she taught in mission schools in Alabama and Virginia, then in high schools
of Central Falls and Pawtucket, Rhode Island for 32 years,
retiring in 1949.   She taught Sunday School in the Primitive
Methodist Church, wrote the lyrics for the Rhode Island
state song, and won prizes in hymn-writing sponsored by
The Hymn Society of America.   She died at Central Falls,
Rhode Island on October 5, 1954.   Her hymn above appeared
in the Methodist (1964); Presbyterian (1955); and Lutheran
(1958) hymnals.

TENNYSON, EMILY SELLWOOD, LADY (1813-1896)
   "Great God, who knowest each man's need. "

She was the wife of Alfred, Lord Tennyson, the poet.   Her
hymn appeared in Gordon Boys' Morning and Evening Hymns
(1885) and then in other English collections.   More recently
her hymn was published in The Book of Worship (Reformed,
1929).

THAXTER, CELIA LAIGHTON (1835-1894)
   "Lift up thy light, O man, arise and shine,
   Steadfast while loud the storms of life assail. "

She was born in Portsmouth, New Hampshire on June 29,
1835.   Her father was a lighthouse keeper on the Isles of
Shoales, nine miles off Portsmouth.   On September 30, 1851
she married Levi Thaxter.   Her stories and poems were
published in the Atlantic Monthly, Harper's, Scribner's and
in all the leading magazines of the day.   From 1880 she
lived on her son's farm in Kittery Point, Maine and died
there on August 26, 1894.   Her hymn was published in the
Christian Science Hymnal (1937).

THERESA OF AVILA, SAINT (1515-1582)
"God alone suffices. "

Born Teresa de Cepeda y Ahumada at Avila, Spain on March
28, 1515, she entered the Carmelite Convent of the Incarna-
tion as a novice in 1536. She founded the convents Medina
del Campo (1567), Malagon and Valladolid, and Duruelo
(1568), and others, also founded several monasteries. She
wrote Life (1565); Way of Perfection; Foundations; Interior
Castle (1577); etc. She died at Alba de Tormes, Spain on
October 4, 1582. Her hymn appeared in her Breviary. St.
Teresa of Avila, translated from the Spanish by Henry Wadsworth Longfellow and appeared in Masterpieces of Religious
Verse (Harper, 1948).

THOBURN, HELEN (1885-1932)
"Father of lights, in Whom there is no shadow. "

Born at Union City, Pennsylvania, she was educated at Stan-
ford University in Palo Alto, California. She spent eight
years in China for the Young Women's Christian Association
(YWCA). Her hymn was written with Elizabeth Wilson.
Helen was a member of the Madison Avenue Presbyterian
Church in New York City. Their hymn appeared in the Presbyterian Hymnal (1933).

THOMAS, CARRIE STOCKDALE (1848-1931)
"Great King of heav'n, our hearts we raise. "

Daughter of Michael and Jane Stockdale, she was born at
Plymouth, England in April 1848 and in 1864 she emigrated
to Utah where she married Richard K. Thomas in 1865.
They had twelve children, eight of whom were living at the
time of her death at age 83. She served as president of the
Young Ladies' Mutual Improvement Association of the Seventh
Ward in Salt Lake City, Utah and attended conventions of the
National Council of Women in Cleveland, Ohio and in Wash-
ington, D. C. She was a charter member of the Reaper's
Club and the Utah Women's Press Club. Her hymn appeared
in Hymns (1948) of the Church of Jesus Christ of Latter-day
Saints.

THOMAS, EDITH LOVELL (1878-1970)
Arranger--ST. ANTHONY'S CHORALE

A composer and arranger born at Eastford, Connecticut on
September 11, 1878, she was educated at Boston University
(B. R. E.; S. R. E.; M. Ed.) and the School of Sacred Music at
Union Theological Seminary in New York City. She also
studied at Wellesley College, and later served as professor
of music and worship at Boston University and for many
years was director of church school music, Christ Church
Methodist, in New York City. She was the compiler of First
Book in Hymns and Worship (1922); Singing Worship (1925);
Sing, Children, Sing (1939); The Whole World Singing (1950);
and other books. She retired to live in Claremont, California. Her hymn tune appears in the Methodist Hymnal
(1964). She died on March 16, 1970.

THOMPSON, IRENE (b. 1908)
    "Come, gracious Lord, to this home."

Irene Thompson was born at Durham, England on June 16,
1908 and served as a Methodist Local Preacher on the Dar-
lington South Circuit in England. In 1958 she moved to Cal-
gary, Alberta, Canada, where she joined the United Church
of Canada. Her hymn appeared in Marriage and Family
Life Hymns (The Hymn Society of America, 1961).

THOMSON, MARY ANN FAULKNER (1834-1923)
    "O Zion haste! Thy mission high fulfilling;
    To tell to all the world that God is Light."

Daughter of an Anglican priest, she was born in London, England on December 5, 1834 and married John Thomson, first
librarian of the Free Library of Philadelphia, Pennsylvania
where he was also Accounting Warden of the Church of the
Annunciation (Episcopal). She wrote more than forty hymns
which were published in The Living Church (Chicago) and
The Churchman (New York City). Four of her hymns appeared in The Church Hymnal (1894). She died in Philadelphia, Pennsylvania on March 11, 1923. More recently, her
hymn above appeared in The American Service Hymnal (1968);
Baptist (1973); Broadman (1977); Christian Worship (1953);
Episcopal (1940); Family of God (1976); Joyfully Sing (1968);
Methodist (1966); Presbyterian (1955); and the Pilgrim Hymnal (1958).

THREFALL, JEANNETTE (1821-1880)
"Hosanna, loud hosanna,
The little children sang. "

The daughter of Henry Threfall, a wine merchant in Blackburn, Lancashire, England, she was born there on March 24,
1821. Left an orphan at an early age, she was raised by
her uncle and aunt, Bannister and Mary Jane Eccles of Park
Place, Blackburn. Later they lived at Golden Hill, Leyland.
She was lamed and mutilated by an accident, and invalided
by a second accident, but she cheerfully endured her suffering. She published Woodsorrel; or, Leaves from a Retired
Home (1856) containing 35 poems; then 55 poems more were
published in Sunshine and Shadow (1873), which included the
hymn above. She died at Westminster, England on November 30, 1880. Her hymn above appeared in Hymns for the
Family of God (1976); Joyfully Sing (1968); Lutheran (1941);
Methodist (1966); and Presbyterian (1955) hymnals.

THRESHER, SARAH B. (1841-1932)

She was born at Zanesville, Ohio on February 20, 1841 and
in 1861 married J. B. Thresher of Dayton, Ohio. "I am
sorry that I am unable to provide much information on the
life of Sarah B. Thresher. The only information available
comes from the William's Dayton City Directory. Sarah B.
Thresher first appears in the 1898-99 directory as married
to J. B. Thresher; she appears as a widow in the 1924 city
directory; and last appears in 1932. " [Information from
Nancy Horlacher, Reference Librarian of the Dayton and
Montgomery Public Library, Dayton, Ohio.]

THRUPP, ADELAIDE (1830-1908)
"Lord, who at Cana's wedding feast Didst a guest
appear. "

It is believed by this author that she was probably the sister
of Joseph Francis Thrupp (1827-1867), who was appointed
Vicar of Barrington, Cambridge (1852) and Select Preacher
before the University (1865), since she was definitely not
his wife or daughter. Her hymn above was published in his
Psalms and Hymns (Cambridge: Macmillan, 1853) and a
new stanza was added by Godfrey Thring in 1882. More recently her hymn appeared in the Episcopal (1940) and Lutheran
(1941) hymnals. She died on July 25, 1908.

THRUPP, DOROTHY ANN (1779-1847)
"Saviour, like a Shepherd lead us,
Much we need thy tender care."

Born in London, England on June 20, 1779, she wrote several hymns for W. Carus Wilson's Friendly Visitor and Children's Friend, often under the pseudonym "Iota," and other hymns for Mrs. Herbert Mayo's Selection of Hymns and Poetry for Use of Infants and Juvenile Schools and Families (1838) under the initials "D. A. T." She contributed to juvenile magazines edited by Caroline Fry. Her hymn appeared in Hymns for the Young (1836). She died at Hamilton Place, St. John's Wood, London on December 14, 1847. More recently her hymn appeared in the American (1968); Baptist (1973); Broadman (1977); Christian Worship (1953); Episcopal (1940); Family of God (1976); Joyfully Sing (1968); Methodist (1966); Presbyterian (1955); and The Pilgrim Hymnal (1958) of the United Church of Christ.

THWAITES, CLARA HEPWORTH (1839-1927)
"The sunset burns across the sky."

Daughter of the Rev. Robert Hepworth, she was born at Tewkesbury, England and in 1869 she married the Rev. H. G. Thwaites, later Vicar of Limber Magna, Lincolnshire, England. She published her poems and hymns in Songs for Labour and Leisure (London, 1885) and A Pearl of Bells: Poems (London, 1888) and her hymns were published in the Church Missionary Hymn Book (Church of England, 1899).

TIDDEMAN, MARIA (1837-1915)
Tune--IBSTONE

A composer born in England, she studied music at Oxford University. Her hymn tune was used for Martin Luther's hymn, "Flung to the heedless winds." She composed anthems, hymn tunes, and songs. Her tune appeared in the Methodist Hymnal (1911) and in Hymns Ancient & Modern (1950). She died on January 8, 1915, at Croydon, England.

TOKE, EMMA LESLIE (1812-1878)
"Glory to Thee, O Lord."

Daughter of John Leslie, D. D., Bishop of Kilmore, she was

born at Holywood, Belfast, North Ireland on August 9, 1812
and in 1837 she married the Rev. Nicholas Toke of Godington
Park, Ashfort, Kent, England. Seven of her hymns, including the one above, were published in the Society for Promoting Christian Knowledge Hymns for Public Worship in 1852
and fourteen more of her hymns were published in the Sunday
School Liturgy ... and Hymn Book, arranged by the Rev. R.
Judd, B. A., Incumbent of St. Mary's (Halifax, Nova Scotia,
1870). She died at Ryde, Isle of Wight on September 29,
1878. Her hymn appeared in Hymns Ancient and Modern
(1939).

TOLLET, ELIZABETH (1694-1754)

The daughter of George Tollet, Commissioner of the Navy in
the reigns of William III and Anne, her father lived in the
Tower of London, England, where she spent her childhood.
Later she lived at Stratford and West Ham. She published
her Poems on Several Occasions (London, 1755). She was a
friend of Sir Isaac Newton who commended her on her early
essays. One of her hymns was published in Psalms in English (1754) and her poems were published in Nichols' Collection and in Frederick Rowton's Female Poets of Great Britain
(1848). She died at West Ham, England on February 1, 1754.

TONNA, CHARLOTTE ELIZABETH BROWNE (1790-1846)
      "Sinner, what hast thou to show,
      Like the joys believers know?"

She was born in Norwich, England on October 1, 1790. She
married a Captain Phelan and resided in Nova Scotia and in
Kilkenny, Ireland, but he died in 1837 and in 1841 she married Lewis H. Tonna. She edited the Christian Lady's Magazine from 1836 and The Protestant Magazine from 1841 until
her death. She published numerous books and died at Ramsgate on July 12, 1846. Her hymn appeared in the Baptist
Hymnal (1973).

TORREY, MARY IDE (1817-1869)
      "When silent steal across my soul. "

Daughter of the Rev. Jacob Ide of Medway, Massachusetts,
she was born on June 29, 1817. Then on March 29, 1837

she was married to the Rev. Charles T. Torrey. She wrote Christian Rule in Dress (1838) and City and Country Life (1856). Her hymn was published in Nason's Congregational Hymn Book (1857).

TOURJEE, LIZZIE S. (1858-1913)
Tune--WELLESLEY

A composer and the daughter of Dr. Eben Tourjee, who founded the New England Conservatory of Music in Boston in 1867, she was born at Newport, Rhode Island in 1858. When Lizzie, at age eighteen, was asked to set a classmate's gradu-ation hymn to music, she panicked and rushed to her father for help. So he had her sit down at the piano with the words directly in front of her, to see what their meaning meant to her. So her tune evolved, and was sung at her graduation high school class in Newton, Massachusetts. She attended Wellesley College for one year (1877-78), and her father named the tune after her college. In 1883 she married Franklin Estabrook. With the hymn, "There's a wideness in God's Mercy, " her tune appeared in the Hymnal of the Methodist Episcopal Church with Tunes (1878) and in Tribute of Praise (1884) for use at the New England Conservatory. More recently her tune appeared in The Pilgrim Hymnal (1958).

TRACY, RUTH (1870-1960)
"I've a Friend, of friends the fairest. "

The seventh child of Plymouth Brethren parents, she was born at Islington, London, England on November 28, 1870 and was educated in private schools in Enfield, Middlesex, where the family moved when Ruth was still a small child. In 1888 she visited cousins in Dorking, Surrey, and one day a drum and fife band passed by the house playing "O you must be a lover of the Lord" and other gospel songs. So one Sunday night Ruth and a friend entered the Salvation Army barracks and attended a prayer meeting. When she returned home, Ruth attended meetings at the Holloway Cita-del at Wood Green, which was a four mile walk from En-field. After becoming a soldier she was sent to the Appoint-ments Department in London. She wrote many songs and hymns which appeared in The War Cry, and was trained as an officer in 1890 at the Walthamstow Garrison. After four years she was transferred to International Headquarters (in

November 1894) where she was an editor's assistant on various publications until her retirement in 1931. She died on September 17, 1960. She wrote over 300 hymns and songs. The hymn above appeared in The Musical Salvationist (December, 1899) and nine of her hymns appeared in The Song Book of The Salvation Army (1953).

TRESTRAIL, ELIZABETH RYLAND DENT (1813-1900)
    "Hallelujah! Praise the Lord. "

Great granddaughter of the Rev. John C. Ryland, A. M. , and a sister of Caroline Dent, she was born at Milton, near Northampton, England on March 24, 1813. She married John Roby, a banker, of Rochdale, and after his death, she married the Rev. F. Trestrail, D. D. , a Baptist minister in 1858. She contributed some poems to her sister's Thoughts and Sketches in Verse and also published, with her sister, Our Darling (1861). Her hymn above was written for the Baptist Jubilee Mission in Jamaica in 1864 and published in the Baptist Psalms and Hymns for School and Home (1882). She died on March 2, 1900.

TURNER, NANCY BYRD (1880-1971)
    "The Word of God shall guide my feet
    Wherever I may go. "

Born at Boydton, Virginia on July 29, 1880, she was raised an Episcopalian, edited the children's page of the Youth's Companion magazine (1918-22) and wrote several books, Zodiac Town (1921); Adventures of Ray Coon (1923); Magpie Lane (1927); and volumes of verse, A Riband on My Rein (1929) and Star in a Well (1935). Her hymn appeared in Hymns for Junior Worship (1927) published by the Presbyterian Board for Christian Worship and Joyfully Sing--A Hymnal for Juniors (1968). "Miss Nancy Byrd Turner, formerly of Richmond, died Sunday September 5, 1971 in Alexandria, Virginia. [Death notice received from Mary Frances Propst of the Southside Regional Library, Boydton, Virginia.]

TURNER, ROSA M. (d. 1951)
    "O dreamer, leave thy dreams,
    for joyful waking. "

She joined the Church of Christ, Scientist on June 3, 1927

and her hymn appeared in the Christian Science Hymnal
(1937). She died on June 15, 1951.

UPTON, ANNE (b. 1892)
        Cantata--Life of Jesus

Composer and hymnist, she was born at Marble City, Arkan-
sas on June 28, 1892 and was educated at the Fred Palmer
Institute. She wrote for radio and composed the opera, Book
of Ruth, a symphonic poem, Cattle at Eventide, etc.

VAN ALSTYNE, FRANCES J. see FANNY J. CROSBY

VOKES, MRS.
        "Soon may the last glad song arise. "

        "Ye messengers of Christ, His sovereign voice obey. "

She was born in England, and her earliest hymns appeared in
a Selection of Missionary and Devotional Hymns edited by the
Rev. J. Griffin, a Congregational Minister at Portsea and
published in 1797; later hymns in J. Dobell's New Selection
of Seven Hundred Evangelical Hymns ... (1806), and seven
hymns in Collyer's Collection in 1812 which included "Ye
messengers of Christ. " This hymn was also published in
the Christian Science Hymnal (1937) and the first hymn above
in the Episcopal hymnal (1940).

WADDELL, HELEN JANE (1889-1965)
        "Lover of souls and Lord of all the living. "

Daughter of the Rev. Hugh Waddell, a Presbyterian mission-
ary and his wife Jane Martin of Banbridge, County Down,
Ireland, she was born at Tokyo, Japan on May 31, 1889.
The family consisted of eight sons and two daughters. They
returned to Ulster in 1899, and she was educated at Victoria
College and Queens University in Belfast, Northern Ireland
(B. A. , 1911; M. A. , 1912). She published Lyrics from the
Chinese (1913), studied and lectured at Oxford and studied in
Paris (1923-25). She wrote The Wandering Scholar (1927);
Medieval Latin Lyrics (1929); a novel Peter Abelard (1933);
Stories from Holy Writ (1949); etc. She became acquainted
with George Bernard Shaw and dined with General Charles

de Gaulle during World War II, Queen Mary, and Prime Minister Stanley Baldwin. She died at London, England on March 5, 1965.

WAKEFIELD, NANCY PRIEST (1836-1870)
"Over the river they beckon to me. "

Born at Royalston, Vermont, she was raised at Hinsdale, New York where she worked in the factories as a child. She wrote her hymn when she was nineteen. In 1865 she married Lieutenant A. C. Wakefield, an officer in a Vermont Regiment during the Civil War. She was only thirty-four years old when she died.

WALKER, ANNIE L. see ANNIE WALKER COGHILL

WALKER, MARY JANE DECK (1816-1878)
"Jesus, I will trust Thee, trust Thee with my soul. "

Daughter of John Deck of Bury St. Edmunds, England, she was the sister of James George Deck, hymnist. In 1848 she married Dr. Edward Walker, Rector of Cheltenham. Several of her hymns appeared in her husband's Psalms and Hymns for Public and Social Worship (1855) and in the Appendix to his Collection (1861). More recently her hymn was published in the Presbyterian Church of Canada hymnal, Songs of Praise (1931) and the Anglican Hymn Book (1966). She died on July 2, 1878, at Cheltenham.

WARD, ELIZABETH STUART PHELPS (1844-1911)
"It chanceth once to every soul. "

Daughter of Elizabeth Stuart and Professor Austin Phelps, she was born at Boston, Massachusetts on August 31, 1844 and was raised at Andover, Massachusetts where she was educated at day schools there. Her young lover was killed in the Civil War, and she brooded over her loss for years. She published The Gates Ajar (1868), which was loaded with Biblical quotations, and the book sold almost 100,000 copies in America and went into 20 printings in one year, but was even more popular in England. The book was translated into several foreign languages. She maintained a summer home at East Gloucester, Massachusetts and on October 20, 1888 was married to Herbert D. Ward and they resided in Newton Center, Massachusetts where she died on January 28, 1911. Her hymn, called "On the Bridge of Sighs," appeared in Whittier's collection Songs of Three Centuries.

WARING, ANNA LAETITIA (1823-1910)
"In heavenly love abiding,
No change my heart shall fear. "

"My heart is resting, O my God,
I will give thanks and sing. "

She was born at Plas-y-Velin, Neath, Glamarganshire, Wales on April 19, 1823. While raised a member of the Society of Friends (Quakers), she joined the Anglican Church (Episcopal) on May 15, 1842. She never married. She visited prisons in Bristol and aided discharged prisoners. She published Hymns and Meditations (1850) and Additional Hymns (1858). She died at Clifton, Bristol, England on May 10, 1910. Her hymn appeared in the Broadman (1977); Christian Worship (1953); Christian Science (1937); Episcopal (1940); Family of God (1976); Methodist (1966); Presbyterian (1955); and The Pilgrim Hymnal (1958).

WARNER, ANNA BARTLETT (1827-1915)
"Jesus loves me! this I know,
For the Bible tells me so. "

"We would see Jesus--for the shadows lengthen
Across this little landscape of our life. "

"One more day's work for Jesus,
One less of life for me!"

She was born in New York City on August 31, 1827, the younger sister of author Susan B. Warner (1819-1885). The girls were raised in Canaan, New York. Anna was a Methodist and Susan a Presbyterian; later they attended the Episcopal Church. She edited Hymns of the Church Militant (1858) and published Wayfaring Hymns, Original and Translated (1869). The women lived on Constitution Island, a rockbound and wooded retreat opposite West Point on the Hudson River, and they conducted Bible classes for the cadets there. In the winter, classes were held at the academy chapel. Mrs. Russell Sage purchased the island from the ladies and

donated it to the U. S. Government. Anna died in Highland
Falls, New York on January 15, 1915, and hundreds of
former cadets returned to the military academy to pay their
respects at her funeral. Twenty-one recordings of the first
hymn above are recorded in Phonolog Reports (1978), and
her hymns are in the Baptist (1973); Broadman (1977); Christian Worship (1937); Family of God (1976); and Presbyterian
(1955) hymnals.

WARNER, SUSAN BOGERT (1819-1885)
    "Jesus bids us shine with a pure, clear light."

The daughter of Henry W. and Anna Bartlett Warner, and the
elder sister of Anna Bartlett Warner, she was born in New
York City on July 11, 1819. Susan was a Presbyterian, but
later attended the Episcopal Church with her sister. They
lived on Constitution Island in the Hudson River (1837-1885).
Susan wrote The Wide, Wide World (1850), which ranked in
popularity with Uncle Tom's Cabin during the 19th century.
She wrote several other novels. She died at Highland Falls,
New York on March 17, 1885. More recently her hymn appeared in The Song Book of The Salvation Army (1953).

WARREN, DELLA McCHAIN (1893-1976)
    "There is a name to me so dear,
    Like sweetest music to my ear."

Hymnist and composer, she was born at Gastonville, Pennsylvania on February 19, 1893 and was graduated from
Douglass College. On June 27, 1917 she married James B.
Warren in Glassport, Pennsylvania, where Mr. Warren was
a butcher in his father's butcher shop. They lived there for
thirty years, then in 1947 moved to Aurora, Colorado, where
she died on August 29, 1976. [Information from her son,
Hugh M. Warren.] Her hymn appeared in Rodeheaver's Gospel Solos and Duets No. 3.

WATKINS, LILIAN BOWYER (1879-1964)
    "O Thou God of full salvation."

Born at Bristol, England in November 1879, her parents
were members of The Salvation Army. Later she resided
in Cardiff, Wales and entered the Army from the Cardiff
Stuart Hall Corps in November 1879. After serving in differ-

ent field and divisional positions in Britain, she was sent to India in 1912. While in India she met and married Staff-Captain (later Major) George Watkins in 1899, where they continued to serve until 1928. The Major later served as Training Principal in West Africa. A number of songs by Lilian Watkins were published in The Musical Salvationist, and the hymn above in The War Cry (June 1895) and in The Song Book of The Salvation Army (1899; 1953).

WEAVER, MARY WATSON (b. 1903)
   Choral--On the Eve of the First Christmas

Composer, hymnist, pianist, and teacher, she was born at Kansas City, Missouri on January 16, 1903 and was educated at Smith College in Northampton, Massachusetts; Ottawa University (B. A.; B. M.) in Ottawa, Ontario, Canada; also private music study in New York City, Paris, and at the Curtis Institute of Music in Philadelphia, Pennsylvania. She gave piano recitals (1927-51), married pianist-organist-composer Powell Weaver who collaborated with her in her compositions and taught music at the Manhattan School of Music and the Henry Street School of Music in New York City from 1957. Her choral works also include All Weary Men; Kneel Down; When Jesus Lay by Mary's Side; Like Doves Descending; Rise Up All Men; etc. As of March 1982 she was enjoying her retirement.

WELLS, EMMELINE B. WOODWARD (1828-1921)
   "Our mountain home so dear. "

Daughter of David Woodward, a soldier in the War of 1812, she was born at Petersham, Worcester County, Massachusetts on February 29, 1828. She was baptized into the Mormon Church at age fourteen and married to a man named Harris in order to leave the state legally and emigrate to Nauvoo, Illinois. Soon afterwards Harris left the Mormon Church, and she married Presiding Bishop Newell K. Whitney and left Nauvoo with his family in the exodus of 1846. They had two daughters when they arrived in Salt Lake City, Utah in 1848, but then her husband died and she married General Daniel H. Wells. They had three daughters. She was assistant editor, then editor, of the Woman's Exponent (1875-1914). Brigham Young University conferred upon her the honorary degree of Doctor of Literature on February 29, 1912, in her eighty-fourth year. She was a member of the Reaper's

Club, the Utah Women's Press Club, and other organizations. She died on April 25, 1921. Her hymn appeared in Hymns (1948) of The Church of Jesus Christ of Latter-day Saints.

WESSON, JAN (b. 1925)
      Tune--MY NEIGHBOR

Composer and hymnist, Ruth Janelle Smith was born at Greenville, Illinois on April 25, 1925 and attended East St. Louis, Illinois city schools. She was married to James Robert Wesson, Professor of Mathematics and Associate Dean of the College of Arts and Sciences at Vanderbilt University, Nashville, Tennessee. They had one daughter and three sons, one granddaughter and five grandsons. She taught Sunday School and is a substitute choir director at the Crievewood United Methodist Church in Nashville, and is also a soprano soloist and handbell ringer there. The text for her congregation's dedication anthem was written by her in 1976. She wrote the music and words for "They asked, 'Who's my neighbor and whom should I love?'" in the pamphlet, New Hymns for Children, published by the Choristers Guild and The Hymn Society of America (1982).

WESTON, REBECCA J. (d. 1895)
      "Father, we thank Thee for the night,
      and for the pleasant morning light."

Her hymn first appeared in Daniel Bachellor's and Thomas Charmbury's Manual for Teachers, and Rote Songs to accompany the Tonic sol-fa music courses for schools (Boston, 1884) and was also included in Kindergarten Chimes (1887) edited by Kate Douglas Wiggin. The following obituary appeared in The Boston Evening Transcript on August 10, 1895:

> Miss Rebecca J. Weston who was widely known as a kindergarten teacher, died suddenly last Wednesday at Concord, where she was passing the summer. She had been associated with Miss Mary J. Garland for a number of years in conducting a kindergarten normal school in Boston, and was twice president of the Eastern Kindergarten Association. The funeral took place yesterday afternoon from Rev. Dr. Hale's church on Exeter St. The Services, consisting of scripture reading, an address and prayer by Dr. Hale and singing of hymns by a group of Miss Weston's former pupils.

She died at Concord, Massachusetts on August 7, 1895. [Information from Patricia Nonamaker of the Boston Public Library.] Her hymn appeared in Joyfully Sing--A Hymnal for Juniors (1968); the Presbyterian Hymnal (1955); and the Pilgrim Hymnal (1958).

WEXELSEN, MARIE (1832-1911)
"I am so glad each Christmas eve."

Niece of Wilhelm Wexels, she was born at Ostre Toten, Norway on September 20, 1832. Later she resided in Trondhjem, Norway, where she died in 1911. Her hymn appeared in the Lutheran Service Book and Hymnal (1958).

WHIDDINGTON, ADA ANNE FITZGERALD (1855-1933)
"Not I, but Christ."

The daughter of Richard Fitzgerald, she was born in England and married Richard Whiddington. Their son, Richard Whiddington, became Cavendish Professor of Physics at Cambridge University. Her hymn appeared in Hymns for the Living Church (1974).

WHITING, MARY BRADFORD (1863-1935)
"Come ye yourselves apart and rest awhile.
The way is weary."

She was born at Bloomfield, Essex, England, daughter of the Rev. J. B. Whiting, later Vicar of St. Luke's, Ramsgate. Seven of her hymns, including the one above, were included in her father's Hymns for the Church Catholic (1882). She died on December 9, 1935.

WHITMORE, LADY LUCY ELIZABETH GEORGIANA (1792-1840)
"Father, again in Jesus' name we meet."

Only daughter of Orlando Bridgeman, 2nd Baron and 1st Earl of Bradford, she was born on January 22, 1792 and in 1810 was married to Mr. William W. Whitmore of Dudmaston, Shropshire, England. In 1824 she published 14 original hymns in Family Prayers for Every Day in the Week ... with a 2nd edition in 1827. She died on March 17, 1840. More recently

her hymn appeared in the Presbyterian Hymnal (1933) and
the Evangelical and Reformed Church Hymnal (1941).

WHITNEY, M. FANNIE (d. 1933)
　　　"We thank Thee, heavenly Father,
　　　　for Thy correcting rod. "

She joined the Church of Christ, Scientist on December 31,
1892 and her hymn appeared in The Christian Science Journal
for July 1894 and in the Christian Science Hymnal (1937).
She died on February 11, 1933.

WHITTEMORE, HANNAH M. (1822-1881)
　　　"How sweet to think that all who love. "

Sister of William M. Whittemore, Rector of St. Katherine
Cree, London, she was born in London, England.　Her hymn
appeared in her Coral Magazine (1845); her brother's The
Short Liturgy; in her uncle Jonathan Whittemore's Supplement
to All Hymn Books (1850); the Baptist Hymnal (1879); and
others.　She died at Worthing, England on July 6, 1881.

WIANT, MILDRED KATHRYN ARTZ (b. 1898)
　　　"Rise to greet the sun. "

Translator and versifier, she was born at Lancaster, Ohio
on June 8, 1898 and was graduated from Ohio Wesleyan University (1920) in Delaware, Ohio.　In 1922 she married Bliss
Wiant and they lived in Boston, Massachusetts for one year
where she studied voice.　The next year they traveled to
Peking, China where her husband taught at Yenching University and she became associate professor of voice there.
Later she was instructor of vocal music at Scarritt College
in Nashville, Tennessee (1942-46; 1961-62), a teacher at the
Biennial Convocations of the National Fellowship of Methodist
Musicians (1957-61), instructor of vocal music at Chung Chi
College, Chinese University of Hong Kong (1963-65).　She
translated 50 Chinese hymns into English, including many in
Worship Materials from the Chinese published by the National Council of Churches of Christ in the USA (1969).　Her
hymn appeared in the Baptist Hymnal (1964).　"We would like
to assure you that Mrs. Wiant is very much alive and resides at 133 West Winter Street, Delaware, Ohio. " [March
1982 letter from Mrs. Sandra L. Fathbruckner of Ohio Wesleyan.]

WIGLESWORTH, ESTHER (1827-1904)
"Father, look upon Thy children. "

Daughter of Thomas Wiglesworth, she was born at Tottenham,
Middlesex, England. She became Matron of the Madgalen
Asylum in Streatham. Her hymns were published in Verses
for the Sundays and Holidays of the Christmas Season (1863);
Verses for Christian Children (1871); Hymns for the Feasts
and Other Verses (1878); Songs of Perseverance (1885); etc.
She died on October 31, 1904.

WILCOX, ELLA WHEELER (1855-1919)
"If my vain soul needs blows and bitter losses. "

Born at Johnstown Centre, Wisconsin, she was educated at
the University of Wisconsin. In 1884 she married Robert
M. Wilcox of Meriden, Connecticut. She wrote A Double
Life; Poems of Pleasure; Three Women; Poems of Power;
Poems of Sentiment (1906); Gems (1912); Lest We Forget
(1915); and numerous other books. Her hymn appeared in
A Treasury of Poems for Worship and Devotion (Harper,
1959). She resided at Short Beach, Connecticut and died on
October 31, 1919.

WILDE, JANE FRANCESCA ELGEE, LADY (1826-1896)
"Jesus, Refuge of the weary,
Blest Redeemer, whom we love. "

Daughter of Archdeacon Elgee, she was born at Wexford,
Ireland. She wrote for The Nation (1845-48), a magazine
advocating independence for Ireland, until it was suppressed
in 1848. In 1851 she married Sir William R. W. Wilde, an
oculist in Dublin, and after his death she moved to London,
England. They had two sons, journalist William Wilde and
dramatist Oscar Wilde. Her hymns are translations. She
once wrote: "It is only tradespeople who are respectable.
We are above respectability. " She died at Chelsea, London
on February 3, 1896. Her hymn appeared in The Lutheran
Hymnal (1941).

WILE, FRANCES WHITEMARSH (1878-1939)
"All beautiful the march of days,
As seasons come and go. "

She was born in Bristol, New York on December 2, 1878 and educated in public schools in Western, New York and at the Normal School at Geneseo, New York. She was an active member of the First Unitarian Church in Rochester, New York when the Rev. William Channing Gannett was the minister. Her husband, Abram J. Wile, was secretary of the Young Men's Hebrew Association in Rochester. She assisted Rev. Gannett in his "Boys' Evening Home" and was active in church work from 1889 to 1921, when she became interested in theosophy and devoted her time to the philosophical and religious cult. She died at Rochester, New York on July 31, 1939. Her hymn first appeared in the Unitarian Hymnal (1912); then in Christian Worship (1953); Methodist (1966); Presbyterian (1955) hymnals and in The Pilgrim Hymnal (1958).

WILKINSON, KATE BARCLAY (1859-1928)
"May the mind of Christ my Savior,
Live in me from day to day."

Born in England, she was a member of the Church of England, and active in the Keswick Convention Movement and conducted a meeting for girls. Her hymn appeared in the Baptist (1975); Broadman (1977); Family of God (1976) hymnals and Hymns for the Living Church (1974).

WILLARD, EMMA C. HART (1787-1870)
"Rocked in the cradle of the deep,
I lay me down in peace to sleep;
Secure I rest upon the wave,
For Thou, O Lord, has power to save."

She was born in Berlin, Connecticut on February 23, 1787, the 16th of her father's 17 children. Her mother, the second wife, bore ten children. Emma attended the Berlin Academy (1802-04), then taught there; later was preceptress of a female academy in Middlebury, Vermont. On August 10, 1809 she married John Willard, a physician. She opened her own school, Middlebury Female Academy in 1814, an academy in Waterford, New York in 1819, and at Troy, New York in 1821. Her husband died in 1825, and on September 17, 1838 she married Christopher Yates, an Albany physician, who turned out to be an agnostic, a gambler, and fortune hunter. She divorced him in 1843. While on an ocean voyage in 1839 she wrote "Rocked in the Cradle of the Deep"

which was introduced by basso Joseph P. Knight, the composer, at a concert in New York City. Later the song appeared in Henry Ward Beecher's Plymouth Collection (1855).
She died in Troy, New York on April 15, 1870. There is
one recording of her hymn listed in Phonolog Reports (1978).

WILLARD, FRANCES ELIZABETH CAROLINE (1839-1898)
  "The hands are such dear hands. "

Daughter of Mary T. Hill and Josiah F. Willard, she was
born at Churchville, New York on September 28, 1839 and
was raised in Oberlin, Ohio and in Wisconsin. She was
graduated from Northwestern Female College (1859) at Evanston, Illinois, taught at schools in Illinois, Lima, New York,
etc., then was president of the Evanston College for Ladies
(1871-74). She resigned to become secretary of the Woman's
Christian Temperance Union in 1874, president of the National WCTU (1879) and president of the World's WCTU (1895).
She wrote Woman and Temperance (1883), Glimpses of Fifty
Years (1889) and died in New York City on February 18,
1898.

WILLIAMS, CLARA TEAR (1858-1937)
  "All my life long I had panted. "

The daughter of Thomas and Mary Evangeline Searl Tear,
she was born at Painesville, Ohio on September 22, 1858
and was raised a Methodist. After three years as a school
teacher in Ohio (1879-82), she joined Sister Mary DePew in
evangelistic work, first working with Methodist Episcopal
groups, then with Wesleyan Methodist congregations. In 1895
she was married to W. H. Williams, a lay preacher, and
they lived in Canton, Ohio, then in Massillon, Ohio, Houghton,
New York, and Philadelphia, Pennsylvania. Besides writing
several hymns, she was also consulting editor for Sacred
Hymns and Tunes Designed for Use in the Wesleyan Methodist
Connection (1900). After retirement, she went back to Houghton. After his family moved to Houghton in 1917, George
Beverly Shea wrote in Crusade Hymn Stories (Hope Publishing Company, 1967) that her appearance reminded him of
Whistler's mother and when he spoke with her, he enjoyed
"the soft, musical tones of her voice. " She died at Caneadea,
New York on July 1, 1937 and her hymn appeared in the
Baptist Hymnal (1975); Hymns for the Living Church (1974);
and Great Hymns of the Faith (1972).

WILLIAMS, FRANCES (1904-1978)
Choral--In Bethlehem's Lowly Manger

Composer, conductor, and arranger, she was born at Caer-
narvonshire, Wales on June 4, 1904 and was brought to
America as a young girl. She was educated at the Cornish
School of Music in Seattle, Washington (on a scholarship), at
Juilliard in New York City on a fellowship, and studied privately. She became Music Editor-in-Chief of Harold Flam-
mer, Inc. and was also a guest conductor at various music
clinics. She wrote Christ is the Risen Lord (cantata) and
the choral works Give Thanks, Night Psalm XXIII, etc. She
died on March 1, 1978.

WILLIAMS, HELEN MARIA (1762-1827)
"While thee I seek, protecting power,
Be my vain wishes stilled."

Daughter of Charles Williams of Aberconway, Wales, she
was born at London, England where her father was an offi-
cial in the War Department. She was raised at Berwick-on-
Tweed and was a Presbyterian. She wrote her first poem
in 1779, and published her first book of verse in London in
1783. She visited the Continent in 1788 and was particularly
attracted to Paris, where she became friendly with the
Girondits and was imprisoned in the Luxembourg Temple by
Robespierre in October 1793 for advocating the Girondits'
cause. During her captivity she wrote many letters, which
have been published, and also translated the Paul and Virginia of Bernardin de St. Pierre, which included some of her
sonnets. After the fall of Robespierre in 1794, she was released from prison and went back to London, but then returned to Paris in 1796. She was renowned as a friend and
admirer of Marat and an ex-Jacobin who took part in the
French Revolution. Her poems and hymns were published
in 1786 and reissued in 1823. She died at Paris on December 15, 1827. Her hymn above appeared in Christian Wor-
ship--A Hymnal (1953).

WILLIAMS, MARIAN (b. 1927)
"Holy Ghost don't leave me."

Black gospel singer, songwriter, and hymnist, she was born
in Miami, Florida. She joined Clara and Gertrude Ward in
the "Ward Singers," then left them in 1957 and joined the

"Stars of Faith, " led by Frances Steadman. She had the female lead in Black Nativity with Alex Bradford, the noted black gospel singer. Two recordings of her song above are listed in Phonolog Reports (1978), plus two for "We shall be changed. "

WILLIAMS, SARAH (1828-1868)
>"Because I knew not when my life was good,
>And when there was a light upon my path. "

The only child of Robert Williams, she was born in London, England. She published Rainbows in Springtide (1866) and Twilight Hours (1868). Her hymn from Twilight Hours appeared in Horder's Worship Song (1905) and more recently in the Presbyterian hymnal (1955).

WILLIAMS, SARAH JOHANNA (1805-1841)
>"Quiet from God! how blessed 'tis to keep. "

Daughter of the Rev. John Williams, Unitarian minister at Mansfield, England, her poem "Quiet from God! it cometh not to still / The vast and high aspirings of the soul" appeared in the Liverpool Sacred Offering (1834) and revised to the above it appeared in Dr. Martineau's Hymns of Praise and Prayer and in J. P. Hopp's Collection (1877).

WILLIS, LOVE MARIA WHITCOMB (1824-1908)
>"Father, hear the prayer we offer. "

Born at Hancock, New Hampshire on June 9, 1824 she was married to Frederick L. H. Willis, M. D. in 1858 and resided for many years in Rochester, New York, and later at Glenora on Seneca Lake, New York. Her hymn appeared in Samuel Longfellow and Samuel Johnson's Hymns of the Spirit (1864) and The English Hymnal (1906). More recently her hymn was published in the Christian Science Hymnal (1937) and in The Pilgrim Hymnal (1958).

WILLS, LOIS BAILEY (b. 1918)
>"Rise, men of destiny, our troubled planet calls. "

Daughter of Albert Edward Bailey, author of The Gospel in Hymns, she was born at Scituate, Massachusetts and was graduated from Northwestern University (B. S. , 1940) in Evanston, Illinois. She married a Mr. Wills and they resided in Sturbridge, Massachusetts. Her hymn appeared in World Order Hymns published by The Hymn Society of America (1958). In April 1982 she was alive and well.

WILLS, RUTH (1826-1908)
"We meet, we part, how few the hours. "

Born at Leicester, England on December 22, 1826, she was raised a Congregationalist. As a child of eleven, she went to work for a hosiery firm in Leicester and stayed there for fifty years, when she retired on a very small pension. She published Lays of the Lowly Life (1861) with a second series published the following year. Her hymn above appeared in W. R. Stevenson's School Hymnal (1880). She died on November 18, 1908.

WILSON, CAROLINE FRY (1787-1846)
"Full oft the clouds of deepest woe. "

Born at Tunbridge Wells, England on December 31, 1787 she was married to a Mr. Wilson in 1837. She published a History of England in Verse (1801); Poetical Catechism (1821); Serious Poetry (1822); and many other books. Her hymn appeared in Kennedy's Hymnologia Christiana (1863). She died at Tunbridge Wells, England on September 17, 1846.

WILSON, ELIZABETH (1867-1957)
"Father of lights, in whom there is no shadow. "

Born at Neenah, Wisconsin on August 19, 1867 she was educated at Lawrence University, Appleton, Wisconsin (1882-1890) at irregular intervals (A. B. ; M. A.). She was an instructor in English and Latin at Lawrence (1894-1900) then at Oxford University, England for one year. She entered the work of the Young Women's Christian Association (YWCA) in 1891 and worked in Chicago and in India for many years. She stayed with the Association until her retirement in 1928, when she returned to Appleton and was ordained a deacon in the Methodist Church. She moved to Los Angeles, California in June 1942 and died there on August 17, 1957, just two days short of her 90th birthday. [Letter from Ray Vignovich, Public Library, Appleton, Wisconsin.] She wrote the above hymn with Helen Thoburn and it appeared in the Presbyterian Hymnal (1933); Brethren; Reformed; Methodist (1935) hymnals and A Hymnal for Friends (Quakers, 1955).

WILSON, EMILY DIVINE (1865-1942)
"Sometimes, when my faith would falter. "

Composer and hymnist, the daughter of John and Sarah Lees Divine, she was born in Philadelphia, Pennsylvania on May 24, 1865. In 1887 she was married to the Rev. John G. Wilson, pastor of the Wharton Memorial Methodist Church in Philadelphia. For years they attended the annual summer sessions at Ocean Grove, New Jersey. He served as district superintendent of the Philadelphia (Methodist) Conference at the time of his death in 1933. She was also a composer, and one of her tunes, HEAVEN, appeared in the Baptist Hymnal (1975); the above hymn was in the American Service Hymnal (1968). She died at Philadelphia on June 23, 1942.

WILSON, JANE (SISTER BEATRICE) (1836-1872)
"A virgin heart she brought to Christ. "

She was the Mother Superior of the Sisterhood of St. Thomas the Martyr, Oxford, England. Sixteen of her hymns appeared in Hymns Used at the Church of S. Thomas the Martyr (Oxford, 1861) and enlarged in 1870, later in Legenda Monastica and Other Poems (Mowbray, Oxford).

WILSON, JENNIE (1857-1913)
"Time is filled with swift transition. "

She was born on a farm near South Whitley, Indiana. When she was four years old a spinal attack (probably infantile paralysis) rendered her a wheelchair invalid. She wrote over 2, 200 poems and hymns, including "Jesus is calling the children, " "There will be light at the river, " "Is it well with your soul?" "Christ is calling you tonight, " etc. She was baptized in 1881, carried on a chair to a stream. She died on September 3, 1913. Her hymn appeared in the Baptist hymnal (1905). More recently her hymn was published in the Christian Hymnal (Mennonite, 1959).

WILSON, LUCY ATKINS (1802-1863)
"O Lord, Thy heavenly grace impart. "

Born on December 28, 1802, she became the wife of Rev.
Daniel Wilson, and her hymn was sung at the Waldbach
Church (England) on June 11, 1820 and later included in her
book Memoirs of John Frederic Oberlin (London, 1829). It
is believed to be a translation from the German, but considered her original hymn by others. There are similar
lines by S. J. Smucker. Later her hymn appeared in Thring's
Collection (1880-82); the Free Church Hymn Book (1882); in
H. V. Elliott's Psalms and Hymns (1835); and others. She
died on January 25, 1863.

WILSON, MARGARET CHALMERS HOOD (1825-1902)
    "We know there's a bright and glorious home."

She was born at Dunbar, Scotland on October 19, 1825 and
in 1869 she married her cousin, the Rev. James Hood Wilson, D. D., of the Barclay Free Church, Edinburgh, Scotland.
Her hymns appeared in her husband's Service of Praise (1865)
and Songs of Zion (1876). She died on a visit to Gullane,
Haddingtonshire, England on July 24, 1902. More recently
her hymn appeared in The Song Book of The Salvation Army
(1953).

WINKWORTH, CATHERINE (1827-1878)
    "Lift up your heads, ye mighty gates."

    "Now thank thee all our God."

A translator and versifier, the daughter of Henry Winkworth,
she was born at Halborn, London, England on September 13,
1827, was raised in Manchester, and later lived in Clifton,
near Bristol. She lived with an aunt in Dresden, Germany
(1845-46). She published her hymns translated from the
German in Lyra Germanica (1855; 1858) and the Chorale Book
for England (1863) which had as its music editors William S.
Bennett, founder of the Bach Society in 1849 and Otto Gold-
schmidt, German born pianist-composer and husband of Jenny
Lind, who founded the Bach Choir in 1875. She also published Christian Singers of Germany (1869); was secretary of
the Association for the Promotion of Higher Education for
Women (1870); governor of the Red Maids' School of Bristol;
member of the Cheltenham Ladies' College (1871); and dele-
gate to the German conference on Women's Work held in
Darmstadt, Germany in 1872. She died suddenly at Monnetier,
in Savoy, France, on July 1, 1878. Her hymns are in the

Christian Science (1937); Episcopal (1940); Lutheran (1941); Methodist (1966); Presbyterian (1955) hymnals and The Pilgrim Hymnal (1958).

WINTER, GLORIA FRANCES (b. 1938) (SISTER MIRIAM THERESE)
"Spirit of God in the clear running water."

Tune--MEDICAL MISSION SISTERS

Composer and hymnist, born in Passaic, New Jersey on June 14, 1938, she was educated at Bayley-Ellard Regional High School in Madison, New Jersey, at Trinity College in Washington, D. C., Catholic University in Washington, D. C. (B. Mus.) and McMaster Divinity College in Hamilton, Ontario, Canada (M. Rel. Ed.). In November 1955 she entered the Society of Catholic Medical Missionaries, also known as the Medical Mission Sisters. From 1963 to 1972 she served as Director of Public Relations for the Northeast District and Coordinator of Public Relations for the U. S. A. and editor of the Society's Medical Missionary magazine. She was both a hymnist and composer, writing over 100 songs and hymns, and also composing the music for them, together with six Mass/Service settings. Her hymn appeared in Hymns for the Living Church (1974). Her hymn "God gives his people strength" appeared in the United Presbyterian Hymnal (1972).

WINTERS, FRANCES WEAVER (b. 1908)
"O Lord our God, whom all through life we praise."

Born at Greeley, Colorado on July 6, 1908, she was educated at Denison University (B. A.), Granville, Ohio; Westminster Choir College (B. M.), Princeton, New Jersey; and William Carey College (D. H. L.) Hattiesburg, Mississippi; and married Donald Winters. She was co-founder, School of Church Music, Southern Baptist Theological Seminary, Louisville, Kentucky, teacher and registrar there; assistant to the Dean and Undergraduate Academic Counselor, Indiana University School of Music; assistant Professor of Church Music, William Carey College. She contributed to The Hymn, The Review and Expositor, The Baptist Record, etc. Her hymn above appeared in 10 New Hymns on Aging and the Later Years (1976) published by The Hymn Society of America. [Information from Frances W. Winters from Hattiesburg in a letter dated July 13, 1982.]

WODEHOUSE, LOUISA M. R. STEAD (c. 1850-1917)
   "'Tis so sweet to trust in Jesus. "

She was born in Dover, England, and at age nine decided she wanted to be a foreign missionary. After coming to Cincinnati, Ohio in 1871 she attended a camp meeting at Urbana, Ohio, and offered herself as a missionary, but was not accepted because of her poor health. She married a Mr. Stead, and they had one daughter (later Mrs. D. A. Carson). While trying to rescue a child off Long Island, New York, her husband was drowned. Shortly afterwards she moved to South Africa with her daughter, Lily, to work as missionaries in the Cape Colony, where they served for 15 years. While there she met and married Robert Wodehouse. In 1895 they returned to America, and he became a Methodist minister. In 1901 they returned to the Methodist mission at Umtali, Southern Rhodesia. She died at her home in Penkridge, near Mutambara Mission, about fifty miles from Umtali, on January 18, 1917. Her hymn appeared in The American Service Hymnal (1968); Baptist (1975); Broadman (1977); Family of God (1976); Joyfully Sing (1968); and Methodist hymnals (1966).

WOOD, KITTY (d. 1926)
   "There He stood amid a crowd. "

She was a cadet in The Salvation Army in Chicago, Illinois when she wrote her hymn, which appeared in The War Cry (April 17, 1886). She then became a missionary in Ceylon (now called Sri Lanka) where she met and married an interpreter to the Supreme Court. Her hymn also appeared in The Musical Salvationist (June 1894) and in The Song Book of the Salvation Army (1899; 1953).

WOODMANSEE, EMILY HILL (1836-1906)
   "Up! Arouse thee, O beautiful Zion.

Daughter of Elizabeth Slade and Thomas Hill, she was born at Warminster, Wiltshire, England on March 24, 1836. When she was only twelve years old, she was persuaded by a cousin, Miriam Slade, to go to a Mormon meeting on foot, six miles away. She returned home converted to their beliefs, but her parents opposed her joining the church. Later a Mormon Elder visited the family and convinced them to allow Emily to go to America. In May 1856 she sailed for America with her sister, Julia. They traveled west, but

when they met a group of Saints preparing for the trip to
Utah, they had no wagon and no oxen. So Emily to pull a
handcart to Utah, a one thousand mile trip. Her sister refused to go along. Those pioneer women were rugged! Emily pulled her belongings in a hand cart for one thousand
miles. Later she remarked: "I never knew what trouble
was until I became a Mormon." After Emily's arrival in
Salt Lake City she was married on June 14, 1857 to William
Gill Mills, but her husband went on a mission for the Church
and never returned. So on May 7, 1864 she married Joseph
Woodmansee and they had several children. She wrote numerous poems and hymns, and the one above was included
in Hymns (1948) of the Church of Jesus Christ of Latter-day
Saints. The lines of her hymn show her tremendous spirit
and determination. She died at Salt Lake City, Utah on Octo-
ber 19, 1906. [Letter of 30 September 1983 from Phillip B.
Dunn, British Correspondent, Genealogical Department, LDS,
Salt Lake City, Utah.]

WOODS, BERTHA H. (d. 1932)
    "Abide with me, fast breaks
    the morning light."

She joined the Church of Christ, Scientist on October 3, 1896
and her hymn, drawn from one by Henry F. Lyte, first appeared in the Christian Science Sentinel for March 28, 1901
and then in the Christian Science Hymnal (1937). She died
on April 15, 1932.

WOODWARD, JUDITH L. (b. 1941)
    "In the beginning, Lord, You made the world in love."

Born in Lincoln, Nebraska on April 17, 1941, she was educated at Kansas State College and at St. Paul School of Theology. She served as a short-term missionary to Japan
(1963-67) and on June 10, 1968 was married to the Rev.
Robert A. Woodward II, or "Tony." She and her husband
served as church and community workers for the United Methodist Board of Missions in Missouri (1969-74). She was co-
pastor of the Boy-Kno Parish in northern Nebraska (1976-
82) and as of May 1982 pastor of the Republican City and
Bloomington United Methodist Churches, residing in Alma,
Nebraska. [Information received from Mrs. Tony Woodward.]
Her hymn appeared in The Stewardship of the Environment
(Ecology) published by The Hymn Society of America (1973).

WOOLLEY, KATE WILKINS (b. 1913)
"Free to be me, God, I really am free. "

Born in Greensboro, North Carolina on December 2, 1913,
she was educated at the University of North Carolina at
Greensboro (B. A.), at Mt. Holyoke College (M. A.), South
Hadley, Massachusetts and at the Southern Baptist Theological
Seminary. In 1942 she was married to the Rev. Davis C.
Woolley, pastor of the First Baptist Church of Palatka, Flor-
ida (1946-53) and director of extension, Howard College (now
Stamford University; 1953-59). They moved to Nashville,
Tennessee in 1959 when Dr. Woolley became executive secre-
tary of the Southern Baptist Historical Commission. She be-
came active in the Nashville Baptist Association and the Glen-
dale Baptist Church, where she was ordained as a minister.
Her hymn appeared in the Baptist Hymnal (1975) and the
Broadman Hymnal (1977).

WOOLSEY, SARAH CHAUNCEY (1845-1905)
"Every day is a fresh beginning. "

A niece of President Woolsey of Yale University, she was
born at Cleveland, Ohio and later resided at Newport, Rhode
Island and wrote verses under the pen-name "Susan Coolidge. "
She published her Verses; For Summer Afternoons; In the
High Valley; A Few More Verses; etc. Unmarried, she died
in 1905. Her hymn appeared in Masterpieces of Religious
Verse (Harper, 1948).

WORDSWORTH, DAME ELIZABETH (1840-1932)
"O Lord our Banner, God of Might. "

Daughter of Bishop Christopher Wordsworth, Headmaster at
Harrow, she was born at Harrow-on-the-Hill, England on
June 22, 1840. She wrote her hymn in the winter of 1884-
85 when the excitement about General "Chinese" Gordon in
Egypt and the Sudan was at its height. Her hymn appeared
in Church Hymns (1903). She was the Head of Lady Margaret Hall, Oxford, England, appointed in 1878 and served
until 1909. She published Glimpses of the Past (1912); Essays Old and New (1912); and Poems and Plays (1931). Her
hymn was included in The Book of Praise (Presbyterian
Church of Canada, 1918). She died at Oxford, England on
November 30, 1932.

WORTH, AMY (1888-1967)
 Christmas cantata--Mary the Mother

Composer, conductor, organist, and teacher, she was born
at St. Joseph, Missouri on January 18, 1888, was educated
in public schools and studied privately with Jessie Gaynor,
Mary Lyon, and others. She taught piano and was an organist and choir director in St. Joseph, Missouri and later
the choral director of the Women's Chorus of the Women's
University Club in Seattle, Washington. She also composed
the choral works: Christ Rises; He Came All So Still, etc.,
and the music for "Little Lamb," "Song of the Angels," "The
Evening is Hushed," etc. She died on April 29, 1967.

YONGE, CHARLOTTE MARY (1823-1901)
 "Into Christ's flock we are received."

Daughter of William C. Yonge and Frances M. Yonge, hymnist, she was born at Otterbourne, Hants, England. She
was well-known as the author of The Heir of Redcliffe; The
Daisy Chain; and other novels. She was also the editor of
the Monthly Packet, and her hymns appeared in her mother's
The Child's Christian Year (1841). She died at Otterbourne
on March 24, 1901.

YONGE, FRANCES MARY BARGUS (1795-1868)
 "Behold a Prophet, yea, and more."

Born on January 13, 1795, she married William Crawly
Yonge of the 52nd Regiment. They resided at Otterbourne,
Hants, England and were the parents of hymnist Charlotte
Mary Yonge. Frances' hymns were published in her book
The Child's Christian Year (1841), with a preface by John
Keble. She died on September 28, 1868.

YORK, SARAH EMILY WALDO (1819-1851)
 "I'm weary of straying, O fain would I rest."

She was a missionary to Greece. Her biography, Memoirs
of Mrs. Sarah Emily York, was published (1853) by Rebecca
B. Stetson Kalloch Medbury (b. 1808), wife of the Rev. Nicho-
las Medbury, pastor of the Baptist Church in Watertown,
Massachusetts and later city missionary to Portsmouth, New
Hampshire. Her hymn was published in the Reformed Dutch
Psalms and Hymns (1847).

YOUNG, LOIS HORTON (1911-1981)
"Christian men, arise and give
Words by which all men can live. "

She was born in Hamburg, New York on April 2, 1911 and
married the Reverend Carl E. Young on April 25, 1934.
They had four daughters. She was educated at Hunter College in New York City, taught in Baltimore kindergartens
(1945-54), and served as Director of Christian Education at
the Milford Mill Church in Baltimore, Maryland, from 1953.
She has written numerous children's books. She was a
member of the United Methodist Church, and her hymn appeared in the Southern Baptist Hymnal (1975) and the Broadman hymnal (1977). She died in Baltimore on February 13,
1981.

ZINZENDORF, ANNA NITSCHMANN, COUNTESS VON (1715-
1760)
"Ich bin das arme Würmlein dein. "
"My Saviour, that I without Thee. "

Daughter of David Nitschmann, she was born at Kunewald,
near Fulnek, Moravia (now Czechoslovakia) on November 24,
1715. The family moved to Herrnhut on February 25, 1725,
after being persuaded to do so by her cousin, David Nitschmann, who became the first Bishop of the renewed Brethren
Unity in 1735. In 1730 she was appointed Unity-Elder with
the care of unmarried sisters, and entered the house in 1733.
Then in 1735 she became companion to Benigna Zinzendorf,
the Count's daughter, and accompanied her to England. During the fall of 1740 she sailed for America with her father,
arriving in Pennsylvania on December 5, 1740. Zinzendorf
and his daughter arrived in 1741, and Anna returned to Germany in 1743. Zinzendorf's first wife died on June 19, 1756,
and a year later, on June 27, 1757, the Count married Anna
at Berthelsdorf. He became sick and died on May 9, 1760,
and she became ill also, and died on May 21, 1760. Her
hymn appeared in the Appendix to the Herrnhut Gesang-Buch
(1735). More recently her hymn was included in the Moravian hymnals (1876; 1908).

ZINZENDORF, ERDMUTH DORTHEA, COUNTESS VON (1700-
1756)
"Jesus God of Salvation. "

Daughter of the Count of Reuss-Ebersdorf, she was born at Ebersdorf, Germany on November 7, 1700. She was married to Count Nicholas L. von Zinzendorf on September 7, 1722. Her hymns appeared in Moravian hymnals. Her hymn was included in the Moravian hymnal (1920). She died at Herrnhut, Germany on June 19, 1756.

ZOECKLER, DOROTHY ACKERMAN (b. 1915)
"When I kneel down to pray. "

Composer and hymnist, she was born at Wheeling, West Virginia on August 19, 1915, was educated at the Cincinnati Conservatory in Ohio, and studied privately with Marcian Thalberg and others. She was organist and choir director of St. Matthew's Episcopal Church in Wheeling. She also wrote "God speaks to me, " etc.

Avery, Gordon. Companion to the Song Book of the Salvation Army. London: Salvationist Publishing Company, 1970.

Bailey, Albert Edward. The Gospel in Hymns. New York: Charles Scribner's Sons, 1950.

Cornwall, J. Spencer. Stories of Our Mormon Hymns. Salt Lake City: Deseret Book Company, 1961.

Covert, William C. & Calvin W. Laufer. Handbook to the Hymnal. Philadelphia: Presbyterian Board of Christian Education, 1936.

Diehl, Katharine Smith. Hymns and Tunes: An Index. New York and London: Scarecrow, 1966.

Douglas, Winfred, Leonard Ellinwood & Others. The Hymnal 1940 Companion. New York: The Church Pension Fund (Episcopalian), 1955.

Dreamer, Percy & Archibald Jacob. Songs of Praise Discussed. London: Oxford University Press, 1933.

Frost, Maurice. Historical Companion to Hymns Ancient & Modern. London: William Clowes & Sons Ltd., 1962.

Gealy, Fred D., Austin Lovelace & Carlton R. Young. Companion to the (Methodist) Hymnal. Nashville: Abington Press, 1964.

Haeussler, Armin. The Story of Our Hymns. The Handbook to the Hymnal of the Evangelical & Reformed Church. St. Louis, 1952.

Hostetler, Lester. Handbook to the Mennonite Hymnary, Newton, Kansas: Conference of the Mennonite Church of North America, 1949.

Hustad, Donald P. Dictionary-Handbook to Hymns for the Living Church. Carol Stream, Illinois: Hope Publishing Company, 1978.

Jones, J. Ithel, et al. The Baptist Hymn Book Companion. London, 1962.

Julian, John. A Dictionary of Hymnology. London: J. Murray, 1892; reprinted, New York: Dover Publications, 1957.

Kelynack, William S. Companion to the School Hymn-Book of the Methodist Church. London: Epworth Press, 1950.

Lightwood, James T. (edited & revised by Francis B. Westbook). The Music of the Methodist Hymn-Book. London: Epworth Press, 1955.

MacMillan, Alexander. Hymns of the Church. A Companion to The Hymnary of The United Church of Canada. Toronto: The United Church Publishing House, 1935.

Martin, Hugh, et al. The Baptist Hymn Book Companion. London: Psalms and Hymns Trust, 1962.

Parry, K. L. & Erik Routley. Companion to Congregational Praise. London: Independent Press Ltd., 1953.

Pollack, William G. The Handbook to the Lutheran Hymnal. St. Louis: Concordia Publishing House, 1958.

Reynolds, William J. Companion to the Baptist Hymnal. Nashville: Broadman Press, 1976.

Ronander, Albert C. & Ethel K. Porter. Guide to the Pilgrim Hymnal. Boston: United Church Press, 1966.

Royal, Samuel J. Sisters of Sacred Song. A Selected Listing of Women Hymnodists in Great Britain & America. New York & London: Garland, 1981.

Seaman, William A. Companion to the Service Book & Hymnal. New York: The Commission of Liturgy & Hymnal, 1976.

Statler, Ruth B. & Nevin W. Fisher. Handbook for Brethren Hymns. Elgin, Illinois: The Brethren Press, 1959.

Wake, Arthur N. Companion to the Hymnbook for Christian Worship. St. Louis: The Bethany Press, 1970.